DIRECTING CONSTRUCTION
FOR PROFIT

Business Aspects of Contracting

Samuel P. Oppenheimer
M.E., P.E., *New Jersey and New York*

McGRAW-HILL BOOK COMPANY

*New York   St. Louis   San Francisco   Düsseldorf
Johannesburg   Kuala Lumpur   London   Mexico
Montreal   New Delhi   Panama   Rio de Janeiro
Singapore   Sydney   Toronto*

DIRECTING CONSTRUCTION FOR PROFIT

07-047646-2

234567890 KPKP 79876543

To my wife Lucille

"And the rain descended, and the floods came, and the winds blew, and beat upon that house; and it fell not; for it was founded upon a rock."

MATTHEW VII, 25

"If you would create something you must be something."

GOETHE

CONTENTS

PREFACE

The quoted price of construction includes the total estimated cost of labor, material, equipment, and overhead—and a profit. Profits establish a means of accumulating resources, progressing to more and better jobs, acquiring necessities and luxuries, and becoming more secure in one's present position and in the society in which one lives. And because the construction field is an uncertain one, it is necessary to make the maximum possible profit on every job. This is difficult when all competitors figure the same plans and specifications and cut profits to obtain a work advantage. On some work, the gain will be small or nonexistent and must be compensated for by a larger return elsewhere.

Profits, however, are only estimated and are considered to be attainable but uncertain. Regardless of how shrewdly a prospective job may have been figured and contracted for, there are numerous ways in which gains may be lost. The misuse of capital, labor, and equipment causes declining returns. The haggling for the low price required to obtain a job against competition may leave little margin for error. A man must know his business before he can price and sell construction service. He must sell successfully in order to survive. *Successfully* means with a profit of some kind, generally a favorable difference between money received and money spent. Or the profit may lie just in keeping a construction organization together when work is scarce. Knowledge of the normal break-even point is essential.

The purpose of this book is to analyze and discover where profits and losses occur and to suggest ways and means of improvement. Where work has been taken with little profit apparent, the profit volume may be increased by good management.

The book is directed to men who are seeking to advance in the construction business. Every man is working for himself, no matter what his status. He must get the best return possible for his time, which means that he must know his business. As an employee and an expert craftsman, he may earn a substantial daily wage. As a businessman, he expects a return better than such wages to compensate for his assumption of responsibility. Many men are limited in attaining knowledge, however, by the restriction of having to earn a living. They become specialists in the execution of that work which is of use to their employer and do not gain knowledge of all necessary phases of their industry. Even men of considerable experience should constantly try to strengthen their insight into this very complex business. To meet such needs, the text outlines explicitly the many functions involved in management. Details are important.

Construction is the act of building, and it is also a service which necessitates management. Ability must be sold against competition, and the price required for a prospective job is a customary indication of productive ability. Such evidence will have to be supported in other ways to obtain a contract. But first a job must be competitively estimated and priced to interest a buyer in negotiating. Even in a cost-plus-percentage job, the buyer will require approximate cost information. Thus, the quoted price is of importance, and the method of developing it is indicated herein.

The price is based on the factual erection and cost summation of all parts of a job. The layout of the text necessarily places job discussion first to give a basis of erection understanding. Thereafter are noted those office functions which must precede the start of the job but which are actually based on previously acquired job knowledge. These include quotation, negotiation, and contractual items.

The concluding chapter discusses possible development of the contracting business. Can developments in large-scale space projects, electronics, atomic energy, and similar fields be of use in regular construction? Undoubtedly, in certain present isolated cases they can—and probably will more fully later, when applications have become more specific. There is presently in these routine fields a vast investment in men, money, equipment, and materials. This investment and the developed technique will not be discarded casually for theoretical reasons. Technical advances will have to be matched with sound financial returns to warrant change. Sometimes, good enough is best.

Construction is a very personal business. True, it reflects the "What's in it for me?" attitude of the men who make their living in this occupation, but there are also belief and faith in worth, achievement, and growth. This book reflects a long-time personal experience with men and methods—and with the fascination of this always interesting and worthwhile business.

Interpretive figures and illustrations by the writer accompany the text. The author would appreciate receiving notice of any commission, omission, or clarification required.

Acknowledgment is made with appreciation to Mr. Seymour Berger, P.E., partner of McKee-Berger-Mansueto, Inc. (construction consultants), New York City, for his review and suggestions with respect to Chapter 9, Take-Off, Preliminary, and part of Chapter 10, Take-Off, Factual and Summary.

The author is grateful also to Mr. P. James Pellecchia, Jr., president of Pellecchia Construction Company, Newark, New Jersey, and former chief magistrate of a Newark Municipal Court, for reviewing and making suggestions for the development of Chapter 12, The Quotation and Other Legalities.

Samuel P. Oppenheimer

1

BEGINNING
THE PROFITABLE JOB

Success in construction comes with applying effort intelligently at a price. Such service is developed by having knowledge of the manner and cost of production of the parts of a structure. Production varies with the type of work done, the location, the material used, and other factors. But basic to all work is the human element. Men guide and do the work and establish the costs. Another basic factor is time. Time can be used and influenced by action but cannot be recovered. Employment of many men may make a job short, but this means can be expensive. Employing few men will possibly be more efficient and less expensive but will result in a later completion date.

The problem of time is complicated by human nature. When men lose the sense of urgency, they tend to act and think more slowly. The reasons for continuous effort are clear. Every working day must be used fully, even if premium time must be paid, to finish a job. The next day may be rainy, and possibly no work can be done. Material trucks may bog down and have to be dug out, so that material is moved. Additional road-repair material must be bought, brought in, and placed. Or even if the next day is fine for working, a key employee may not show up, a subcontractor may be undependable and not arrive to start, or promised material may not be delivered.

There is no substitute for knowledge, push, and actual field experience. What is required is competent leadership.

1-1   *Importance of the Superintendent*

Costs are of importance on every job. Because the superintendent of construction directly affects the development of costs, and hence the profits or losses, the choice of a competent person is of vital importance to a construction company. His actions are subject to many outside influences. Strength of character is as necessary as intelligence and some education.

Whenever and wherever a construction company does its own work, the superintendent must know local limitations and try for the maximum productivity. There may be restraining factors, such as a limit to the quantities which may be produced, as determined by the local union; a jurisdictional requirement to employ a specific trade to do certain work (thus affecting payroll); a location in a structure that physically restricts the size of the work force; or a local building department requirement.

Even when work is subcontracted, the superintendent should be familiar with the trade practice in order to know the difference between a workmanlike job and an unacceptable piece of work. The later repair or replacement of defective work is always expensive in reputation and cost. Upon the job superintendent depends the character of the work developed.

Production information also has estimating usefulness. Occasionally a new plan for estimate or a specification may require the pricing of something different. Such a piece of unusual work can be valued with reasonable accuracy by calling in the superintendent. He will infer a price from his experience with the productive rate for a similar item. This price may not be exact, but it will give the estimator a good practical answer.

The superintendent's job is indefinitely defined, and the man himself must appropriate many of the functions and responsibilities which he exerts. His company confirms his authority by allowing him to speak for them in matters such as hiring, firing, and paying; ordering material, tools, and men; interpreting plans and specifications; correlating trades; and managing production. The true measure of the extent of his position is what he successfully does and the backing accorded to him by his organization.

The health and work habits of the superintendent must be good so that he is regularly on the job every working day before starting time.

He must also be there when work resumes after the short luncheon break. He must be actively on the job so that he knows what goes on at every hour of the day. He always carries keys for necessary locations. He should keep the work time book and make up the payroll, even though he may utilize the office help or a job subordinate for its final composition. He is the authority for whom the men work. On a construction job, as elsewhere, men will exert themselves when they must. And on a construction job it is the superintendent who represents and controls the power of the payroll.

The superintendent needs the mental strength to stand up to others. A union shop steward may claim certain undue work in an endeavor to get all the benefits possible for the men of his trade and local organization. Or a subcontractor may try to avoid doing certain preparatory work by claiming it is another's responsibility. Or an inspector for the buyer may interpret the specifications in a manner unjust and expensive to the contracting organization. If it is necessary to block such demands, the temporary strife which is occasioned will not last. All are too interested in getting on with the job and making a living and will adjust as necessary. On the other hand, weakness leads to other troubles and cannot be condoned. Because his decisions are subject to question, the knowledge of the superintendent must be such that he is in the right on his facts.

He must be resourceful. If, for example, a water-hose junction were to start leaking on the job, a good superintendent might devise a paper washer out of a morning newspaper. He must be self-reliant and self-confident, observant, and of a retentive memory. He must also be a good technician and manager, so that an adequate but not excessive number of workers are on his payroll. In Westcott's novel *David Harum,* when a cat in a general store fell into a barrel of molasses, David Harum remarked, "The cat is working very hard but getting nowhere." There is an obvious comparison to be applied. Men moving things around a construction site may also be working hard but not necessarily effectively. They are getting paid for such action, but their employer is not.

The superintendent is responsible for the welfare of his firm and the well-being of the men under him. But he needs the supervision and help of his organization. All actions must be coordinated. Although the activity of the office is necessarily concentrated on getting work and supervising the business in its entirety, detailed production items are also very much its business.

In the final analysis, much of the superintendent's success depends on the foremen on the job. Each foreman's job assignment should specify what is to be done, how long it should take to do it, and what equipment and material will be supplied. The foreman is expected to maintain a good level of progress and to improve in efficiency by proper utilization of his manpower. Specifically, the questions of what, when, where, and how become practical realizations at this point—one of the key areas in which dollars are made or lost.

Of course, the superintendent does not always have the power to pick or control his own assistants. Key men have usually been tested in their positions for a long period of time and are worthy of trust. They are apt to be fixtures with their organization and to move from job to job. But men are subject to the limitations of their overall knowledge, education, and training and are motivated by self-interest. The superintendent must believe that all men, including himself, are fallible. He must constantly check.

1-2   *Understanding the Job*

Of primary importance is knowledge of what is included in plans and specifications, contracts, subcontracts, and other job documents. Every detail and description must be studied in advance of need. There can be no error-free and profitable erection without a complete understanding of what the designer is trying to convey by representation, symbol, and notation, and of what the buyer asks for by documentation. The following examples demonstrate this point.

A. A partition can be used as a bearing wall to carry a floor load above. To indicate this condition, the plan for that partition will show that the masonry-block voids are to be filled with concrete during construction. The masonry foreman must be warned at the proper time to install the correct construction and material; otherwise, the load-carrying ability of the structure will be affected. Often, with no attempt to skimp, a foreman will omit something of importance through ignorance or carelessness. An inspector will note the error or the part as built, will show weakness leading to failure and condemnation. The damage to reputation is irreparable, and the additional cost of replacement is a distinct and unnecessary loss.

B. In certain cases, particular structural members must be completed before others can be installed. Interpretation of a layout will have to be modified to meet actual job conditions of clearance, interference, or commercial tolerance. Curing or drying time will require delay.

C. Information shown on one plan will be used elsewhere. For large-scale clarity and to save drafting time, all room finishes of floors, walls, and ceilings in a number of locations will be indicated in columnar form on one plan. Such information, however, will be used throughout the structure. Cost differences compel close attention to such architectural shorthand. Working drawings should be additionally marked in crayon where necessary. An exposed wall with a tooled (smooth) joint, later to take a painted finish, will cost more to produce than a wall to be plastered by another trade, where the joints will be hidden and can be unfinished. For a contractor doing his own masonry, these details are of importance and should be noted on the locations referred to.

Even when the details are clear, several trades may be involved in what at first sight may appear to be the work of only one contractor. A partition may include a metal door buck (frame), to be set by the carpenter; plumbing pipes, to be included inside the wall only after their installation has been approved by the local inspector; conduit for electric switches; and pipe sleeves for later installation of radiators by the steamfitter. Because the expenditure of a minimum of construction time and money can be achieved only by advance planning and coordinated effort, understanding of construction procedure and notation and proper notice to workmen are necessary.

Notation:

A. The specification is a vital and complementary part of the plan (the plan, of itself, can indicate only form and dimension). Material, however, has variable properties, such as density, elasticity, hardness, strength, texture, color, granulation, friction, and fluidity. Different types or grades of similar material may be required at different locations of a job. The same material may be uniform or varied, new or old, original or an allowed substitute, with permissible manufacturing variations, in quantity or in some other per-sales-unit size—all as a basis of comparison. Dimensions shown on plans may be modified by the allowed interval between objects, the required number of layers, the maximum or minimum heights and depths. Time enters into consideration with the ability to traverse distances and the duration of drying periods. The specification gives information of this nature and thus controls price.

B. There are also general specifications, which give bond and guarantee responsibility, safety measures required of all trades, cleanliness obligations, and requisition information and which define many other topics of contractual importance.

C. Other documents are necessary for understanding the job. Copies of contracts give not only typewritten modifications but printed requirements agreed to during negotiations that are nowhere else indicated. (Such copies, for job use only, sometimes purposely omit monetary values as a security protection.)

Understanding the meaning of the trade terms used in these documents can be very important. *Flemish bond* is not a Dutch insurance policy but an arrangement of brick in a repetitive design. A *door buck* is not a type of male deer found on construction jobs but a metal doorframe. Extra-heavy pipe, referring to plumbing, is a material grade designation.

This construction language is in common use among journeymen of various trades, specification writers, and supply sources. It is necessary to acquire a knowledge of these expressions. The field is so extensive, however, that new terms are always appearing. It is no disgrace not to know what something means. It is customary just to ask and continue to learn.

D. Approved installation plans give essential information for and by associate trades. For example, steel-erection plans will show locations and dimensions of niches to be built into a masonry wall so that steel bearing plates can be set. Electric-light-post details will include anchor bolts and conduits to be built into precast concrete foundations provided by others. Plumbing-fixture plates will require hanger irons fastened to stud partitions for future support. It is simple to take care of such items at the proper time but costly to omit them.

The plan and specification must be considered together. Each has an effect on cost. In addition, the requirements must be included, even if not mentioned, of the following: local jurisdictional authorities, trade-union working conditions, site existence of service utilities.

1-3   *The Job Headquarters*

Whether it be only a toolbox on a small job or a complete complex of buildings on a large site, there must be a focus of activity. The superintendent of construction spends considerable time referring to plans, specifications, contracts, and pertinent supplementary documents, such as subsoil boring plans or shop details. He must plan his actions in advance and must have a place to work and to stow documents, tools, and material.

In preparing for work, he establishes job headquarters of suitable size in a site trailer, a rented store, or some other accessible, unobstructing, and relatively secure location. On sizable construction jobs involving detail work extending over a considerable period of time, establishing the headquarters is worthy of some thought and expense. It entails installing loud-ringing telephones, fire-resistant and lockable files, medical supplies, paper drinking cups, survey instruments, steel tapes, and job tools, such as portable saws. It includes an inclined-top table on which to spread out plans and the use of stationery and scrap pads for figuring, telephone directories of numbers to call for supplies and equipment or for the use of men of various trades for emergencies, and means of heating and lighting—in short, anything which may be needed for a specific operation.

The working plans and specifications are brought to the job. If not previously done by the home-office employees, the first duty of the job superintendent is to reinforce all edges of plans with transparent adhesive tape. Sets and details which are not to go out on the job should be mounted on slats supported by wall brackets so as to be out of the way and yet accessible and should be marked for office use only. All the working plans and specifications should be kept up-to-date by marking on them in colored ink confirmed written and dated changes as shown in addenda or other documents. (Personnel sometimes change also, and this is a reason for writing every change on the plans as it develops. When an "as-built" plan is required for the owner at the end of a job, such modifying detail is most helpful.)

Because the superintendent keeps on file his copies of the contracts as well as other confidential documents for requisition purposes, the payroll records, and similar material, a locked file is an essential. This precaution is particularly necessary because every construction shanty is the nerve center of a particular job. Many visitors passing through will pick up any information available and will broadcast it. Possibly this action builds up their sense of self-importance, but otherwise it does no one any good.

All communications of any nature should be filed and locked away.

1-4 *Progress Planning*

As a rule, the office will have made up a tentative erection-order schedule to determine subcontract delivery dates for trades requiring lead time. Many trades, such as structural steel, elevators, and toilet partitions have to go through a lengthy procedure involving shop detailing, architectural approval, material procurement, fabrication, delivery, and erection. Even the delivery of a range of colors of face brick will involve delay for the mason and, thus, for others as well. These trades are the keys to progress and must be given out first in subcontracting. The delivery dates, therefore, are very important. The superintendent should get this schedule at once, as the progress of the job is set up around production time. Manpower will be varied up or down as appears necessary for any particular function to mesh with others. Revision is inevitable, and follow-up information is essential during the actual progress of the job.

For the present, however, the tentative schedule will determine the times of appearance on the job of the various trades involved. This leads to requests by the superintendent to such trades for job consultation on the location of housing, material, and equipment at the site. The decisions are complicated by the amount of space available, the need for access, and the necessity of not interfering with the work of others. Many construction jobs are limited in some of these respects. Even when there is plenty of room, a contractor wants to be close to the scene of action. In the best of circumstances, his own workmen customarily use expensive time in getting from and to his shanty or material location. Naturally, he wants to cut this time down. This is true both for the general contractor and for all subcontractors.

In addition, there are times of the year or other conditions of the labor, material, and equipment market when shortages develop. This situation is particularly noticeable just before the opening of schools or when several large projects are under way in one locality, when transportation facilities are interrupted, or when special types or sizes of equipment must be acquired. Unfortunately, such shortages sometimes lead to premium pay, express and delay charges, or inefficient erection. All such items cause pay in excess of what should be made, and many of them can be eliminated or the effects alleviated.

Weather also is a big factor in job progress and overhead expense. To salvage time, a contractor must prepare to get in every possible working day even though conditions may require extra effort and expense.

Tradesmen will show up for work during inclement weather if they are assured that work rules allow them to be paid a certain number of hours for waiting time if they are unable to start. This lost time can be minimized by advance preparation. For example, supplying raincoats, hats, and boots for the few laborers who must bring in mortar or other material from an outside location will help to ensure that they work effectively. Rolled-back tarpaulins or pliofilm can be hung from many structures and braced with studs, if necessary, to form enclosures in rainy or cold weather. Temporary electric power and lights should be in place and activated to furnish heat and light.

The need for material supplied by other trades must also be foreseen and supplied on the job in advance, preferably in place. Interior partitions to be built might require steel doorframes, electric conduits, and a definite thickness of a certain hollow masonry block. The various trades should have this material and equipment on the floor and set up, where possible, in advance of need.

Advance preparation puts appreciated payroll in workmen's pockets for otherwise lost working days and gives a reputation for efficiency. Such a reputation spreads among tradesmen and sometimes makes the difference between being able to hire competent journeymen and those not so good. Planning progress in advance is worth all the thought that can be given to it.

1-5 *Site Layout*

It is evident that the layout of locations for the field office, subcontractors' shanties, delivery storage, material access and elevator, toilet, rubbish-disposal facilities, and sources of water, light, and power must be carefully projected. The gain or loss of hours of reiterative field payroll throughout the course of the job is affected. Although the office may have made up a preliminary layout for the superintendent as part of the original estimate of equipment and overhead, the actual layout should be subject to consultation on the job. Also, few jobs are big enough to permit all to have a favored location.

When space on the site is limited, it is sometimes better to store in a location off the site (such as on a rented trailer) than to risk damage to material which cannot be adequately protected. If reinforcing rods in long stock lengths can be stockpiled only in driveways, where they may be run over and bent out of shape by truck wheels, a possible alternate means or time of delivery or location is indicated. When finished trim must be stored in the open, it must be adequately protected. And when small fastenings or other objects may become lost or damaged, the purchase of tote trays or other methods of material filing may actually result in a saving of time and money. All material-storage requirements should be checked.

The progress schedule will only in part determine who is to get preference. A steamfitter's storage trailer must be accessible for both heavy highway delivery and the continuous replenishment of job use. It would seem to rate first. Yet in a limited area, the very considerable space required to put a construction-crane boom together may militate against prior possession by the steamfitter of this essential space.

The progress schedule is not an infallible directory. The weather is always unpredictable, material and equipment deliveries vary and are complicated by individual problems, and available manpower fluctuates. The actual progress of the job varies from day to day and requires constant attention. The job superintendent, therefore, must sit down with everyone in turn, find out the needs, and attempt to be impartial in his space decisions.

1-6 *Method of Operation*

Erection methods and approximate costs also will have been tentatively formulated during the makeup of the estimate. The actual site, the plans and specifications, the contract documents, and the construction market, however, will offer choices of methods of operation. Some one of these differing methods (not necessarily the estimated choice) will do the most work for the least money.

As an example, concrete can be raised to the proper height by some type of elevator and then sluiced into place by a chute system. Alternatively, the concrete can be conveyed in hand-powered or machine-powered buggies or machine-powered conveyor belts, can be pumped through hose into place as a liquid, or can be deposited by crane and bucket. Members can even be precast and hoisted into place. The determination and use of the most profitable method are necessary to get the most out of the contract.

Usually, both the contractor's office and the superintendent will continue to use customary methods of operation—particularly on smaller jobs. Beneficial factors exist, such as easily and quickly obtainable equipment, labor which is used to handling the equipment, and cost experience which will foretell the production rate and size of crew which will be needed. Such advantages, however, may be added to in special cases by special answers, as indicated in the following examples.

A. A steel erector might be called in to stiffen existing beams with welded steel cover plates. He will ordinarily hire a steel journeyman, who is licensed, in order to obtain the necessary welding penetration between old and new members and will rent the necessary equipment. Yet possibly a licensed commercial welder of proper labor affiliation can be found. As part of his regular business, the welder should own a generator and leads for welding already mounted on a truck and should employ steady specialists in this one trade. His costs and subcontract price will be cheaper.

B. After studying a problem, a superintendent may be able to suggest methods of expediting the work. These may involve architectural or engineering design changes, ordering of material and equipment, changes in procedure or personnel, or other approvals and coordinated actions. For example, an inexperienced draftsman may use an architectural reference book to copy and detail the space between a concrete-footing top and a steel-column bottom baseplate. He shows the plate set on movable steel shims resting on the footing; the shims are to be set individually by surveying machine during construction to bring the plate to the correct height. Later, the space under the base is to be enclosed in an individual form, filled in with liquid grout (a concrete mixture), and worked on by passing a flexible steel strap back and forth under the base and through the grout. This procedure removes any entrained air bubbles and is necessary for heavily loaded columns when the load must positively be carried to the concrete footing below. This is a really good detail, and the architectural checker will undoubtedly pass it. But these are small columns carrying a light load, which does *not* warrant this individualized and expensive operation.

Here, what can and should be done is to request approval of architect or engineer of a revised and adequate, yet less expensive method of operation for lighter loads, with the erection saving predetermined with the steel erector and split in some fashion between buyer and general contractor. Thin steel plates (known as templates) are set by surveying machine and tapped down all at one time to the proper level of the bottom of the column plates, on stiff concrete grout. There is no necessity for formwork or hand strap motion as described above. The operation is done considerably in advance of steel erection, and the grout is allowed to harden. When the erectors and equipment do get on the job, the columns can be set immediately, with no expensive delay of crew and equipment while individual columns are held in place by the crane and set for height. There is also no further top-of-footing cost.

C. The plan may indicate what work is to be done but give no detail of what is actually involved. This situation frequently occurs in alteration jobs, when the designer wants to be contractually covered yet cannot specify all the job conditions because these will not be known until the section is actually opened up. Here the estimator for the construction firm must "guesstimate" a price for the work based on the limited knowledge available. The price must be conservative so that money will not be lost and yet not so conservative that the job will be overpriced and consequently not even obtained. In such a case, the superintendent is in a position to make money for his firm or to minimize loss.

For example, there is no question that shoring is required at a first-floor location, and it is distinctly noted on the contractual plan. But if the present floor construction proves strong enough to bear the concentrated load of the shoring safely, one cost will be developed. If the shoring load must be spread or carried through the opened floor to a firm cellar foundation below, another cost will be developed. The profit left over will vary.

D. An erection problem may develop. The laminated roof trusses of an auditorium are to be delivered by highway trucking facilities, unloaded by crane, and swung into place. They are carried by a masonry bearing wall and buttresses, which have to be preerected.

Due to the required lineal erection coverage of the auditorium, a long-length crane boom will be used from a setup adjacent to the street. Practically, the swing of the boom will be prevented by the presence of the front wall, and the wall will have to be left down until the roof members are in place. Should this involve any front-wall bearing locations, temporary erection shoring may have to be provided during erection. There may also be power lines over the crane location, which can be hazardous as well as damageable.

As indicated, the superintendent will have to foresee such contingencies. He is in a position legitimately to improve the profit possibilities of a contract. He can also protect his firm against possible losses.

E. Or such a simple thing as the order of doing work may be varied with considerable effect. In a choice between exterior and interior work, the former will always get the preference for a working day and the latter will be saved for bad weather. But there are other considerations. For example, other trades may be affected.

Before the tinsmiths can start their essential roof work, the carpenters must form and block for a built-in gutter. This work requires the erection of an outside scaffolding. And when this perimeter scaffolding covers locations where areaways or entrances project from the main structure, the scaffold will prevent for some time any further construction work there. It might, therefore, be advisable to complete masonry work outside of the main wall line before finishing other outer work.

And on interior partitions, the toilet rooms will affect the time of starting of lath and plaster, tile, plumbing fixtures, and other specialties, in addition to such trades as are regularly involved in normal work. There is no question about which interior walls should be erected first. Yet here the question arises as to what essential items must be built in with the wall so that they will be in place when needed.

1-7 *Timing of Operation*

In addition to the determination of method, men, and material requirements, there are problems connected with equipment and coordination which remain to be solved.

A. Erection is frequently dependent on special machines, such as an erection crane with a long main boom and a jib boom to reach from the place of truck delivery and unloading over the entire operation. There may not be many of these machines and skilled operators available on the rental market, and just when wanted they may not be obtainable. Or they may be available for a limited time only, subject to a prior obligation.

In a busy construction season, when manpower is in scarce supply, skilled erection crews to run such unusual machines may also be unavailable. Inexperienced men may be willing substitutes, but they may work scared and be accident-prone, placing an inordinate safety load on a foreman in such a potentially dangerous situation. The result of attempting to ensure safety by slowness of erection leads to overtime and premium pay so that the machine can finish and proceed to the next promised stop. Extra unfigured payroll, of course, means a necessary cost overrun.

Thus, timing involves making advance arrangements.

B. There is also the problem of wanting to install one trade but having to wait for another. As an example, from a boiler-room ceiling are suspended sheet-metal ducts carrying tempered air from an air-conditioning unit to diffuser and return locations. These members are hung from the construction above and are located within a few inches of a fire-retarding ceiling designed to be affixed to wire lath. The ceiling must be lathed and cement plaster finished before the ducts are installed so that the plasterer's trowels will work clear of obstructions which would prevent making a firetight job. Yet before this work is done, the roof may have to be on or a temporary structure may have to be installed on the floor above to protect men and material from the weather as the ceiling is being installed.

C. Advance planning should take cognizance of work rules in a particular locality. A local union may have a ruling that the laborer operating the mortar mixer and the men supplying mortar to the masons may start work ahead of time. They are permitted to get material loaded up on the working scaffolds prior to the customary working time. There is, however, a premium-time payment required. This additional payment may be well worthwhile when there are many masons involved who would otherwise lose expensive working time because of any delay in starting.

D. Timing of work may also involve the seemingly simple but cumulatively expensive operation of day-to-day management of labor. Rubbish accumulates from masonry walls, carpentry cuttings, plaster droppings, and many other causes. When the superintendent is obligated to keep the site clean, he could carry cleaning labor on his payroll every day the job continues. Such expense is partly avoidable. Instead, when necessary, he might have rubbish collected in isolated piles to prevent tracking dirt over the job. He would then hire labor at one time only at such later date as he has a dump trailer parked at the job so that he can wheel directly into it for disposal.

It will be noted that irrespective of the progress schedule, certain things must be done as soon as possible. As the job progresses, certain unfinished places become absolutely inaccessible and occasionally are workable only at considerable extra expense. Or damage may be caused later in the job to finishes or equipment already in place, and these may require refinishing or replacement. Or some preliminary work may have to be installed to allow other trades to move ahead.

Emphasis is placed upon alertness.

2

PREPARING
FOR PRODUCTION

The job site is now ready to be set up for the advent of that most expensive and irretrievable of costs—the labor-force payroll. Part of the money spent will be wasted unless adequate preparation is made. To forestall this loss, work is generally started with a few men and manpower is built up as production proceeds. Of itself, this method is no guarantee of efficiency but merely limits losses until a problem can be solved. Tools, equipment, material, and power and other utilities must be checked out as available on the job before men are brought in to work. Attention to detail in getting such items is most necessary.

2-1 *Material*

Supply houses and specialty companies provide the construction trade with the variety, quantity, grade, size, and cost of material which use and competition make advisable. It is necessary, of course, to order specifically in advance of need. To avoid delays due to weather, shortages, or prior preliminary delivery requirements, it is advisable not to proceed until the job is stocked up to some extent. Some construction material is carried on hand by the local hardware store in small quantities for the homeowner trade. But many specialties are not carried at all, prices are high (being based on retail rather than wholesale selling), and quantities are adequate only for emergency use.

It may be inexpedient to order large and complete quantities for immediate delivery. Possible contingencies are lack of storage space, need of payment for previous deliveries, and overordering. (The result of overordering is material left over to be paid for and then stored for use on some future job.) However, when something is to be color-matched, is hard to get for any reason, or must be specially manufactured, it pays to order in advance. Such material should be ordered in adequate quantity and with specified delivery dates.

Occasionally a construction-material salesman will offer a new development—to do something better or cheaper or both. Such a consummation does not happen often. Before being ordered in quantity, a sample of the item should be delivered to the job for testing under actual working conditions. For example, material to connect old cement floors to new ones or to featheredge patches together may adhere not only to the old construction but also to the journeyman's trowel during application. Waterproofing material used in mortar may cause efflorescence to appear on the wall. An additive used to prevent freezing in a concrete mixture in normal winter temperatures may cause an unacceptable loss of strength in the finished mass. The side effects will sometimes cancel out any advantages.

A close watch must be maintained on the material on hand. Not only must the quantity be adequate, but the material should be protected. Previously wet and frozen brick cannot be laid on an otherwise workable winter day and for this reason should be covered against the weather. Rough racks should be built to store reinforcing rods according to size so that they can be checked readily and will not be run over and bent. Bags of lime and cement and plaster stored in waterproof and heated shanties will remain usable. A small preventive cost returns a great deal of savings (particularly when men and equipment are delayed in completing a task because of lack of a few additional pieces of usable material).

Unfortunately, material stored on a job has a tendency to become diverted to other uses or to be spoiled. Lumber in long lengths or expensive-quality grades for particular locations will be thoughtlessly sawed up or used because it is available. Bags of cement, plaster, and common sand will go home with the workmen to patch or repair something. Glass in stock sizes will be broken. Because of this problem, unprotected material should not be stored on a job or accumulated too far in advance of when it is to be used.

The superintendent must also be mindful that he is responsible for the work and coordination of others. Necessary material of theirs should also be on the job. Coordination is particularly important when the work involves building in items that will be required by a trade which may not yet even be on the job. For example, pipe sleeves furnished by the mechanical trades may have to be installed by the concrete subcontractor in the basement walls. There may be a radiator niche which requires a steel angle to be built into a masonry wall to carry the top of the recess. Or fixture frames may be needed by the lather to build into the hung ceiling construction for the future use of the electrician.

Note that the subcontractor, too, must be given every opportunity to make money. His problems must be considered, so that he also can cut his payroll charges. From a purely selfish viewpoint, thoughtfulness pays.

2-2   Tools and Equipment

In some trades, the journeymen furnish all their tools and the employer provides only heavy machines. In other trades, custom or necessity causes the employer to supply everything. In either case, attention must be given to attaining the utmost production at the least cost by supplying what is necessary. Generally, if a machine can do the work, it pays to use it to supplement the work of a man. There are exceptions to this rule: Rentals may be high. When additional manpower is required to operate the machine, the expenses may be disproportionate to the savings. It is necessary to check.

The machines and equipment used in construction are of diversified types and involve many trades. The carpenter will need several sizes of hand-operated electric power saws for different thicknesses of material. (Additional blades are provided for rip or cross-grain sawing or for replacement when the teeth get dull.) The mason will require two mortar-mixer machines, allowing one machine to make regular laying mortar and the other to mix filling for concrete-block voids. (Such different compositions will be carried by the same laborers for the same operation to the masons making a bearing wall out of cement block and concrete fill.) The heating contractor will use several sizes of electrically driven pipe-threading machines.

Effective tools are not necessarily power tools. For the laborer used in every trade, there is a round-edge shovel designed for earth digging and moving and a square-edge shovel used for cleaning up a finished floor. Regardless of the trade, the right tool at the right time is essential.

But just being there is not enough. Tools must be in first-class operating condition. Motors should start immediately so as not to keep a whole construction gang idle waiting for action. Chisels should be sharp in order to penetrate the location efficiently. (Chisels used with sledges should not have the end broomed over; this might cause flying-steel accidents or absorb driving effort.) Electric-power connections require the correct adapters to fit outlets at the site.

When tools require power, fuel, or supplies of any nature, these must be on hand, and they take time to obtain. Temporary power and light outlets must be in place and connected to an electrical source. When a public utility does not exist in the area, the power source may have to be a motor-generator set (fueled and ready to go). Special cartridges for gun-type penetration tools should be purchased where available and brought on the job. Tanks of oxygen and acetylene for welding or burning should be rented and on hand.

Maintenance and inspection of tools and equipment are also problems. Construction workers, because of their status as transient employees, have little or no feeling of responsibility toward the material and equipment of their employer. Tools, equipment, and unpainted trim will be left exposed to the weather overnight. Fastenings will be wastefully used. Lumber will be uneconomically cut. Mortar tubs will not be cleaned after use. When company machines are sent to a job, they may have been overhauled and the oil changed, but it is no one's business, in a changing labor force, to check whether the oil should be changed or added to after constant operation in order to prevent a burned-out bearing. Or, without someone's interest and inspection, a scaffold plank may crack from misuse—and not be discarded. Expensive and dangerous conditions develop. Loss of construction time occurs. It is up to the superintendent to maintain control of this essential problem—for example, by appointing a regular employee to include inspection in his work.

Tools and equipment should be protected against misuse and theft. Concrete pumping machines, chutes, and ordinary tubs will need to be washed clean after every use. Small portable chain hoists should not be loaded beyond capacity, as this might result in a bent axle. An electric light-duty jackhammer should not be used when a large motor-operated air compressor and heavy-duty jackhammer is needed to break through mass concrete.

Ladders, wheelbarrows, and even motor-driven buggies should be chained together (with electric wiring removed). Picks, shovels, hoes, marking crayon (known in the business as *keel*), and similar material should be placed in a locked toolbox. Surveying machines, steel tapes, plumb bobs, and other tools used by the superintendent should be kept under lock and key in the job office.

Although the cost of thievery may be substantial, the loss of working time by not having the proper tools when needed is what hurts. Labor hours must be paid whether efficiently or inefficiently used, and time does not return.

2-3   *Equipment and Facilities*

Through common construction usage, the term *equipment* has come to mean almost anything furnished by an employer to advance production. He furnishes equipment for trades whose work he does directly. It may be masons' mortar tubs on detachable legs to vary the working height. It may be electrically driven diamond-blade saws to cut expansion joints in concrete floors. A vibrating roller may be required to tamp and compact fill. For contractual conditions for which he is responsible, such as safeguarding the premises, he must furnish barricades, streetlights, or warning signs.

Equipment may already be owned by the general contractor, may be rented for a particular job, or may be purchased. But use must be planned and arranged for in advance. Any equipment may be in demand at certain times, and supply is not unlimited. Arrival of equipment at the work site before or at the same time as tools and men is essential.

Conditions of equipment use occasionally require erection and installation of temporary structures as supplements. Supporting truck ramps will have to be built if the elevation of the work and the size and character of the operation warrant direct access. Or a hoist to supply buggies at different elevations may be required. Or a protective bridge to protect passersby may be needed before production starts.

The needs of the men themselves must be provided for in advance of their arriving on the job. Enclosures for natural or chemical toilets should be in place and operable. Drinking water, cups, and washup facilities should be available. Shanties for changing clothes and safeguarding them during working hours should be in place. First-aid kits, accident forms, names and directions for medical assistance must be on hand.

2-4   *The Labor Force*

When the superintendent is sure that preparations are complete, he will proceed to get the necessary manpower on the site. He should first check with his own organization and then with all other contractors to determine if the insurance or other contractual coverage is effective and satisfactory. Even when his firm has merely taken a brokerage contract and all work is to be subcontracted, he is, nevertheless, obligated to furnish labor for contractual necessities, such as cleaning, maintenance, and protection. Whether work of trades is to be done by the general contractor or by other contractors, manpower is, of course, required. Insurance coverage in the form of a written notice from an approved insurance company to the general contractor *must* be on hand for *all* contractors prior to their starting work.

The superintendent must make it his business to become acquainted with the local labor market. When help can be acquired readily, he may get men on a day's notice at a hiring hall. At other times, he may have to scour every possible source to locate tradesmen in advance. When there is a local union available, the number of its men employed on any job will necessarily depend on the regional employment-availability situation. When local men are unavailable, the contractor may use union men from an outside local organization with the permission of the local delegate. When there are several local unions in one district, they probably control different trades but may be in competition with one another in claiming the right to do certain work for men of one trade as against another. These jurisdictional disputes are adjudicated by representatives of the unions, who meet regularly to consider and settle any problems.

Requirements that enforce the employment of certain categories and rates of pay are part of the work rules which differentiate union from nonunion labor. The determination of the class of labor to be employed is the settled policy of the contracting organization, arrived at after consideration of many factors. For unionization, these include a belief in the right of men to unite for strength in the mass bargaining of their labor pay, rates, hours, and other conditions of work and benefits to be obtained. For nonunionization, these include a belief in the individual right of a man to work where, as, and for as much as he personally chooses and can bargain for.

There can be no price competition between companies employing different types of labor because there is no wage or work-rule comparison. There is, therefore, also no labor comparison since union men refuse to work with nonunion members. This custom includes all employees on a job. Both general contractor and subcontractor must employ the same class of labor.

If the job will proceed as a union operation, the superintendent will have to obtain knowledge of those local union work rules which he must observe. When he is under the necessity of hiring different trades, he must get information about all the trades involved. Such requests can readily be made to any of the building-trades unions available, which will, in turn, recommend the right party to contact.

Rules and regulations are far from uniform, even in adjoining districts. They may be purposely vague to meet variable conditions. Actually, the shop steward (who is appointed by the delegate) interprets the rules for the job and acts as representative for his union. By the nature of his job, he is a person of importance during the course of his employment. Because his rulings are generally favorable to his union position, he frequently causes his employer additional payroll expense. And because this exposed condition sometimes causes a certain amount of antagonism and strain between shop steward and employer, the employee's position is somewhat protected by his union. He can be laid off if his work is unsatisfactory, but his delegate is the judge of what is considered unsatisfactory work and has to be shown that vindictiveness was not involved. In practice, the shop steward is retained for the length of time that his trade is employed on the job. Because a certain amount of his working time is spent looking after the interests of the union, such time becomes necessary overhead, which cuts down production effectiveness.

2-5   *Management Problems*

Many of the same questions arise on every job:

A. A prospective piece of work always involves an estimate on the part of the person in authority as to how many men will be required to do the job. Some smaller number of workers will be used to start. Thereafter, the working force will be built up to obtain maximum supervision with a minimum of nonproductive overhead and a maximum number of producing journeymen with a minimum of supporting labor. This result is subject to balancing the operation so as not to be overmanned or undermanned in any category. Each extreme leads to loss of maximum production for the money expended.

B. Men who are about to finish a prospective piece of work must have another phase laid out for them and stocked with equipment and material. Local work rules may require a full day of pay for men who have started, regardless of how long they have worked. But efficient management and the minimizing of losses will want to utilize men who are working and available. Also, men who are to be laid off must be notified in advance so that they can clean their tools, pack up, and be paid before quitting time. As a practical matter, there is little incentive to do productive work during the necessary lapse of time between notification and ostensibly stopping work. Thus, there is a loss.

C. Some jobs require many men to start and only a few to finish. In the laying of a concrete floor, both cement finishers and laborers are necessary for spreading and leveling. But thereafter, although the finishers are busy for an extended period of time, the laborers have nothing further to do with completing the slab. If the laborers, therefore, can be shifted to some other concurrent job, considerable payroll time will be saved. Such work can be thought out and laid out in advance. For the trade in question, there are hand grading and tamping of earth for future work locations, stripping and cleaning for reuse previously poured and hardened concrete in forms, and backfill and tamping around completed concrete to form finished subgrade elevations.

D. As work progresses and needs for manpower vary, there comes a time when even keymen may have to be laid off. The superintendent may be unable to shift men from one job to another because of lack of work in the organization. Or because local manpower is available, he may be limited by union work rules as to who, of his most competent workers, can be taken from district to district. A working organization, which has taken time and effort to put together, may have to be broken up. This economic loss is a part of the business, a fact that is keenly realized and fought against. In addition, there is the chronic unavailability of all-around workmen. Thorough apprenticeship and grounding in a trade are not always available.

In trying to forestall this situation, the job superintendent should consult the office in advance. The latter may then attempt to take work at a price low enough to induce a job but still allow a break-even or better return on costs. Thus, in addition to new methods and materials of working, the construction sales-market situation can have an effect on prices and profits.

E. Supplementary considerations, such as taxes, become part of this situation. For example, social security laws oblige every employer to contribute a fixed percentage of each employee's wages, up to a maximum yearly earned wage. Once the employee has earned this maximum within a given year, there is no further contribution from either party for the tax year. But the estimator for any construction firm must figure transient labor conditions and cannot deduct a doubtful overage from a job price. For every estimated job, therefore, the social security contribution is figured as a percentage of the total wage estimate, and this amount is included in the quotation and obtained with the contract price.

Now, should the yearly earnings of the employee exceed that maximum set by law, both employee and employer can stop contributing for the balance of the tax year. Any excess time coming in the work period of a particular job, therefore, appears as an additional unfigured profit which accrues to the employer. This welcome profit increase occurs reasonably often with high-priced labor which is steadily employed. Here is a further reason for attempting to stabilize employment.

As a reverse situation, when employment is unsteady and short-time employees are used, an employer must contribute to their social security premiums regardless of what they have obtained previously (or will earn later) from others and, further, regardless of what they may be entitled to later as a rebate from the government for overpayment of tax. The employer gets no rebate. He must pay until the individual workman has earned on the employer's payroll the maximum which the government can obtain in a year. That is the law. For this reason, among others, short-term and discontinuous employment is economically unsound.

For a possible tax saving, as well as for reusing capable manpower, a record of names, addresses, and telephone numbers should be kept in order to reuse employees from job to job.

F. Grouping of effort as to time of work can also be a saver of money. As an example, demolition, cutting, rubbish removal, and any related functions of some one class of labor can be planned for *one economical period of payroll time.* The men will alertly note that there is considerable steady work planned for a relatively long period of employment. It is because of self interest that the men work efficiently and make money for their employer. They want to keep working in an uncertain business.

There are many, many management devices for obtaining good cost results using what one has on hand. Sometimes an apparent hindrance, such as having a hand-operated erection tool instead of motor-operated equipment, may work out to a cheaper final cost. The hand-operated erection pole, when used for a small number of pieces of light steel, requires only four journeymen and a foreman. The mechanical crane would require five men, plus a foreman, an engineer, and an oiler, plus a rental charge. The time spent would be one day for the small gang; and whereas less time would be spent in erection by the large gang, a minimum necessary one-day charge for their labor would result in the same payroll time and therefore in a higher cost for the same results.

There should be no preconceived ideas; rather, there should be a willingness to consider, compare, and then do what seems best.

2-6 *Payroll Supervision*

In any location where men are working, the superintendent must be there, too. There are always differing methods and procedures and, sometimes, minor antagonisms, even under competent foremen. The superintendent is responsible and must be on hand, since a guiding and forceful intellect is necessary. In addition, any particularly sensitive location will be one in which the pocketbook nerve of a firm is located. This is true for trades which are handled not only directly by the superintendent's organization but also by other contractors on the job.

A firm's own men tend to lapse into poor work habits—because of trying to save effort, wrongly directing energy, or playing along with wasteful habits to win favor. For example, a very common masonry practice is to allow mortar to remain in tubs or wheelbarrows over the lunch period; the hardened mortar is then partially reactivated by putting water into the material and mixing vigorously. Although, debatably, a small amount of mortar is saved, the quality of the work suffers and the masonry labor is increased. (The laborers do save some effort in throwing out and getting new material.) In another case, not enough mortar is mixed near quitting time. This is to avoid its being left over in the tubs at the end of the working day (and having to be cleaned out each evening as requisite additional work by the laborers). The mortar generally runs out considerably before the actual quitting time, and the result is a wasting of masons' and laborers' pay, which is given for a full day although a full day's productive work is not received.

Many of these habits are customs of years and can only be kept to a minimum, not eliminated altogether. One of these practices might be the essential ten-minute breakfast coffee break, in which one man is sent out to buy for all the men on a job. When men come to work without eating, such a practice is really necessary to keep up their strength. But when the time spent is overdone and the custom deteriorates from a necessity into a social function at the expense of the employer, the superintendent is responsible.

There are many locations where contingencies or work rules require additional payroll with some justification. For example, while a concrete floor slab is being poured, there should be a carpenter present to repair and maintain the installation in the event that the previously built wood form sags and leaks. This slab has reinforcing bars, previously laid by ironworkers. One man of this trade will be required on the payroll until the slab concrete is poured to ensure that the reinforcing does not shift in position during work and remains in the designed location.

Note that other contractors affect the cost of the job and its progress. In the case of the floor slab, the concrete cannot be poured until the electric conduit is placed in position by others, no matter how many waiting days (such as for the carpenter and ironworker) are required by other trades for contingent operations.

There is no justification for neglectful supervision and needless loss.

2-7   Payroll Records

The record keeping in connection with the hiring and firing of transient labor requires strict attention to a routine. There are a few details which must be handled correctly for every employee. Only by meticulous attention to such particulars can the bookkeeping be handled with a minimum of time spent and without the aggravation of incorrect totals. It is necessary, therefore, that the construction organization have its accountant set up a simple procedure for recording facts as men are employed. This method will take cognizance of deductions for local taxes, federal and union fund contributions, unemployment insurance, and other needs as they materialize.

Even if the aim is to transmit all information to the office for relative safety of computation and payment, situations requiring on-site payroll makeup and payoff will arise. Men may have to be laid off after working overtime, when the office is closed, or because of insubordination or some other contingency. The superintendent must enter these individual computations as they occur in order to know what is required and to keep his office in touch with the current situation. There may be a local union rule calling for the inclusion of a percentage of prepurchased stamps in every pay envelope. This device allows men who move from employer to employer to accumulate a vacation fund, a sick benefit, or a pension. Sometimes there are penalties for incorrect payment *and also for not paying on time*, plus unnecessary further overhead in straightening out such matters.

The superintendent, therefore, should be furnished by his firm with a certain amount of money and with payroll tables for various rates of pay to enable him to reckon the net amount to be paid. He should also be supplied with the forms used in obtaining the requisite tax credits (such as number of dependents) and other withholding deductions, with envelopes, and with duplicate record computations to be signed and to act as money receipts. He must be sure that his office instructs him in its requirements and procedures so that his emergency measures will match the office records. The fund should be replenished constantly to maintain its full value.

2-8   *Layout*

Proceeding simultaneously with labor, equipment, and material arrangements is the establishing of the actual construction line and grade. Especially when, seemingly, there is nothing tangible to start with, this process is deservedly fascinating to both experienced individuals and the novice in construction. The technique for checking the location of initial points and elevations is of utmost importance. Success or failure depends upon initial correctness. Succeeding intermediate dimension points are added to or subtracted from starting points.

As with all property rights, ownership of the location is asserted and enforced by the society to which men subscribe and under which they live. There is always a starting point, going back to some original, assumed granting authority. The right to a particular location is established by an original survey of the property with respect to certain landmarks and elevations. This process develops the contours and boundaries of the area, and a recording of the survey details and of successive transfers and transactions establishes a chain of title and legal encumbrances dating back to the starting date. To assist in creating reasonably permanent and fixed locations for establishing property rights in an impermanent environment for a man-made system, recourse is had to fixed reference points known as *datum points*. Because datum points are interrelated, supporting points will reestablish one which is lost. Such datum points may already exist when a property is developed. These points, among others, may be a cross mark cut into a sidewalk, a verticle arrow cut into a curb, or a horizontal line established by the invert (bottom) of a sewer manhole.

In any case, the designer in the course of his development will establish on the plans the linear and height dimensions that are required for the particular job. These dimensions are referred back to a plot plan made up in accordance with the ownership deed description of the property. This description will also be used by a surveyor, who physically establishes on the site any points or elevations, if such are necessary, to delineate the actual property location and the height starting locations where they do not previously exist. Note that elevations are as important as lineal dimensions in carrying out the concept of the designer. Thereafter, as part of his job, the surveyor will furnish a plan showing where and in what form all locations are established. One of the first jobs on a site of anyone representing a contracting organization is physically to protect such survey marks with small solid fencing or other barricades so that they are not run over, lost, or shifted in any manner.

The layout process is part of the stock-in-trade of the competent superintendent. He may do it himself, or he may use others, but he must know layout technique and be responsible for constructing exact locations in accordance with general and detailed plans.

The technique must be studied and learned under an experienced teacher. There are sound reasons for every precaution taken. Instruments used, such as the transit and level, go out of adjustment or are inadvertently knocked out. Steel tapes sag and do not indicate linear feet and inches exactly unless corrected. They must be cleaned after every use to remain legible and usable. Even the customary 6-foot folding wood rule should be properly opened and closed to ensure that it is not broken just when most wanted. Mistakes must always be anticipated, and precautionary checking taken.

Mistakes in setting corners, in widths of footings, in heights, in the location and screw-thread-length dimension above a set bearing elevation for anchor bolts, and in the location and insert dimension of beam pockets required in new bearing walls are typical errors of omission and commission. Such costly mistakes are caused by a lack of familiarity with every detail of the job. A conduit must be set up in floors and walls long before it is built in. Wood floor beams, supporting heavy tile floors, should be provided with cleats and cross planking at the proper dropped elevation to take deafening (filling) concrete. Sprinkler piping openings must be left in walls and floors as they are erected.

Errors in such work are difficult to correct, costly in wasted time and money, and damaging to the confidence placed in the estimator, superintendent, and supervisor.

In any trade, good layout is a sign of a man who knows his business. A tinsmith cutting into ceiling ducts for a diffuser location must be accurate the first time, with no snipping and filling. In carpentry, the pitch of the sloping roof beams must be exactly the same each time so that the finished roof surface is flush and uniform. In erecting miscellaneous iron stairs, the starting and finishing rough risers of the undertread must be variously dimensioned so that the finished risers will all be the same.

But any workman, no matter how competent, needs the forethought and effort of the superintendent. Future metal windows require that masonry openings be left with adequate space on all sides for insertion and blocking. Formed-metal roof gutters will have to be mounted on shaped framework material previously built into the structure. Recessing of medicine cabinets, while framing partitions, requires foreknowledge of the rough size and method of application for the type of unit which has been ordered. Such details may be given on the plans. Or information may be outlined from approved catalog cuts or shop details which are sent to the job or to other interested parties or at the request of the superintendent. Every plan or document of any nature on a construction job carries information. Details should be given close attention and used.

Depending on who is doing the contract work, the superintendent will arrange for men to install the beginning footings and walls.

After permanent footings are set and walls are laid to establish corners and elevations, a "survey in possession" will provide a check by a competent surveyor. When a permanent mortgage will be required to refinance the final structure, this procedure may also be required by the buyer, who will pay for the survey.

3

CONTINUING THE JOB

All the preceding effort is aimed at getting started in a manner which will allow obtaining the greatest possible profit from a job. Such action is taken with full knowledge that erosion of profits does take place, and constant vigilance is needed throughout a job and in the office.

3-1 *Some Sources of Loss*

Some of the many possible sources of loss are noted in the following paragraphs.

A. The supervision may be at fault. As an example, location stakes at each end of a trench to be excavated for a footing and a wall may be properly placed, but layout is not completed until further work is done. Regardless of how experienced the machine operator is, the excavated trench will tend to wander out of line or up and down. This result will lead to the operator's having to retrace part of his travel. There may then be loss of machine and payroll time, excess excavation, backfill and material to be replaced, and sometimes, not enough excavation or other work done, requiring hand work at a later time.

Marking out a line on the ground with powdered lime, following a stretched string, or using a surveyor's transit is a help. And as height itself is important, flagged and protected grade stakes, set for the machine operator, will take but little additional layout time. But the best manner of handling such situations is to give them personal attention. If the superintendent is right on top of the work, he is checking constantly and can immediately correct any operational error. Men should do what is marked out for them. Unfortunately, they do not always follow instructions. Knowing this, there is no excuse for failure to check work as actually done.

B. Loss can be caused by carelessness. A plasterer's laborer, mixing material on an upper floor, may leave the water-barrel hose feed flowing and unattended. The overflow, running down to the basement, may flood an electrician's conduit in which operating wires have been pulled. The resultant short circuit will cause damage and time loss.

Or nut-and-bolt fasteners may be left out at night, unused. The threads rust together, and the union becomes unusable.

Or a trenching machine may cut through a location where a new construction waterline has been installed but has not been protectively staked.

Carelessness in the operation of a machine can be costly. A caterpillar tread may cut up unprotected sidewalk and finished lawn, which will require later surface repair. Or a steel erection crane may contact unprotected low overhead electric wires, electrocuting a workman touching both the charged frame and the ground.

There is no end to what can and does happen. The only possible help is forethought and attention to detail—and constant alertness to everything that is going on.

C. Pilferage is present on some jobs. Equipment, material, and tools disappear. The cost of a missing object may, in itself, not be large, but the cumulative effect of a series of losses can amount to a considerable sum. And the really serious matter is that an item may then be missing at the particular time it is needed. Care is worthwhile. If something is chained or locked in place, the average workman will not jeopardize his job and reputation by deliberately trying to make off with it.

A cheap chain and padlock passed through ladder rungs, wheelbarrow spokes, or shovel handles will deter most men on a job from taking these tools. But material in bulk, such as bags of cement, sheets of plywood, or sand, which can easily be loaded into cartons, is more difficult to control on a job. The workmen's psychology seems to be that since there is so much of it, a little will not be missed. Such items are controllable only by clearly and definitely establishing a job rule and publicizing it: *No con-*

struction material is to be removed from the site. This dictate must be enforced.

Of course, in some neighborhoods a watchman may be necessary.

D. Specification evasion does occur. This type of dishonesty is sometimes due to the specification writer himself. The latter cannot know every trade and relationship completely and, therefore, may adopt some previous wording which does not apply. The wording offers loopholes and substitutes, which are taken advantage of in the bidding. The superintendent must guard his organization and obtain what is aimed for and bought.

If the job copy of an office purchase order indicates that a specific item has been ordered, that is what should be furnished on the job. Regardless of whether a cheaper item will do the job satisfactorily, it may *not* be installed unless the construction organization has approved the substitution and has obtained the cost reduction to which it is entitled. On its part, the construction organization must be strictly honest. In most cases, if the buyer is advised through his architect or engineer that a good substitute is contemplated at a definite money saving to the buyer (if approved), such approval will be forthcoming. The goodwill built up is worth a lot of money. As a practical matter, if the approval is not obtained, no saving will pay for a loss of faith when a corrupt action is discovered.

Occasionally a subcontractor will attempt to evade the specification. For example, a grade A glass may be called for but a grade B is furnished and installed at a money saving. These grades, of differing price, are factory-determined by the manufacturer, dependent on the physical characteristics of the sheet of glass, as sold. Allowable bubbles, scratches, or other defects and production-finish allowances are taken into account by the manufacturer's plant inspector, who affixes a label giving the marketable grade of the material. If this label is removed after job receipt and installation, it is difficult to tell a difference in grade.

The job superintendent must be alert to check promptly any and all grade-marked material and delivery tickets sent to the job. The supplier's original records may be relied on to give the facts. When an unauthorized substitution has been made, an option then exists of accepting the material with knowledge of what was installed and receiving a definite credit from the subcontractor or of having the substandard material taken out and replaced as specified.

Obtaining material and workmanship *as bought* is as much a part of the construction profit picture as getting the job itself.

E. Plan changes do sometimes occur without permission. Because structural safety may be involved, this is both a dangerous and an uncommon practice. The criminal liability involved makes this an unusual stratagem.

For example, a suspended concrete floor system is constructed 4 instead of 5 inches thick, as indicated on the original plan and as estimated. Both the equipment and the material involved are considerably decreased, as is the amount of installation labor time. The strength, however, is also lessened. Again, it is the job superintendent who guards the well-being of his construction company. He must be alert to bring any such attempt to light. The action taken will depend on the particular circumstances involved.

F. Items of work may not have been finished before the men and material have to be moved to another location. This action may be taken for a very good reason, but it results in payroll loss since men lose working time by job movement. The move may be necessary because of other essential work progressing overhead with another trade, with consequent danger to men working underneath. The situation necessitates their moving for safety and returning later.

Or work may have to be discontinued on a scaffold so that the frame can be raised as work progresses upward. In this case, lost motion might be minimized by having several adjoining scaffolds available and loaded so that the men can move from one to the next.

Or there may be a simultaneous necessity for several similar jobs, with only a limited number of men available. A boiler-room wall may have to be erected to support piping; a first-floor vestibule wall may have to be raised to close up the building; and toilet-room block partitions may have to be installed as a base for tiles. All this work may be needed at about the same time with only a few men to do it. This will result in some lost motion and lost profit.

G. Loss may be caused by ignorance. On one job, the metal flashing members over the window heads were carefully provided and built into the masonry wall with the necessary protrusion for later waterproofing. The summer employment of a young relative as boss of the small isolated job led to his snipping off the projections to make the job look trim and one to be proud of. This was a very laudable but expensive ambition. Every organization should train men, but under strict supervision.

H. A telephone call in advance will alert a subcontractor as to job progress. It is necessary for him to have men, material, and equipment on the job to start correlative work immediately.

A union shop steward should be alerted in advance to obtain manpower for the following day. Otherwise, assuming that men are available, there will be an unnecessary loss of time for men traveling to the site of the work from the hiring hall during working hours.

Advance planning and action are necessary on every job. New locations should be stocked with material and equipment prior to moving workmen. Location layouts should be made and checked. Every possible interested trade should be advised and asked to cooperate. Foreseen problems do not usually become emergencies, and spending money properly leads to saving money. (Old stuff, but still applicable.)

I. Work being consciously slighted to save labor and material is another source of loss. In masonry, header brick holding the wall together gives strength to the wall. In rare instances, headers may be consciously omitted to save a small amount. That the wall is weakened and may later become defective and crack under use means nothing to a venal subcontractor, provided he can be paid before discovery. Or the nailing of a floor in a carpentry subcontract may be the minimum to hold the floor together, without the necessary number of nails to give holding power and to prevent displacement. Or expensive plaster may be mixed with too much relatively inexpensive sand to make a cheap but quickly deteriorating material.

The best time to forestall expensive replacements is to check work as it is being built.

3-2 *Dealing with Job Conditions*

On every job, conditions arise and must be corrected as work is done. These unforeseen contingencies require expeditious and economical solutions—and not necessarily by the most obvious means. Such circumstances seem to recur with regularity. *They also involve responsibility and payment.*

A. *Existing Site Conditions*

The excavation of one old building site for a new foundation uncovered:

1. An unmarked city water main under high pressure within the new basement location

2. An old cistern excavation and leaching field within the new planned parking-lot location

3. Masonry walls (originally figured as openable at the joints by a hand wrecking bar) with cement mortar so hard that the brick, and not the joints, had to be split piece by piece for jackhammer and air-compressor demolition

4. The intersection of a constantly flowing subterranean stream, which necessitated collecting and automatically pumping water out of a sump pit

These items involve payments and responsibilities among the buyer and his agent, the architect, the general contractor, and probably other subcontractors. Responsibility and cost vary with the individual contract documents and in many cases cannot be estimated accurately in advance of opening up. Provision should appear in every contract for fairly adjudicating a site condition and confirming the judgment in writing. The cost can be appreciable as a profit-and-loss factor.

When the language of a specification or a request to bid is so broad that it obligates a general contractor to responsibility for anything and everything, the documents must be changed before a contract is accepted. The buyer needs the contractor as well as the latter needs the work— but not work at a loss.

B. *Existing Structural Conditions*

The particular job may entail the resting of shoring or even concentrated loads of new building material on an old intermediate floor slab which was never designed for such a concentrated load. It may be necessary to shore or otherwise strengthen the questionable floor down to a solid foundation to carry the construction load safely. Again, who pays?

C. *Incorrect Material Deliveries*

In one case, a large steel girder arrived on a job with some of the holes for a bolted connection obviously mispunched and then repunched in the correct position, a half-bolt diameter away. Clearly, the bearing bolts would not support the designed weight and might fail by crushing. The member could have been left on the delivery truck and sent back to the shop for correction, but this would have been very costly in loss of time. A steel-erection foreman, a six-man gang, an engineer, an oiler, and an erection crane, plus the truckmen and trailers, were waiting to unload and erect.

Consultation by the superintendent with the steel-subcontractor foreman developed the information that the beam connection could be, and would be, repaired in place with no loss of time. This expedient was adopted. The girder, as delivered, was erected in place, and the connecting beam was temporarily hand-clamped to it near the proper location but apart from the defective connection. After the erection crew and equipment had completed this section and moved on with no delay, one additional man reamed out (drilled accurately) a large-size hole encompassing the 1½ diameters of both the girder and the beam framing into it. Thereafter, the larger-size holes were filled in with especially large-diameter machine bolts, which, of course, gave greater size and strength than required. Note that there was no loss of erection time and a minimum of money loss for the subcontractor directly responsible.

D. *Errors in Plans and Specifications*

When a number of trades are involved in the same location, there are often noticeable differences in the plans and specifications of the different trades. A heating plan, for example, may show a vent duct at a particular location on a ceiling, while the corresponding separate electric plan indicates a ceiling light outlet at this point. Something has to move.

Or a hung-ceiling plan will show an access door and a ladder in such an inaccessible location that the crawl space under the roof could not be reached for maintenance.

Or a boiler-room door should be changed from an unrated door to a rated and fire-labeled door to reduce the yearly fire insurance premium.

In any such case involving architectural or engineering functions, judgment, and payment, the designer must issue a modification order before any work is done.

E. *Conflicting Operations*

The work of one trade necessarily affects that of others. For example, suppose that the temporary electric service being supplied during construction is adequate. As the construction advances, however, and the large permanent service is connected through a new switchboard, there will be a period when no service will be available due to the changeover. This would cut off power for apparatus, such as sump pumps, electric lights, or room heaters, which necessarily must continue to operate. It would also forestall the operation of subcontractors' hand electric tools, such as power saws, drills, or electric hammers. A portable generator may have to be installed in advance of the turnover for essential electric power.

Or the plumbing contractor may have to extend a vent pipe through the roof to equalize the air-pressure changes in the system during use of the fixtures. This piping installation must be completed, however, before the roofing contractor arrives to start work. There can be no delay of the tinsmiths in installing the requisite flashing around the piping through the roof.

In any case, the superintendent must anticipate such needs. He must prevent loss of construction time for his own firm and for his subcontractors.

3-3 *Overcoming Interferences*

The avoidance of loss of time by the subcontractors is worthy of effort. If subcontractors foresee that they will make money out of a contract, the general contractor will get a good job and good bids on the next job. If the subcontractors are losing money, they may tend to skimp and save wherever possible. As a matter of self-interest, therefore, the superintendent should help them make money if possible. Overcoming obstacles and interferences for subcontractors is a method of gaining friends and securing cooperation—and, of course, of speeding up the job.

When the designers for different trades are not the same (and even when they are the same), errors will occur despite close coordination. A space conflict might happen easily in a room occupied by a number of trades, all trying to get their work completed in a limited space. For example, an equipment room is designed for the building heating and ventilating apparatus and ducts, the electrical switchboard and conduit, the water main, the sprinkler system, and the sump pump. Every mechanical trade will be involved, including three different sets of engineering plans. Each trade is entitled to consideration in working out the mutual problems involved, in order to obtain maximum facility of installation.

In a specific case concerning an equipment room, after consultation with all trade foremen involved, a practical solution appeared to be that of obtaining more vertical space than the plan indicated. This revision allowed the new runs of ducts and piping to pass at different elevations. Acting as an intermediary, the job superintendent contacted the architect and explained the situation. The solution involved no extra work or extra orders since only design headroom was to be decreased. After consideration, the architect agreed and commented, "Maintenance workers at the sides of the room will have to be a maximum of 7 feet 2 inches in height; elsewhere they can be 8 feet 0 inches tall."

The superintendent will also have to take such action for any part of the entire job as is called for in overcoming interferences for any trade. A hornet's nest in the attic of an alteration job will stop all work until quick recourse to a drug store produces a can of poison spray for exterminating the insects.

3-4   *Subcontract Relationships*

The subcontractors are members of the construction force supplied to the superintendent for the purpose of producing a profitable job. Their proper coordination and progressive functioning are necessary to achieve this result. But also necessary is their realization that they have contracted to do certain work for which the general contractor is primarily responsible. He has a direct interest in their quality of workmanship and timing of installation. His supervision is necessary.

The job superintendent is the person in charge for the general-contracting organization. He should promptly receive copies of every subcontract and order (such copies customarily omit prices as being confidential information). The wording of these contracts and orders is of importance as modifying the plans and specifications in accordance with the negotiations of the construction-office purchasing agent. Vital information will be given, such as delivery dates, required tests, payment requirements, and similar mutual obligations. Details will be outlined of any specification variations to be furnished. Subcontractors will be asked to do what they have contracted to do. They are not expected to do more or less.

With these documents goes a purchase progress schedule. This is a simple time schedule to outline the date and manner of delivery and installation for all trades which have been settled upon and purchased by the office personnel. As additional subcontracts or purchases are negotiated, the information is promptly transmitted to the job. This key schedule is made up with the master progress schedule as a basis. It takes account of shop drawings, approvals, seasonal shortages, and other delays. It is, of course, susceptible to changes, follow-up or other means of expediting, and additional action to correct an error or supply an omission.

Because of the volume of money involved, the physical method to be used by the superintendent in checking requisitions should be the subject of considerable forethought by the office organization. The superintendent's working hours are heavily engaged, and the purchasing agent should attempt to word documents to give a simple checking procedure. A preliminary requisition breakdown for approval can be obtained from every subcontractor immediately after contract signing (Figure 3-1). These requisition breakdowns are approved by the architect in advance

---

PROJECT

ARCHITECT

SUBCONTRACT (PLUMBER)

1. Contingency for repairs to present installation	Price
2. Outside storm drains	Price
3. Roughing installed, tested, and approved	Price
4. Pipe installation tested and covered	Price
5. Fixtures set and approved	Price
6. Sump pump installed and operating	Price
7. Areaway and floor drains set and wall hydrants set	Price
8. Chemical job toilet installed and removed	Price
Contract total	Price

figure 3-1. Requisition breakdown for subcontract.

Description	Material	Labor	Total
Project			
Architect			
General Contractor			
1. Bond	-	-	Price
2. Temporary fence, 800 lin ft @	Price	Price	Price
3. Job sign	Price	Price	Price
4. Supervision, 32 weeks @	-	Price	Price
5. Field office, telephone, stenographer	Price	Price	Price
6. Excavation (a) Strip and clean 450 cu yd @	Price	Price	Price
(b) Excavate and trench 800 cu yd @	Price	Price	Price
7. Concrete (a) Footing forms 4,000 sq ft @	Price	Price	Price
(b) Footing concrete 160 cu yd @	Price	Price	Price
(c) Slab on ground 8,000 sq ft rein. mesh @	Price	Price	Price
280 cu yd stone conc. @	Price	Price	Price
9,600 sq ft finish @	Price	Price	Price
8. Carpentry and millwork, subcontract	-	-	Price
9. Finish hardware, allowance	-	-	Price
10. - - - - others	-	-	Price
	Contract total		Price

figure 3-2. Requisition breakdown for general contract.

and are established as a basis upon which percentage-completion observations by the superintendent may be determined and requisition prices arrived at with a minimum loss of working time.

For the subcontractor, requisitions are cleared with the superintendent so that disputes are ironed out in advance of typing invoices. Thereafter, there is no time loss. For the general contractor, there is always the power of the purse behind the superintendent's actions; his authority is therefore seldom questioned. As such requisition records become payable, of course, they are promptly forwarded to the office and become part of the job file for succeeding applications. A general contractor's requisition is shown in Figure 3-2.

To ensure good relationships with subcontractors, the job superintendent will help them at every opportunity to arrive at a profitable job. He will consult their representatives in advance concerning delivery and installation. He will arrange good working conditions, such as temporary light, a clean and unobstructed space for working, and easy access for materials. He will coordinate all trades for mutual action. He will try to accumulate items for work so that labor can be fully utilized when it is on the job.

When installation requirements entail the matching together of the work of several trades, he will ensure that it is done as needed. The window-frame erector needs carpentry jamb blocking. The plumber requires metal hangers to be built in as part of the new partition. The tile journeyman wants a cement scratch coat on wire lath as a base for the application of the ceramic ware. The superintendent acts to coordinate the efforts of all.

But the superintendent must realize that the interests of the subcontractors and his own interests are not always the same. He must think for himself and for his firm and must require complete cooperation from his subcontractors in properly expediting the job. Should such participation not be forthcoming when requested, the superintendent should immediately call the attention of his organization to the situation for follow-up. Upon job completion, he should definitely notify the office purchasing agent of the subcontractor's actual job performance. In future dealings, a low-price subcontractor can be a loss rather than an asset.

There are such things as subcontractors who skimp on work. This practice takes many forms. The dishonest subcontractor will change both plans and specifications when a saving in outlay is possible. He may change or even eliminate parts of the plans if his experience indicates that the cheapened revision will function safely and will stand up unnoticed until the final payment on the contract can be obtained. He may leave undone contract work that is basic to several trades if he believes that someone else will do it to expedite the job. Such dishonesty and delay debase any contractual relationship between subcontractor and general contractor. It should not be permitted.

3-5 *Material to Be Built In*

On every job, material for a particular trade is required to be built into work in progress by other trades. To avoid loss of time and money and a later blemished appearance, it is essential that such material be available when required, plus information for setting and installation, if necessary.

Built-in wall radiator niches require the installation of angle-iron lintels to carry the closing construction across the top of the niche. Wall bearing plates for structural steel must be built into the wall under construction not only at the correct height but with the proper dimension allowed for the height, depth, width, and erection clearance of the beam to be inset. Sleeves must be built into the construction for the future passage of piping at precise locations. Electric conduits must be laid out and placed in position so that they will be properly positioned and enclosed in slab construction when floor arches are poured.

These details, particularly, will be shown or indicated on architectural or shop details sent to the superintendent. On the handrail detail of the miscellaneous iron contractor will be shown inserts to fit the rail and to be built into the floor or wall. On the drawings of the metal grilles to ventilate the attic, the carpenter will be shown the necessary cutting and setting. On the erection plan of the steel contractor will be shown the column anchor-bolt details and the locations for the concrete footings.

Emphasis must again be placed on safeguarding such stored material. Not only is intrinsic value involved, but also loss of time because of unavailability. Items such as hardware in shipping containers, full cans of adhesive, or plumbing fittings are easily gotten away with. Long stock lengths of material stored on the sides of driveways to be job-fabricated can be ruined by being run over by passing trucks and equipment (see Section 2-1).

There are, of course, many more details involved. The party in charge must study the problem and confer with all available trade foremen. Contact of subcontractors and other suppliers by the superintendent and follow-up by the office are obligatory. Omissions are unnecessary and expensive for everyone.

3-6   Buyer-Contractor Relationship

During construction, the plans (obscure to the layman) materialize into actuality. A buyer frequently wants something changed or something added to the plans and specifications which were originally prepared but perhaps not completely visualized by him. Yet when the bills come due later, he may be disinclined to pay for such work. He may use the specious premise that his original contract called for a complete job and entitled him to such items or that the work was not properly authorized —or some other self-interested excuse for not paying.

Of course, as in purchasing anything under a delayed contract, the buyer should get what he bought, but he is not entitled to unilaterally obtain more than he bought at the expense of the seller. The contract is based on the work shown and specified, and that is the only way a lump-sum price can be arrived at.

Yet good relations between purchaser and contractor are of such value that every effort must be made to avoid strain and bad feeling. Good relations can be attained by the job superintendent by keeping the buyer out of temptation. The superintendent does not have to refuse requests and can even adopt a sympathetic attitude toward their development. He can and should act only, however, if he receives *a written order from one with authority to act for the owner*. This order should give details or a plan of the work involved, the price, the time, and anything else pertinent to the change. The superintendent's reason for so acting is very simple. He is on the site only to do the work contracted for. Anything else must be presented to his office and authorized. This method allows his office the final say in accepting or rejecting or changing an extra order and permits entry of the prospective transaction so that it will not be overlooked or wasted. There have been cases in which the person in authority who has verbally given out an extra order is not present at the time of completion of a job or denies a verbal authorization.

Extra orders offer an opportunity to improve the percentage of profit, although this contingency is rarely figured in an original bid. The buyer is presumed to have gotten the lowest possible price for his own benefit. In the give-and-take of doing business, it is, therefore, up to the contractor, in turn, to increase legitimately such portion of any overage as is possible. Should the buyer, without compulsion, decide that he wants something, he should get it at a price which will not be at the expense of the contractor.

Suggestions to the buyer's representative might amplify this source of business. During the course of drawing up the plans and specifications, the designers are confronted with so many problems to solve that some small improvement will possibly be overlooked. For example, in the outer vestibule of a commercial building, the ceiling was to be inexpensively decorated by using square perforated sheets to form a honeycomb effect, which would also allow recessing the light bulbs between the hung ceiling and the floor above. Unfortunately, the vestibule then could not be kept warm because of the constant leakage of heated air to the ventilated space above the honeycomb. A simple and inexpensive cure would be to construct an inverted-dish effect of fire-proof board over the perforated ceiling and light bulbs so as to retain the heated air. This solution was suggested, priced, and adopted.

Another type of change might be a suggestion for decreasing maintenance or overhead expense. The fire and liability insurance premium rate is established by inspection after the structure is completed and will, thereafter, be in effect repetitively for years. A particular installation may have something simple and inexpensive added during construction which will decrease the yearly premium cost by a sum out of proportion to the small first cost involved—for example, a fire extinguisher on a wall bracket or a safety pipe fence adjoining a parking-lot exit door from a factory. In this case, the small profit involved is far outweighed by the large advantage to the contractor in establishing a reputation for intelligent thoughtfulness.

Occasionally the buyer will divide his construction project among a series of prime contractors as well as a general contractor. When a lengthy time period (*lead time*) is required for the design, approval, obtaining, and fabrication of a structural-steel framework, a high-speed elevator installation, a special fire-alarm system, or something similar, the buyer may purchase these trades separately. They are very much part of the complete project and must progress under one supervision and in unison with all others. If their work were included in the contract and responsibility of the general contractor, he would be paid for their supervision. But unless the buyer furnishes his own supervision, there is no influence over the prime contractors. Should such a circumstance materialize, there is an opportunity to acquire an additional supervision fee with little additional overhead. The general contractor would be the obvious coordinator.

3-7   *Safety Practice*

In addition to the humanitarian reasons for safeguarding workers and job visitors, there is a very practical aspect to maintaining job safety. The compensation insurance rating (also used in estimating) varies with the actual experience in every trade and occupation as developed by an individual firm. The fewer the number of accidents in any trade rating classification, the less the premium that will be charged. As considerable payroll may be involved in a classification, a premium change up or down can have appreciable results (very noticeable in estimating).

The time to think about safety is before the inception of a job—and every day thereafter. Accidents can happen in so many ways. The jagged edges of a cold chisel, mashed over by repeated blows of a maul may break off and be the cause of permanent eye injury from a flying piece of steel. A concrete-form stripping job, improperly performed, may cause a rusty-nail puncture, blood poisoning, and death. Holes in floors, when not barricaded, can cause serious accidents and fatalities. These cases, unfortunately, are not exaggerated and do happen.

It should seem obvious, but many jobs do not have even a rudimentary kit of first-aid supplies to clean out and sterilize cuts, wash out eyes, protect wounds from dirt, and offer some relief until help can be obtained. Medical articles should be among the first essentials to be sent to any job. This action should be followed up by a prominently placed listing of who is available in the neighborhood to reach immediately for medical service.

Accident report forms and carbon paper should also be on the job before the first employees arrive. A duplicate of a report may have to go immediately to a hospital or to a doctor with an ambulance call. An employee job-card file giving the home address, telephone number, next of kin, and social security number is invaluable for emergency use. A card should be made out for each employee when he starts work.

The office should be notified immediately by telephone of any accident which has been handled in any way, followed immediately by written detail as called for.

Many localities have safety laws covering obvious conditions. These may include requirements for planking over skeleton steel floor framing, enclosing unfinished stairwells, or erecting scaffolding with no unsupported ends of planking. But exterior doors and windows may be left open, a job wire fence may be lapped so that jagged edges can injure passersby and tear their clothing, or the loose storage of form lumber on an upper floor may allow wind damage by permitting the material to be blown off.

Because the law protects children and passersby from the consequences of their own actions as well as those of others and because public liability claims are limited in the amount for which insurance companies will write them, an award may exceed the amount of coverage. An additional damage claim will then be levied, which may be serious in its effect on the contractor involved

Again, *constantly thinking and acting for safety is the only way to attain it.*

Part of safety procedure is to prepare in advance for job mishaps. Not only doctors and hospitals but also police and building departments should be listed. A water main may freeze and crack open, be damaged by an excavating shovel, or leak in some manner and flood the site. Or an oil burner may stop functioning in the middle of winter and need immediate attention to prevent a freeze-up. Or a short circuit of some nature may blow a power fuse and render inoperative every electric machine and light on the site. The superintendent should keep an up-to-date address and telephone list of subcontractors' offices and a list of emergency numbers for after working hours. There should also be a list of addresses and telephone numbers of all job foremen. The complete list should be carried home at night and kept safe with wallet and automobile driver's license. Such precaution is invaluable when the need arises. A duplicate should be prominently posted in the job office for the use of others.

4

JOB AND OFFICE

The job and the office are essential to each other. Each is a mutually dependent part of the organization. Each does some share of the work, makes contacts, transmits information. The job functions primarily in a productive capacity. The office functions as the location of management authority and guidance. But these functions overlap one another to the extent that certain information and action are of interest to both job and office.

4-1 *Communications*

Transmission of information should be given the importance to which it is entitled. Interoffice memos of the kind shown in Figure 4-1—full-size, printed sheets of paper in duplicate—will not be treated as unimportant scraps of paper and lost. The printing will act additionally as a reminder. The cross-section backing is a standard stock, which can be readily purchased, and enables formation of sketches to clarify the memorandum. A copy is retained by the maker, so that there can be no question about what information was furnished on a particular day.

43

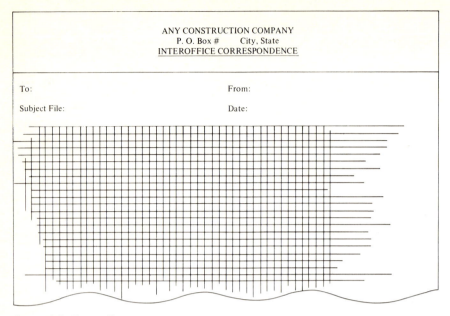

ANY CONSTRUCTION COMPANY
P. O. Box #   City, State
INTEROFFICE CORRESPONDENCE

To: From:

Subject File: Date:

figure 4-1. Interoffice memo.

Using the interoffice memo as a record to be filed, information will be directed both ways. The office will transmit to the superintendent changes of plans and specifications, progress schedules, extra orders, or directives of any nature. The superintendent will transmit factual evidence for use in disputes and in the making up of change-order estimates, progress reports, and actual production records.

This factual information should be studied immediately by management to determine the exact relation between the originally quoted estimate of production and the actuality. If it is found that production must be improved, the only possible time to do this is immediately. Construction will still be under way, and only at this time can progress be affected by corrective action. Entry of new records on old sheets, of course, should also be done at this significant time.

Because the job superintendent is human and therefore fallible—subject to constant interruptions and many demands for his attention—it is conceivable that he also can and should be reminded of something and assisted by the office whenever possible. As an old cookbook[1] noted to the lady of the house in the era of many servants, "Visit your kitchen daily or as often as occasion requires."

[1] *Aunt Babette's Cook Book*, The Bloch Publishing Co., New York, 1889, p. 8.

4-2   *The Clipboard (A Simple File)*

Certain important original documents come into the possession of the job superintendent to be transmitted to the office. These might be a series of ready-mix concrete tickets giving a record of ingredients and the yardage delivered for the day, a lumber delivery receipt, or a social security form made out by a new employee hired on the job and giving pertinent tax and other information for the office bookkeeper. They represent an obligation of some nature to be transmitted to, and taken care of by, the office personnel. Whoever visits the job regularly can pick up these documents, or they can be mailed in. But until then they should always be simply, visibly, and safely hung on a clipboard in one place on the office wall.

4-3   *The Daily Report*

The daily report is actually *a continuous record in ink in a bound, ruled ledger book* of some nature. Occasionally it must function as the primary factual record of what actually happened. It then has the status of an impartial, unchanged daily record which carries credibility and influence. Such a book might be a surveyor's logbook for a small job or a series of numbered and lined ledgers for larger jobs.

Of course, the flyleaf carries the name of the job, the location, the name of the general contractor, the name of the job superintendent, and a request to return the book to a definite address should it accidentally be found elsewhere than at the site. Normally it should never leave the job. Carbon copies of daily entries are made for transmission to the office.

The beginning sheets, to the extent required, serve as a permanent reference record of who participated in construction, including addresses and telephone numbers for emergencies or later reminder. These might be associates, such as the architect, his office manager, his field representative, and his secretary; the owner (buyer) and his agent; the various contractors and subcontractors; utilities, such as telephone, water, gas, and electricity; emergency services, including hospital and ambulance, police, fire department, and municipal maintenance; supply companies for materials, such as ready-mix concrete, lumber, masons' supplies, builders' equipment; labor sources, such as names and addresses of individual journeymen or of local headquarters and delegates of unions; equipment and maintenance sources.

This information is a valuable later record when something needs attention and the original employees are gone. Particularly, a long-surviving maintenance bond or a guarantee may be invoked by an owner at a much later date. The record function is entirely different from the customarily used names, addresses, and telephone numbers on the tacked-up job telephone index.

The daily report is generally made up every morning after a walk through the job to determine what is going on. To be worthwhile, it must be more explicit than simply a marking of the weather. As shown in Figure 4-2, the report should specify the location of the trades at

---

DAILY REPORT

Day—   Date—   Weather—   8 A. M. Temp
                                                12 M Temp
                                                4 P. M. Temp

Genl. Contr. —Name—   1 Superintendent

1 Mason frmn, 7 masons, 5 laborers; basement boiler room.

1 Carpenter frmn, 3 carpenters; completing 1st fl forms.

1 Ironworker frmn, 1 journeyman; laying mesh in forms.

Plumber—Name—   1 Frmn, 1 journeyman; installing roughing for first floor.

Received preliminary requisition for inspection of supt.

Heating—Name—   1 Frmn, 1 journeyman; setting boiler fire brick; installing circulating lines for radiators.

Sheet-Metal Subcontract—Name—1 Frmn, 1 journeyman; receiving air-conditioning unit and moving it.   2 additional journeymen started work at 12:30 P. M. ; complete gang setting unit.

Electric—Name—   1 Frmn, 2 journeymen; installing conduit and outlet boxes on 1st fl forms for pouring of slab.

Steel—Name—   1 Frmn, 3 journeymen; receiving and setting material for pin shoring old party wall at location of new opening.

Accident Report—   Approximately 11 A. M. carpenter
(Name and address   )
(S. S. number   Age   Wage   )
Stepped on rusty nail and punctured foot. Sent immediately to doctor (Name and address), received antitoxin, and returned to work after lunch. No lost payroll time. Made out accident report and mailed to office.

On Job—   Inspector for architect, Mr. (name), approximately 2 P. M.   Progress and work approved.

figure 4-2. Daily report.

work as well as any other details which may be pertinent later. The record may also include those who visited the job, decisions made and orders verbally given to be corroborated, contractor's and subcontractors' actions and number of men employed (a basis of credits, extras, and completion expectations), and insurance information. As many things can change during the course of a day, the record is reviewed early in the afternoon to determine what job conditions have changed and whether additional entries should be made.

This enforced daily review is a very important reminder. *Telephone calls will be made for subcontractors to show up the next working day.* Follow-up calls may be made when promises are not kept. Material and men can be ordered when needed.

4-4   *Tax Records*

New employees are regularly added to the payroll on the job. The existing laws covering these men in connection with tax returns are of importance to every construction company. Tax records must be developed, and percentage proceeds must be paid to the federal government on behalf of both the employee and the employer. Unfortunately, evasive or careless or transient workers will occasionally furnish an unreadable or even fictitious name, address, and social security number on the forms universally used to obtain such information.

When quarterly tax records are sent to the collection agency, a scanning machine attempts to match names to account numbers before the master record itself is altered. But when such pairing does not take place, the machine rejects the information, which is returned to the construction company for further verification. This results in difficult and costly attempts at completion or correction of records, which adds needlessly to the overhead. Particularly at certain times of the tax year, a heavy concentration of work already exists for the office personnel, and such additional work is a real burden.

The job superintendent can be of help. At the time of hiring he can and should check job-furnished information and require legibility of name and address, correspondence of information given with passport, union dues book, driver's license, or other reasonably trustworthy information, and *inspection of original social security card*. Missing information need not prevent a journeyman from being placed on the payroll and started to work, provided he is notified that this information and evidence must be brought to the job prior to some set closure date before payroll is received and paid out.

Particularly when labor is scarce, this leeway will allow the daily working force to be built up. Individuals who are avoiding alimony payments, who are unwilling to be identified for garnishee orders, or who have similar nefarious reasons for withholding personal information will move on promptly before fouling up the records. Those who are merely illiterate or careless will be helped at the inception of their payroll experience but before they cost the contracting company money for verifications. There is a further advantage to a scrutiny of the payroll as it is built up. Such a procedure minimizes the addition by anyone of fictitious names for purposes of payroll padding.

Tax records covering material are, of course, handled in a different way. They will show up on invoices sent to the office or in other accounting department procedures. The job function is to verify delivery before payment is authorized and to send receipt tickets to the office.

4-5   Cost Records

Few jobs are large enough to support a timekeeper and cost clerk. Yet when work is self-produced, the recording of accurate unit-price cost records is an essential job contribution. Cost records provide information for future estimating and the obtaining of profitable work.

Different trades and companies require different kinds of information and use different methods of recording. It is apparent that there is a lot to do in the course of a day, and the superintendent must conserve his time as much as possible. Therefore, he should be informed by his office as to what units are required and whether it is possible to combine certain operations in one unit. For example, when a firm does masonry work, the basic unit might be the cost of laying 1,000 bricks to a certain pattern and in a certain thickness of wall. To this might be added the cost of renting and erecting the required scaffold, the cost of moving the brick from the street storage location to the place in the structure where it is to be used, the cost of material and labor for cleaning the wall, and the cost of removing the scaffold and cleaning the floor. The office estimator will use this composite unit to save time in estimating new work, and this figure is what the company requires.

One way to save the superintendent's time is to obtain a separate set of floor plans to use only for making up cost records. The extent of each day's production is measured at the location and then dimensionally marked off and dated in colored pencil on the appropriate plan. The color of the pencil is varied so that successive days of work can be readily distinguished. The superintendent in his job office then scales the plan to determine the quantity produced for a particular day and combines this information with his daily payroll time book to obtain the complete labor cost involved. The information is entered in duplicate on an interoffice memo, and the office copy sent on immediately for timely action if wanted.

The office has the facilities and the office machines (such as electric calculating machines, payroll tables, and other timesaving, accurate devices) to take over the work of extension and division. The records will be computed at regular intervals, kept safe, checked, acted upon immediately, and filed. There are, of course, other ways of keeping costs, which will be developed if required by the accountant.

4-6 Detail Approvals

A. In addition to the plans and specifications, which outline all the work to be done, information is given to the superintendent about details. Such information is necessary to make individual members fit together in the proper place and as intended.

This knowledge is transmitted to the job through a rather time-consuming process which yet has the advantages of accuracy and of affording agreement with the wishes of the architect or design engineer. By contract, the prime and general contractors and their subcontrators must submit to the designer for approval all working drawings, catalog cuts, hardware lists, or similar elucidation. These approvals assume no responsibility for dimensional accuracy or strength of material; this determination remains with the contractor. Such approvals, however, are a prerequisite to fabrication and delivery of material to the job. As such, they are transmitted in copy form to the job superintendent as a preindication of what is coming, where it is to go, and how it is to be installed.

If this preliminary material is not received promptly by the job superintendent, there will be delay. The concept of "promptly," of course, varies with the length of lead time required for any particular trade. Advance delivery should be the aim. When received, details should be studied by both the job superintendent and the office to ensure that there is correlation with all other trades *and that they are approved.* No delay is permissible for certain items, particularly for material to be built in. It is, therefore, distinctly within the responsibility of the superintendent to anticipate any contractor or anyone else in authority to obtain such information and material as will be necessary.

Any trade can affect any other trade. The installation of standard steel storage shelves seems to be free of relationship. Yet the approved layout affects the location and design of electric wall outlets and of radiator enclosures. This, in turn, may hold up masonry, plastering, and painting.

B. There is another type of approval required which can also affect job progress. The actual manner of installation of certain trades must be approved by jurisdictional authorities before such work can be enclosed or used. A primary case in point is the plumbing piping (known as *roughing*), which is one of the first items to be taken care of on a construction job. Not only is piping generally enclosed in partitions or other walls, but lead bends for waste connections and vertical piping for other uses affect floors and roof construction. Inspection, tests, and written approval are generally a requirement of the local building department. The department must be notified, an appointment made by the trade involved with their representative for inspection, and the job signed off as approved to the building superintendent or other representative of the construction company.

In other cases, the electrician and the duct installer for the heating contractor might each require examination by the inspector for the fire underwriters and also by the local fire department for code compliance. There are other special cases for special jobs, in which installations must be tested and approved while accessible.

4-7   *Extra and Credit Records*

The extras or credits on any job are a contentious item. Naturally, the buyer wants to get as many items covered in the original contract price as a broad interpretation of the contract plans and documents will permit. His job, as purchasing agent, is to save money.

The contractor, however, feels that the purchasing agent has already taken full advantage of his competitive position to get a low price for the work originally shown and specified. Also, by specification, the contractor is usually held responsible in meeting job conditions at no extra cost to the owner. To stay in business, if the contractor must absorb contingencies, he must charge for extras. And if he must eliminate certain work and give a credit, he should at least get some return which will help to recompense him for his previous overhead. This expenditure will involve not only estimating the work which is now to be eliminated but also planning and, often, prior purchasing and delivery of material (which will now not be used).

As is apparent, the interests of buyer and contractor are here at variance. It is not the business of the buyer to permit the contractor to make more than is necessary. It is the business of the contractor to increase his margin of profit and to try to get back some portion of the profit and overhead that he might have made on work now eliminated.

In accomplishing such results, the contractor cannot come right out and ask for permission to attain a more profitable job. He therefore adopts a procedure which will allow the buyer to manifest attention to duty and yet permit him justly to issue an order for some additional amount. Note that for this extra only one bidder is possible until the general or prime contractor finishes his work, gets off the job, and is paid. Common building-business conduct prevents any other than the contract holder from bidding or working for a buyer on some one particular job until the present contract is completed and paid for. In addition, labor unions will not supply men for any conflict of trade interest on one job. There is, however, a reasonable expedient limitation placed on a quotation given by a contractor in that there is a necessity to maintain good relations in order to be paid promptly and to obtain future business. Practically, one extra order or credit will not change the outcome of the job. Not only the present parties are involved; reputation is conveyed by word of mouth. There is, therefore, a practical limit which prevents an excessive charge.

Should notice of the proposed change come through job contacts, the superintendent will notify the estimator in writing of everything involved before a change estimate is made up. Should the notice come through the office, it is necessary to get the superintendent's opinion about what is involved. In any event, an itemized change-order list is roughed out by the job superintendent and transmitted to the office estimator. The latter now has more leeway in estimating quantities, overheads, and profit percentages than when figuring the original estimate.

In presenting an estimate and request for a written order to the buyer, an opportunity is allowed for a fair interplay of ideas. After all, there is no compulsion for either party to make any change. The original plan and specification are still in effect and were good enough to pass close scrutiny at the time of contract. The change and estimate must be sufficiently better to warrant action.

After the responsible parties have agreed that there should be a change, a signed order, and notice of it, should be gotten to the job as soon as possible. The work originally contracted for is continuously under way and progressing. News of change-order discussions can justly hold up progress of the work only for a limited period of time. If the change is not received reasonably quickly, the original design may be installed and later may have to be taken out. Other costs will also be affected by delay, such as changes in material and labor costs during the time of negotiation.

The cost estimate will often hold up an agreement. Few agents, whether school committee members in charge of construction or the purchasing officers of a manufacturer, feel competent to estimate and authorize a change in construction. It just is not their business. If the designer, however, will first examine and approve the proposal as part of his work and with full knowledge of what else is involved, the buyer cannot be criticized on price or procedure.

A stratagem working toward this effect and saving time for both job and office is worth trying. The American Institute of Architects publishes a change-order form, G701 [1] (Figure 4-3), in sets of four copies, each of different-colored paper. In effect, this is a definite proposal to do

---

[1] American Institute of Architects, Washington, D.C.

CHANGE ORDER

AIA DOCUMENT G701

OWNER ☐
ARCHITECT ☐
CONTRACTOR ☐
FIELD ☐
OTHER

PROJECT:
(name, address)

CHANGE ORDER NUMBER:

TO (Contractor)

ARCHITECT'S PROJECT NO:

CONTRACT FOR:

CONTRACT DATE:

You are directed to make the following changes in this Contract:

The original Contract Sum was . . . . $.
Net change by previous Change Orders . . . . $.
The Contract Sum prior to this Change Order was . . . . $.
The Contract Sum will be (increased) (decreased) (unchanged) by this Change Order . . . $.
The new Contract Sum including this Change Order will be . . . . $.
The Contract Time will be (increased) (decreased) (unchanged) by ( ) Days.
The Date of Completion as of the date of this Change Order therefore is

ARCHITECT	CONTRACTOR	OWNER
Address	Address	Address
BY	BY	BY
DATE	DATE	DATE

AIA DOCUMENT G701 • CHANGE ORDER • APRIL 1970 EDITION • AIA® • © 1970 • THE AMERICAN INSTITUTE OF ARCHITECTS, 1735 NEW YORK AVE., NW, WASHINGTON, D.C. 20006 — ONE PAGE

figure 4-3. Change order (AIA Form G701).

certain additional itemized work at a fixed price or not to do certain contractual items at a fixed rebate. Seemingly, it is the same as any proposal made on the letterhead of the construction firm. It has, however, certain very definite advantages:

A. The four copies of the change-order form are for (1) the owner or buyer, (2) the architect, (3) the contractor, and (4) the field. Thus, when these are distributed, all interested parties are fully informed immediately. Should the proposal later be approved and signed, it can be placed into effect by a telephone call and still incorporate all written provisions.

B. When signed both by the architect or engineer and by the buyer and dated, the form becomes an immediate contract, with one exception:

The form, of course, is made up to satisfy the architect, and it has one defect when used as a general contract, for which it was not designed. As the architect is supposed to use it following letter details of a proposal which was not received from a contractor, it has no place for the contractor's *written acceptance*. This must be written in before mailing for future use.

In cases in which the agreement includes any kind of time or material agreement, the source of such information is the job superintendent. The information must be obtained, summarized, and transmitted to the office for invoicing.

The job superintendent must, therefore, be in a strong position factually. If he is doing fixed-price work, the complete change is satisfactory. But if he is working on a time-and-material basis, regardless of for whom he is doing work, he must keep a separate daily record of labor, material, and equipment used. If an itemized daily receipt can be signed for in duplicate by the representative of the other party as a means of verification, such evidence needs no further checking. But in any case, the superintendent should maintain a separate large notebook for the sole purpose of entering extra work facts. Payroll, bills, and rental charges can be readily transcribed. And supporting pages and signatures for verification can be photocopied without being removed from the original binding.

4-8 *Job Meetings*

Coordination on a construction job is essential. Due to the fact that the general contractor acts as a broker of service, he is responsible for all the organizations that are contractually under his control. In addition, under his contract he has tacitly or actually agreed to work with such others as are not under his control to such extent as is practical and possible. Also, as a matter of cost saving, it behooves every separate contractor of any status on a job to be familiar with the planning of every other contractor so as to have foreknowledge of interrelated actions. Only by acting with others can their actions be influenced and can expense be minimized. One self-interested party is not concerned with the expense of others but only with how their work affects him.

Whoever has the duty of supervising the work for the buyer—whether it be architect, engineer, or general contractor—customarily fosters coordination. But because everyone is interested, such action may be called for by anyone at interest. The method used is the job meeting.

The party calling the meeting notifies all other interested people in advance of the place, day, and time of meeting, with someone to be present to represent each interested party. In addition, a stenographer, furnished by the person calling the meeting, is present to note, transcribe, and send out to each party at interest whatever action transpired. In particular, the progress schedule acts as a guide to determine required dates. There is thus a permanent record of who said what, for the common aim of action toward expediting the work.

As a matter of procedure, there must be a directing personality at every meeting. Each party present is called in turn for a report on his specialty, with particular attention to progress and expected action. Every other trade present is asked to comment, if desired, on the previous statement, noting items, such as adequacy, interference, or inadequacy. The result is an open discussion of progress or lack of progress, a general understanding of the status of each trade, and a definite commitment toward completing certain phases at definite times. Figure 4-4 is a simulation of the minutes of a job meeting.

As records, the minutes act as constant reminders of what was discussed, promised, and achieved. In cases in which a trade must take an action that might affect other trades, preliminary planning will outline the problem and what is necessary for continuous job progress. For example, in order to cut over electric service from the preliminary wiring to the final switchboard, new electric service meter, and permanent conduit and wiring, the electrician anticipates an interruption of service for several days. Until he brings this event to the attention of a job meeting, however, there is no reason for other trades to be aware of this disturbing contingency.

Discussion, however, emphasizes that other trades are constantly using electric equipment. Discontinuance of power supplied to the automatic sump pump of the plumber would lead to flooding of the equipment room. Subsequent damage to circuiting and controls might be caused to the basement heating and ventilating apparatus. Electric light should also be maintained at this location to afford accessibility and safety. And this is only one specific location. In every general location the various trades use electric tools such as portable saws, drills, pipe-threading machines, and electric hammers.

In short, if all other work is not to stop for the period of the cutover (with incipient damage to everyone, including the electrician), a temporary or supplementary source of power of the correct size and phase must be arranged for and furnished in advance of need. It may be a temporary additional feed from the public service company or a separate motor-generator set with the requisite connections. Whether or not the contractual agreement covers such a cost contingency, the job meeting affords time to consider and act upon any particular problem.

The advantage of such foreknowledge to the job superintendent and to all others responsible for job progress is self-evident.

Note particularly that there is considerable leeway in this joint meet-

MINUTES OF JOB MEETING

Date—   Time—

Re—   Job and location

Present:—Architect   Contractors:— Plumbing
    Architect's Inspector   Heating and ventilating
    Other   Electric
    General Contractor   Concrete
    Job Superintendent   Carpentry
    Stenographer   (Mail copy also to tile
    Other   contractor)

The meeting was called to order by Mr._____(architect). He stated that he had received a call from the owner asking for the cost of an additional fireproof service door from shipping platform to warehouse. His staff was completing a small addenda plan for pricing which would go out to necessary contractors shortly.

Architect asked Mr._____ of General Contractor for progress report. Demolition complete, all foundations in place, basement walls in place. Started interior partitions (basement), but has not yet received approval of plumbing inspector so that toilet partitions can be enclosed. Expect to pour first floor slab concrete in two days.

Architect asked Mr._____of Plumbing Contractor for report. Has foreman and 1 journeyman on job completing roughing installation so as to obtain city inspection approval for enclosure of piping in walls. An appointment has been set up for building inspector to be on job in two days. Expects approval immediately. Architect asked for copies of original for himself, the general contractor, and the owner. Note that masonry partitions are under way, and approval necessary to enclose toilet walls and to start tile work. This item on Progress Schedule barely on time.

Architect asked Mr._____of Heating and Ventilating Contractor for report. Latter has foreman and 4 journeymen on job. Installing and welding 4" diameter circulating pipe from water tower to heat exchanger. Sheet Metal subcontractor for duct runs will start tomorrow. (At this point, Electrician asked for immediate completion of duct installation in meter room so as to install the meter board. He is to be ready for test operation in three weeks time.) General Contractor reminded Heating Contractor that galvanized dummy sleeves were not yet placed on floor slab form to make radiator riser pipe holes in concrete.

Architect asked Mr._____of Electrical Contractor for report. Has foreman, journeyman, and apprentice on job finishing conduit and floor outlet boxes for slab, and also installing conduit runs from and to meter board location. Progress Schedule on time.

Architect asked for general comment. Carpenter at meeting merely to check progress. Job Superintendent asked Architect for notification of approval or disapproval of proposed changes to plans and specifications. Some of the subcontractors already working in locations affected by changes, and would have to use original design unless otherwise directed. Architect stated he was cognizant of this problem, and was in process of arranging extras and credits involved. He expected to have change orders and revised plans out in several days. If there is any trade involved in an immediate decision, he will be available after the meeting for discussion as to how to handle the problem.

There being no further business, the meeting was adjourned after setting the next meeting date as of _____at _____ A. M. in the construction shanty.

Respectfully submitted,

cc: All noted

figure 4-4. Minutes of job meeting.

ing. If there has been a design change in the roof trusses, the carpenter subcontractor may ask his own laminated-wood supplier (sub-subcontractor) to come to the meeting to answer questions regarding details and delivery. Or if work changes of any nature have been decided upon, the physical changes can be discussed and provisions decided on as may be necessary. Or if contingencies have caused a change in the progress schedule, offsetting action of some nature may be possible.

The job meeting, of course, is also fallible in that changes may be decided on but not followed up or executed. Or they may be followed by some but not all. Even the designer may fail to follow up an approved change with a written specification and plan to all parties, and the tradesmen on the job will then not receive instructions in working form. No contractor is responsible for what is a new but very vague contract without details. In such a case, the work, although authorized, will not be done.

Written records are most important, but men who will follow up and carry them out are also essential.

4-9. *Requisition Approvals*

An essential to stay in business is money. Money may be due for work incorporated, material stored, or other contractual agreement fulfilled. Money is needed for subcontractors' and the general contractor's requirements. Because of the large sums of money to be invested and the length of time involved in completing a construction project, payment is generally not a simple transaction. The mechanics of getting money, the amount of consecutive payments, and occasionally the percentage of retainer pending some subsequent happening should all be spelled out in detail in the contract.

A general contractor invoices the buyer as the contract provides. There are types of construction, such as an apartment building based on a construction loan, in which certain of the proceeds are released for payment in stages, such as when the roof is on or the plumbing fixtures set. Additional money is released at fixed subsequent points of completion. Here a certification of progress by the representative of the mortgagor to his company may be required and adequate.

When, however, the contract permits payments to be consecutive and at regular periods of time (usually every month, at a fixed period of time for each month), a question arises: Is the invoice correct?

Because of the continuing necessity of meeting payroll requirements in cash, any contractor with work installed has actual money invested in the job. His material and equipment bills must be paid, even though some of these items may be reasonably delayed. Such delay is limited by the requirement that credit must be maintained to stay in business. (Also, a cash payment within a short time after being billed earns a material cash rebate, which is a real factor in making money. And the contractor may have other payment obligations.) Unquestionably, then, the tendency is for the contractor to invoice the full amount to which he is entitled and, occasionally, to overinvoice.

The buyer is perfectly willing to pay such amount of the contract as can be justified. One of his aims, however, is always to have enough money left in his possession to complete the job at whatever stage it may be in at that time. Therefore, the buyer requires that the requisition be approved as correct by an independent party and someone worthy of belief. That someone may be the architect or engineer or his agent, the general contractor, a resident representative of the buyer, or anyone familiar with the plans, specifications, and other pertinent documents and capable of estimating construction.

Thus a trustworthy general contractor may represent both himself and the buyer. This conflict of interest is recognized and minimized by acceptance of worth and verification. The major items of work in every category are submitted as contract percentages to the architect or engineer before starting the job (Figure 3-2). This list is then approved or corrected for payment purposes only by the designer. Each contract percentage of the whole thus acquires a money value which, in turn, needs only an estimate of percentage of completion at the time of a requisition to check its correctness approximately. This procedure also permits visual checking by the superintendent of the work of others with little loss of time. Because there is generally a lapse of time between the makeup of a requisition and the time of payment, the buyer benefits financially by the additional work and material incorporated in the job during such passage of time. This additional safety margin renders unnecessary any very correct estimate at this time, as the buyer is protected.

Even when the general contractor does the complete job and there is no requisition to be approved except his own, this method of prearrangement and percentage approval can readily be checked by anyone familiar with construction and inspecting the job for the purchasing agent. Of course, the weakness of this particular method is that the correctness of the installation in material, workmanship, and functioning is not taken into account at every inspection. Dependence is placed on reliability.

There are times when a subcontract requisition seems inadequate or may be missing altogether. This is not a good sign. The purchaser is not getting a month's work for nothing, and the superintendent must start immediately to look for a reason (if he is not already aware of it). The amount of work done may have been inadequate to invoice. Or the organization of the seller may be inefficient, insufficient, or incompetent.

Or it may be that the necessarily expedient favor will be asked of an emergency payment at an uncalled-for time to meet a delayed requirement. Whether the superintendent is the representative of the owner or not, he must be aware of everything that goes on. He and his firm are very much affected.

At all times, also, a requisition must bear with it a record indicating the amount of the contract, previous payments, the amount of this requisition, the amount or percentage to be contractually withheld, and the balance remaining. All the carry-forward information required for approval of payment will thus appear on this requisition, with no reason for loss of time on anyone's part.

4-10   *Job Completion*

As a job approaches completion, the momentum which it has developed tends to be lost. Final details must be included in the structure, systems and operating equipment must be tested and adjusted to function properly and as designed, and other contractual requirements must be complied with. The completion of the production phase will be signified by the act of approval of the buyer or his agent. This termination is not a simple matter, however, but involves foresight and continual effort during the entire course of the work—not only in the closing weeks of a long process.

A. The production of changed styles of construction points out the problem. When taxpayers balk at school construction costs, the designers may make savings by eliminating the plaster. The interior masonry is finished by tooling (rubbing) the joints and then painting directly on the masonry surface. Where necessary, enamel paint is used for washable corridors or toilet rooms. The journeymen for the various trades, however, are the controlling factors. The appearance of the undersurface that they produce shows right through the paint. Therefore, unchipped edges, machine-cut and square openings, unblotched and clean surfaces, and evenly tooled joints have to be obtained from the masons. And because no spoiling of future facial appearance can be tolerated, every other trade involved will have to work right with them. This means that the electrician will be required for neat conduit installation leading to switch and outlet boxes, the plumber for accurate piping, and the sheet-metal man for neatly installed ducts—among others.

Because the job superintendent is obligated to anticipate and obtain the desired results by the use of available labor, material, and equipment, he must start his finishing work at the beginning of his job. He will have to get many of the desired final results at an early stage in the course of construction. Attempts to alter inadequate basic appearance for a final approval can be prohibitively expensive.

B. Defects may occur during construction which, while not structurally serious, are objectionable. Such conditions might be indicated when the forms are stripped from concrete walls and floors. Occasionally surface pitting of the concrete face, known as *honeycombing*, will appear. This may be due to improper mixing, inadequate puddling (agitating), or the use of a particularly dry mix to obtain finished concrete strength. These flaws only require the return of the mechanics for refinishing. Where the surfaces are as yet unobstructed, this is simple. But access becomes progressively more difficult and costly as building construction advances. And as locations become obstructed, they may still remain visible for criticism and have to be refinished.

C. An error in layout or design may cause a very minor yet objectionable conflict in space requirements. For example, the heating plan indicates that the breeching from boiler to chimney stack will be in a certain location. An entirely separate plumbing plan may indicate a hot-water line adjacent to the breeching and with an installed shutoff valve. The plumber installs first and cannot consult the heating foreman because the latter is not yet working on the job. He places the valve so that the stem projects into the breeching location.

Of course, this particular interference is readily solved when the steamfitter does get on the job for his installation. The plumber turns the bonnet of the valve body 90° by altering the connections between piping and valve, thereby carrying the stem away from the breeching. As every trade depends on every other trade for help and cooperation, there is a spirit of necessitous give-and-take and no question of responsibility or cost for any minor job. Cases do occur, however, in which cost is so high that a charge must be made.

D. There may be poor weather conditions or a delay for some other reason. Precast footings, preformed light poles, prefabricated alarm boxes all sound fine and in the modern manner but give old-fashioned delays in delivery. An outside site plan is as important to completion as the structure which it serves and may include a number of trades and installations. There are the layout and planning for the footings, excavating, forming, trenching, installation of electric conduit from the building to the aforesaid precast light-pole footings (complete with anchor-bolt rings and bottom connection boxes). Thereafter, the light-pole fixtures and the exterior fire-alarm box must be erected, installed, and fused and the walks and parking pavement installed—all as specified.

E. Incomplete items in every trade occur for no good reason. These are noted in a so-called "punch list," generally made out by the architect and added to by other interested parties. Until the listed items are completely checked off as being finished and are approved in both material and workmanship, final payment will not be made. It is time- and energy-consuming to get any trade back on the job once it has left. The superintendent should therefore, considerably in advance of completion, formulate and have completed his own punch list.

F. Extras and credits may have occurred during construction. The extras will appear not only as orders but as physical changes to the structure. They will be completed as necessary to obtain payment. But credits sometimes also come into being. A piece of work specified or shown on the plan may have been omitted by error or intent, with the omission agreed to by the buyer or his agent. Or the general contractor may feel morally obligated to repay certain verbal modifications of the contract made by the buyer.

It should be emphasized that credits are as much a part of the contractual relationship as contracts and extra orders. Credits should be figured and presented as offsets against a subcontract before final payment is made by or to a general contractor. And the latter should invoice the agreed-upon revised amount with the final invoice.

G. The establishment in writing of a definite date *when the work will be considered completed* is a contractual necessity. The completion date fixes final payments and the time of release of retained money, gives the start of guarantee periods, removes liability by passage of title, and has other specific contractual effects. Possibly the letter claiming an actual work-completion date should be preceded by a contractual final-payment arrangement. Such prearrangement might be a contractual clause establishing approval by the buyer within thirty days of the date of the terminating letter or a written specification of claims of failure to complete. Neglecting to specify such claims will constitute final acceptance. Such contractual agreement will prevent any tendency to stall final approval by the buyer.

4-11   *Possession*

When the time finally does come for the purchaser to take possession, the new construction should be turned over to him only after verification and approval by the general contractor's office. The original agreement and any subsequent modifications all have significance. They determine possession time, payment, ownership, furnishing of certain supplies and equipment, transfer or cancellation of insurance, condition of property, and other contractual matters.

Possession time, for example, may not be synonymous with completion time. The contract may permit a buyer to take possession of a structure for use even if it is only partly complete. In this case, there is no onus on the buyer to make complete payment and the obligation still exists to complete construction. There may also be possible expense involved in maintenance labor and material, which the buyer has not assumed.

When a construction job has been and is being erected by union labor of one wage scale and is to be turned over to a different union or to non-union labor of a lower wage scale, there is the question of who, physically, does the succeeding work on the site and who pays. If this problem can be solved by granting a letter of possession, the letter must state that the construction is accepted as complete by the buyer, subject to the contract. And this latter clause means nothing if the union labor must still come back to the job to complete unfinished work. Such union labor is under no obligation to work on the same job site as nonacceptable or nonunion labor. Labor conditions must be satisfactorily arranged before the turnover.

If a temporary partition must be erected to separate finished work safely and cleanly from work still in progress, this is an added expense which may or may not have been originally shown and estimated. It may have been only a contractual contingency thrown in during negotiation. Certainly it might be avoided. And during an extensive interim period of occupation, lamp bulbs burn out and must be replaced, windows get dirty and must be cleaned, safety of personnel and equipment and material is a problem—and there are other items of expense.

Who pays, and where does it come from?

There are no final answers on how to handle such widely varying circumstances. Rather, the job superintendent must foresee the development of such situations and attempt to preclude or minimize their effect. The office must work closely with him to handle the cost and legal aspects involved.

5

MOTIVES OF THE BUSINESS

The construction business is founded upon a specialized knowledge of production, but it is also affected by other influences. While the basic principles of operation are similar for all businesses, considerable variations do exist among different kinds of businesses. In the study of profitable operation, it is essential to realize the similarities and also the differences between the building business and other businesses. Such variations affect operations.

5-1 *The Profit Essential*

For every business, the profit motive is basic. In the construction field, however, a particular job will finish but an organization or an individual must continue working. Constant work and the resultant wages are what cause the earnings to accumulate and total to a satisfactory yearly return for employer and employee. This sequence requires that successive jobs be obtained with reasonable frequency to ensure continuity of operations. In addition, the management and individuals must show a yearly profit above what they can earn elsewhere to justify and stay in the particular business. In the case of the employer, this return must exceed that which his capital would realize if it were deposited without work and risk in a savings bank.

In construction, *profit is not fixed by establishing a sales price.* It is increased or decreased by the actions of many people, interested and disinterested. Profit must be construed as a measure of the alertness, efficiency, and desire of involved individuals.

Monetary profit is not limited to any preconceived and fixed amount. Rather, it is the maximum obtainable. Consider why this policy is necessary. Risks are entailed, such as the cost of doing business, the weekly payroll and monthly bills to be met, the contract retainers withheld by others, the contingencies to be met and paid for (but which competition may not figure). The price which the general contractor can obtain may not be adequate for such costs, let alone for making a profit. In addition, because of the necessity for individual attention and the scarcity of desirable jobs at any one time, there is a limit to the number of jobs which can be estimated, obtained, and properly handled.

The buildup of a reserve contingency fund becomes a necessity.

5-2 *The Selling Problem*

The construction business is a specialized service, delivering in tangible form some definite arrangement which is contracted for in advance, generally under definitive plans and specifications. Construction selling differs in some respects from other selling. The sales price quoted for successive jobs will not often be the same even though the work may be similar. It may vary in detail and technique required, in location, in small or large monetary values, in the number and kinds of competition, and even in tangible and intangible possibilities. Thus estimating, pricing, and quoting are on an individual job basis. The sales problem is technical in scope, demanding in ability and responsibility, and subject to outside influences.

One must first sell in order to get work so as to earn food; otherwise, one will get painfully hungry.

What, then, is selling? It may be simply defined as the transfer of something of value for a present consideration or a future contract. Added to this definition, the exchange not only must provide for such supply of services, material, and equipment as are requisite for the job in question but also must allow for the prior knowledgeable marketing of these items. The contract work must be earned to be obtained—and the obtaining of the contract is the first essential of the construction process.

Also, the field of effort must be limited in scope to those jobs offering the best possibility of attainment as well as of making a profit.

5-3   *Influences on the Buyer*

From the buyer's viewpoint, he must justify his action to himself and to those others to whom he is responsible. Therefore, he solicits and welcomes bid competition and comparison. He hopes to obtain a choice of competitors of equal competence and reliability—at a low price (which occasionally happens). But the erection of structures is a complex operation involving a high degree of technical and supervisory skill, financial ability, personal effort, and moral integrity. Everyone hopes to make a profit, but not everyone figures to do it in the same way or even to deliver what is called for. All contractors are not the same. Knowing this, the purchaser can be and is influenced in favor of a particular seller.

The buyer is well aware that a variation in bids is normal and to be expected. Individual pricing is one of the bases for the separate bidding of work and leads directly to this result. Assumed production rates differ, as do material prices and equipment requirements. Wage rates and working conditions will make a difference.

In addition to the actual cost of the structure, the purchaser is paying for the services which he is hiring. These services are represented by an indefinite fee approximating some locally recognized and added percentage of the total cost. The fee will vary with the services of the individual contracting company. Cost factors will include quality of workmanship, adherence to specifications, reliability of contracted completion time, and later freedom from excessive deterioration. There may also be other factors involved in some particular job. These might include financing by taking part payment in notes, reduction of overhead (and profit) because certain major subdivisions of work are to be given out by the purchaser, who will do his own coordinating, or alternates to the base bid which offer a possibility of an extensive change of some nature.

There is usually some similarity in pricing, but occasionally a bid much lower than the others will indicate something requiring special attention. It does not always indicate an error; it may be a very definite sales strategem. Work may be scarce, a method may have been devised for cutting the cost of construction, or the written bid may specifically exclude some required item. There is usually a reason for a variation.

5-4   *Special Influence of the Bid*

The buyer is occasionally pressured by his own interests into disregarding danger signals. He will adopt an attitude that he can put up with and can handle faults if a money saving reverts to him by using a certain contractor. The best comment on this prevalent posture was made by John Ruskin: "The common law of business balance prohibits paying a little and getting a lot. If you deal with the lowest bidder it is well to add something for the risk you run, and if you do that, you will have enough to pay for something better."

Most buyers seem to believe that they can successfully manage any situation which will arise if it is to their interest. Even when they will not negotiate with a very low bidder, they will use his price to hammer down the price of competitors. It is evident that *the quoted price for doing a job relative to the price of others is a major premise toward influencing a purchaser.* The base bid becomes translated for the buyer into a measurement of the charge for the management services of one competitor as against another.

Even in that special and unjust case in which there is undue influence in favor of someone, such price comparison will be used. The favored bidder will first have to satisfy the buyer that the proposals of others have been met.

Thus, the value of a construction quotation is its comparison with competition. Which bid offers the most for the least money? A sales inducement is of interest, but only as an addition to such an appraisal.

It is only after the price obstacle has been successfully passed that a bidder will be called upon to negotiate. And negotiation is the general method of placing nonpublic contracts. Any construction job is sizable in money value compared with any ordinary daily purchase, and direct contact is necessary to make such a large sale. Because of his determining position, the buyer has the option of whom to see. *And until and unless a bidder is called in to negotiate actively with a buyer, all prior work toward getting that particular job is wasted.* There are so many items of expense involved for a contractor that this is a real problem. There are, for example, limitations on work available, the cost of obtaining entrée against other competitors, and the time and expense required to bring together the multiplicity of details which must be assembled.

Estimating just to get one's name on the bidders' list does not pay the bills. And quoted prices occasionally bear little relationship to a cost but only to what must be bid to get on a bidders' list to see the buyers. The responsible party must anticipate actual negotiations and make every possible effort to get to the bargaining table. And when he does get there, he must be in a position not to "leave his profit on the table" because the buyer knows his business and the contractor primarily knows construction. The contractor must have the facts in readily obtainable form to protect himself properly and to emerge with a profitable contract.

5-5   *Other Sales Arguments*

To reiterate, it is generally only after an influencing price is quoted to the purchaser that an opportunity is afforded to the low or otherwise influential bidder to negotiate and present additional sales arguments. (Of course, there are exceptions.) Here is the opportunity to marshal pertinent advantages. For example, a company may do much of the basic craftsmanship on a job (concrete work, masonry, and carpentry) with their own workmanship and material. This controls to a large extent the timing of the job and the quality of the workmanship and therefore can be an asset.

Another organization gives all the work to subcontractors, eliminating everything except such fundamentals as supervision and coordination. Working as a broker, this type of contracting organization limits its own liability and capital investment by making use of the credit rating and financial worth of the subcontractors. Larger jobs may be possible than would otherwise be safe to go after. There may, however, be a loss in quality of workmanship, material, and time control. Here, price may be of predominant influence.

During negotiations with the buyer, should the two preceding types know that they are in competition, undoubtedly each will attempt to disparage the other without offensive criticism. The contractor type may not have the finances for a continuous payroll and may require cash advances at frequent intervals. The broker type has no journeyman organization in being and cannot service a building owner by meeting minor requests for maintenance or alteration.

At the right time during negotiations, arguments such as these do carry weight with a purchaser, depending on his needs. But sales arguments to be effective must be utilitarian. They should include practical items, such as personal relationships, suggestions for cost cutting, advantages of labor obtainment, time of completion, bondability (or credit rating), and a reputation and references imputing honorable dealing. But again, to reiterate, the bid price is basic in its influence.

5-6 *Obtaining a Profit*

Business existence is finally determined not only by getting work but by the amount for which it is obtained. If he profitably could, the buyer would do his own construction to save money and as part of his own business effort. It is only because benefits accrue to him in actual money, know-how, and time saving that the letting out of the contracting operation pays for him. And as the principal reason for such action is the amount of money accruing to the purchaser, the simplicity of the problem becomes a difficulty for the contractor. The pressure of competition forces the latter to offer an attractively low price, yet at the risk of obtaining a profitless job.

How does one get a profitable construction job when everyone figures the same plans and specifications and the buyer seems to be purchasing low price only?

A solution presented here is to find ways to reduce construction costs of every nature, in estimating and in actuality, and to obtain that corollary elimination of losses which leads to an increase of profit. This entails the development not only of good job functioning but also of good office and job procedure.

5-7   *The Search for Costs*

The points previously emphasized in this chapter have all been facets of what might be called the *sales problem.* Yet in their turn these become part of a cost problem.

The importance of knowing production costs as a foundation of pricing has long been recognized in the extensive literature devoted to this subject. In general, emphasis is placed first upon obtaining an adequate knowledge of the business, sufficient to understand the particular production problem involved. The use of existing techniques and the possible application of new theories of design, new machines, new methods, and new materials are considered.

But what is not emphasized is the effect of existing relationships, procedures, equipment, and trends of thought on the success of the business. *Where costs are increased and where they are saved is not in one place but in many places throughout the organization.* Saving excessive and unnecessary losses and preventing the diminution of profits are fully as important as developing new methods or materials of production. (Note that the specification often prohibits any type of substitution without the prior approval of the buyer or his agent. How does it profit a contractor to develop something new and be unable to get it adopted without the necessity of giving away most of the benefits to the buyer?) The emphasis must be on getting the maximum return by improving every part of the existing business itself.

For example, examining the question of subcontracting policy will indicate that doing one's own work has elements of both advantage and disadvantage. There will be a gain in quality and a time saving, but the necessity of meeting weekly payroll and monthly material bills prior to receiving a payment may impair working capital. This will necessitate a costly loan at high interest rates. Thus, subcontracting may be more advantageous from a total monetary viewpoint.

Similarly, the contract as first written by the purchaser may be very inequitable. Payment approvals and amounts of retainers may be unfair, unreasonable, and inflexible. The time to change the wording and to save loss and aggravation is before agreeing to and signing the contract. If to the purchaser the contract is worth signing, he will agree to a reasonable change. Once a contract is signed, no one is willing to modify the details, terms, and price unless convinced that his interests will be served by so doing.

Furthermore, job costs will vary with the relative experience of the construction superintendent, the amount of supervision he is given, and the individual circumstances surrounding a job. Inclement weather can always be expected, and it is good practice to forestall periods when work is not possible with whatever additional labor time can be applied beforehand. The saving in overhead will be appreciable.

Petty thievery is equally harmful. A missing plumb bob does not represent very much money lost, but the consequent time loss in laying out work is serious. And the theft of a gasoline-motor-driven mortar buggy can be disruptive of production when there are not enough laborers available to service the masons by hand-wheeling mortar to location.

Individual trades and labor management offer problems also. The mason who has too much mortar mixed at the end of the working day has material left over to harden in the mortar tubs. On the other hand, unless there is an adequate amount for the men to finish up with, their production will drop. Their final so-called "working" hour can be more costly than the others. And the steel-erection subcontractor who examines the work site at the end of the day can always pick up expensive steel-connection nuts and bolts dropped from the frame and left out overnight to rust tight. Quite often he also finds costly tools exposed to weather and theft. Careless losses by journeymen are a profit hazard.

Therefore, discussion of these functions is necessary to the full development of the profit yield of any job. To cover every contingency is manifestly impossible, but additional personal investigation will be worthwhile. The reason for being of the contractor is cost saving with good workmanship. He *must* devote his attention to this basis of his business existence.

5-8 *Special Influence of the Individual*

A machine, even if it has as many possibilities as a computer, is inflexible. It can only do the work for which it is set up. An individual, on the other hand, can realize, learn, remember, reason, and act. He can think to put a machine to work. In motivating an organization, he can build up himself. And in serving his organization, he serves himself.

Consider a particular form of simple organization chart (Figure 5-1).[1]

[1] *Organization and Management*, LaSalle Extension University, Chicago, 1923, p. 22.

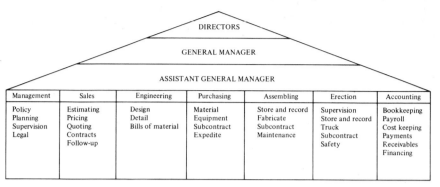

Management	Sales	Engineering	Purchasing	Assembling	Erection	Accounting
Policy	Estimating	Design	Material	Store and record	Supervision	Bookkeeping
Planning	Pricing	Detail	Equipment	Fabricate	Store and record	Payroll
Supervision	Quoting	Bills of material	Subcontract	Subcontract	Truck	Cost keeping
Legal	Contracts		Expedite	Maintenance	Subcontract	Payments
	Follow-up				Safety	Receivables
						Financing

figure 5-1. Organization chart.

It has a functional basis which can be expanded or contracted or otherwise changed to meet the needs of a particular enterprise. The chart form is a series of columns designating departments and held together by lines enclosing management functions. The departments are spelled out in detail to conform to the requirements of the construction business being analyzed.

Although the creation of these separate parts of a going business is the work of management, their performance is the result of the work of individuals. The location of employment can be in any department and yet can lead directly to the management function, provided that there are two additional factors present: knowledge and opportunity.

Logically, the education of anyone employed in construction work should include considerable knowledge of that business. When earning a living, however, the work of the individual is specialized in some function of importance to his employer. He is being paid for specific work. This may not include outside job supervision (which includes noting what men actually produce), paying out money, bringing it in— all the practical facets which a manager should know. An employee gets little chance to increase his knowledge by direct experience with other operations. But supplementing information by study and the use and observation of the services of others is one way to maintain and advance income, position, and the ability to earn. And if an employee wants to learn and to make an opportunity to advance himself, his employer is more than happy to help him. Continual improvement of manpower functioning is a necessity of the construction business.

5-9   Delegation of Authority

Referring again to Section 5-1, the item of profit, or even just the meeting of overhead, is not fixed by establishing a selling price. The work contracted for must be properly installed and completed despite inopportune circumstances. These may include cost modifications, such as the necessity of meeting competitively low prices to get work; the unallowed (although not unexpected) expense of bad weather conditions; mistakes in office, shop, and job; delays in delivery and installation by others.

It is physically impossible on any job above a bare minimum in size for any one man to take care of all the details involved. Through the authority gained by paying salaries for necessary assistance, the management outlines duties and establishes departments and staffs them, as finances permit and require. Even on small ventures, the additional aim is to obtain competent and reliable assistants for every important position. Volume of work, accidents, sickness, religious holidays, retirements, and other replacement contingencies must always be considered. Here is where the growth of the individual becomes of interest and advantage to management.

5-10 *Developing Assistance*

The proper direction of energy is an important function of both management and employee. The development of ability is a necessity of management.

To management, developing capable assistance is essential for many reasons. Profit must be guarded and enhanced by the current personnel. For example, labor can be used efficiently or can be wasted. Materials purchased may show a price saving against the estimate and yet carry an overriding and offsetting loss due to lack of quality, poor type of finish, or delay in delivery. Pilferage and carelessness are sources of loss. Poor supervision of safety practices may increase accidents, which will not only lose manpower but increase premiums unnecessarily.

In contrast, the purchasing of both material and subcontracts may be achieved at prices below those used to obtain a job. Plan and specification changes during construction may lead to extra orders at better-than-normal prices. Changes developed in construction procedure may effect economies in production.

The individual often makes the difference between profit and loss.

The construction business is thus seen to be, in considerable part, a series of individual actions. These actions are influenced by an upper price maximum determined by contract and owner price resistance and a lower cost limitation enforced by labor, material and equipment prices, and overhead. Although most items are available to all at about the same price, they are not used in the same way. And because profit is so small in relation to the total job value, the individual successive actions of every employee affect the management in the pocketbook nerve. The effect is very noticeable and serious.

The enhancement of the organization in any manner is of importance. For example, the construction business is unusual in the use of the contract for almost every job. This method of delaying monetary payments pending the fulfillment of other conditions depends primarily on credit. Surprisingly, however, credit ratings are not often continuously checked by management, and over periods of time they sometimes deteriorate. Adverse credit conditions do give some indication of developing, such as a visitor's comment or a telephone call requesting information. Vigilance in this or any other field is necessary. Management must depend on its employees to be watchful in its behalf.

5-11 *Employee Advancement*

There are two methods of manpower growth available to management:

1. They can build up from inside the organization. This method supplies the insurance factor of substitute available help at a minimum immediate payroll cost and offers to the individual the advancement so essential for hope and perseverence.

2. They can recruit from outside the organization. This procedure might be necessary for expanding the size or character of a business when the management is dissatisfied with the present personnel or wants to add to it.

In any case, the source of help is the individual. The location of that person on the organization chart is immaterial. What is fundamental is the desire to learn and the will to study. What pays off is the ability to make money legitimately for the employer and for oneself.

5-12 *Technical Advancement*

The contractor who can devise a simpler and less costly way of accomplishing an operation will gain a benefit. The construction supply business, in general, is attempting to satisfy this need with new management techniques, new products, and new machines and equipment. These include, for example, special steels in which the surface will protectively and pleasingly coat itself with oxide, thus eliminating the painting part of the cost of erection and also later maintenance. The new techniques involve the use of computers in the critical-path method of job analysis and follow-up. New products require a diversifying of selling objectives and skills, such as going after air-pollution-control business or something else which is new. This entails changing not only construction techniques but also sales methods if necessary, so as to act as a sales representative for a manufacturer. Although much of this development is in the control of the specifying designer, the contractor must personally do what he can to help himself.

5-13 *Interrelationship of Office and Job*

Another factor that is important to any business which has grown beyond the one-man stage *is the necessity for communication and cooperation* in action. The contrast in efficiency between a cohesive organization and an assemblage of loosely knit, autonomous departments is very evident. A condition of concordance must be developed.

Any method which will have this effect in practice is of value. A simple and effective means is a regular weekly office meeting, with management and every department represented, a written agenda prepared in advance, and a stenographer present to take notes and to furnish a permanent record to all the participants (similar to the job meeting). This procedure affords an opportunity of reviewing progress schedules against actual progress reports for every job. It shows up deliveries and delays requiring action and pressure, results obtained since prior discussion, and previously initiated but still open items. In general, it acquaints the entire organization with the current status of operations and what must be done on every job. Just the necessity for preparing factual disclosure showing progress or lack of it for every job, every week, compels regular review by every interested party.

Along these lines, an adjustable time stamp and a good copying machine are essential for proper coordination. Every letter that is received should be stamped with the date and the initials of each key department head. These initials for each interested person are checked by whoever reads the incoming mail, and a copy is made for that person. Photocopies of outgoing mail, actual specifications, or bidding documents can be made as required.

In addition, there should be a record in writing of the transmission of facts between departments. Letter-size interoffice memos (Figure 4-1), in duplicate, establish dates and facts which can be filed and referred to. Such simple means act as reminders, eliminate disputes, and assist cooperative effort.

5-14 *Interdependency of Job and Office*

Because the actions of each person in an organization have an effect on every other person, there can be no such thing as an independent entity. Take the very common case of a buyer who calls up some member of a construction organization and asks for a deduction change in a work contract which is underway. On the face of it, granting this small matter might eliminate something, save money for the general contractor, please the buyer, and redound to the credit of the subordinate; but this is not so.

Further checking indicates otherwise. The engineering department has completed and given out working drawings considerably before this date. They have already been acted on in the form of bills of material by the purchasing department, which has ordered mill delivery and pricing so as to save money by advance placement. Certain stock material has already been fabricated and stored by others. The job has already progressed to considerable layout work, which at present appears only as position stakes at the site. Already involved are these expenditures of manpower, material, and overhead, which cannot be correctly billed and may become worthless except as lost time and scrap material.

There are possibilities of discordant relations with the client and with coworkers as well as monetary loss. What seemed at first to be a very simple request has proved complicated. Each department has worked as well as it can to save time and to make that share of the profit for which it is responsible. Any change involves everyone, and all must be consulted.

A few of the many facets of the construction operation have been briefly outlined to show their intercorrelations as a business. The development of the text hereafter will discuss individual factors in detail.

6

PLANNING FOR SALES

Due to the necessity of obtaining work against competitive opposition, it is requisite to plan and limit the selling program. A construction organization has a good chance of getting a job with profit if the work that it figures is limited in extent to that which it knows well. This detailed knowledge involves labor and productivity and equipment and supplies particularly relevant to the work upon which it is figuring.

6-1 *Advantages of Limitation of Scope*

Organizations having experience and past success in such fields of work as earth moving will confine their bidding, when possible, to earth dikes surrounding fuel storage tanks, to irrigation and drainage canals, or to something similar. When bids include, in part, some new type of work, the same organization can, without too much risk, estimate directly or by subcontractor such additional items as concrete spillways, cast-iron pipe, or bituminous roads. In this way the primary organization gets added experience, but it starts with what its men know—and where it should have a price advantage. Elsewhere, a competitive advantage may exist in the formation and control of a skilled group of experts, the reuse of formwork paid for on a previous job, or the application of modern machines and erection techniques.

The effect of the competitive advantage of limitation may be enhanced by the mental tendency to look for and recognize unusual job aspects in any bid. For example, in bidding fill material a contractor allowed for purchasing an actual hill of bank-run gravel within a short trucking distance of the job on a good highway. He got the contract. His own equipment excavated and delivered material at the low cost which he had figured to get the job. Upon completion, he also had obtained a desirable level site upon a highway, which he sold to an industrial developer. The total amount realized made a sizable profit on the entire transaction, although there was little benefit on the construction job alone.

There is no limitation on flexibility in thinking—thinking ahead of competition—about how to make a profit and yet get a job, even if this involves something just a little different from what one has done before.

6-2 *Disadvantages of Limitation of Scope*

Although as a general rule bidding will be confined to the type of work which has previously been successful, this need not always be the case. Bidding is a crucial function with much at issue. It cannot be treated as a routine matter, for to stand still in mental use is to be overtaken by others. As an example, public works, such as schools, libraries, and municipal buildings, will usually be bid by some of the same group of competitors for each successive job. The jobs are always competitive and may be of little profitability. Yet the same firms will bid the same type of work time after time. They do so to make money, to get to know the architects or the public agencies, such as the school boards, or because it is easy to get in the rut of habit.

But in such a case, broadening the scope of bidding to include the general business community will change the customers and the method of bidding rather than the type of work done. It will show up any lack of breadth of contact, which can be a distinct weakness. This does not mean that every available job should be bid just because the element of diversification in bidding is present. Judgment is still very necessary. The profit is still the aim.

Every possibility should be examined on its own merits. A firm may be well known by good repute and may be asked to figure a prospective job. The proposed contract may be advantageous. The site may offer a construction asset. Whatever appears should be examined and handled as indicated.

6-3   *Which Jobs to Bid*

The buyer may be an owner, his purchasing agent or designer, a public agency, or any other economic entity. Naturally, he is primarily interested in obtaining his own objective at as little cost as possible. This involves the comparison of bids and bidders; provided the competitors are equally reliable and competent, a reasonable number of bids is to the interest of the buyer.

But what about the contractor? Bidding is costly, time-consuming, and limited in the number of jobs which can be properly quoted. Of these jobs, only some small percentage will be obtained. Obviously, nothing should be bid to increase weekly payroll unless there is a fair opportunity of obtaining a profitable job. Every effort should be made thereafter to get the work which is quoted. Bids are made not for practice or for the benefit of the buyer but to get work and stay in business. Selectivity thus becomes immediately necessary in order that prospective work be figured which one has the best chance of obtaining and doing profitably. Jobs must be compared with each other as to their relative worth for the contractor.

Such comparisons lead to many pertinent questions. Of a choice of prospective buyers, for whom should one bid to get equitable bidding treatment, fair supervision at a later date, and cash payment? For what type of work is an organization best gaited? Are there bidding limitations which may cause difficulty, such as the necessity of a large-volume certified check to accompany the quotation (and become unusable working capital)? Are there contractual terms anticipated requiring the withholding of an excessive amount of working capital (which can be dangerous later)? Does lack of work for key employees make the obtaining of a single large job represent a future problem for the organization?

There are other questions, of which only some are discussed here. The reader must be alert for those additional ones which are pertinent to his own business.

6-4   *Types of Bidding*

The instructions to bid, which classify the requested quotation as either *closed* or *open* bidding, are of primary importance to a construction firm. They help to determine if a job is of interest and worthy of investigation and how it should be bid. Although they seem to refer only to the manner of quoting, actually they lead to a preferential choice of job and customer in estimating.

A. *Closed Bidding*

In closed bidding the amounts of the various quotations *are not* disclosed to general knowledge. After delivery to the buyer, the bid becomes his property. He may use it for what he considers his best interests. He may choose the low bidder, the high bidder, or no bidder. He may have the plans and specifications revised and returned to some or all of the contractors for rebidding if the figured costs are in excess of what he wants to pay. He may accept suggestions, financial help, or other variation from one negotiator and not from another.

The so-called "select list," compiled by the owner, buyer, or designer, includes some bidders who should be excluded—and omits some who should be included. Favoritism is occasionally suspected. Actual monetary fraud is sometimes indicated, when a consideration passes to a buyer who is also a self-seeking individual to ensure that work is given to a certain bidder. The credit rating of owners extends from very good to speculative and even dangerous. And, worst of all, the presumed buyer may not even have authority to act. After negotiations are supposedly concluded, the documents may go to the actual party who gives out the contract (after further bartering).

Yet for all its disadvantages to the contractor, closed bidding is the method most used in obtaining quotations. It can result in an advantageous fixed-price contract for the buyer. For work of any value, this procedure allows financial arrangements to be set up far in advance of the need for payments. It gives bargaining power to the buyer.

It also has advantages for the contractor, which is the reason it continues in use. The number of bidders is limited to a selected list, which allows better pricing to the individual. The vast majority of purchasers are reputable businessmen of stability and known character. In negotiation, the contractor need only exercise common business prudence. Buyers are themselves subject to the pressures of their own going organizations regarding standards and the successful maintenance of structure after completion. This restraint tends to make the purchaser buy quality and good workmanship rather than price alone. Above all, buyers want good contractual relationships. Their own future reputations depend on their present actions, whom they choose, and how the business experience develops.

True negotiation can and does take place. Everything about the contract is subject to open discussion and can be mutually modified because of the pressing need of both participants to come to an agreement. As some changes are inevitable in every complex human endeavor, there is a good possibility that the contract, if obtained, may become more profitable to the contractor. (As a practical matter, the contractor who is actually doing the work at the time of change is the only one who can quote. If he wishes to retain the buyer as a future client, the charges of the contractor must be reasonable, but not necessarily low. He thus has an opportunity to better his contract.)

B. *Open Bidding*

In open bidding the amounts of the various quotations *are* disclosed to general knowledge. The buyer is usually a municipal, state, or federal agency—although some large entities, such as public service companies, occasionally follow this practice.

This procedure developed because of frauds which were commonly and notoriously perpetrated against the public interest. Public servants in positions of trust were privately determining the amount of each quotation. Regardless of who offered the best proposal, bids were changed, manipulated, awarded, and administered so that a sizable profit reverted to a favored few. Such situations became so scandalous that an open method of bidding was adopted as being most conducive to honesty and protective of the public interest.

In essence, work is publicly advertised and may be bid by anyone capable of meeting certain nominal fixed prerequisites. The quotation must be delivered in writing in a form that makes every bidder meet the same conditions. The quotations, all in sealed envelopes, are publicly opened at a specified time and place. If a quotation conforms to the requirements, the amount of the bid is read aloud and openly compared with others in the presence of competitors, press representatives, and the general public. This method is not perfect. For example, credit statements can be misleading, supervision may vary with prearrangement, or workmanship may be thoroughly uncomparative (also by prearrangement). But it is as good a system as has been developed for protecting the public interest.

From the contractor's viewpoint also, open bidding has some distinct advantages. Hidden influences (as in closed bidding) rarely succeed in getting a job away from a contractor who has been publicized as being the low bidder. There can be no negotiating not participated in by all. The awarding agency works in the spotlight of public notice and has little leeway in the choice of a contractor. As a result, the low bidder who has complied with the technicalities of the invitation to bid usually gets the award. (When other types of work are scarce, public bidding is generally available.)

There are other advantages. The payments are quite safe and loss by nonpayment is almost unheard of. Unreasonable demands are limited by what was in the original specification. This gives rise to the inevitable written extra order, which offers an opportunity to improve the contract. When unit prices must be divulged in the quotation by the terms of the bidding, an opportunity is afforded to compare competitive costs directly with other like bidders under known and similar conditions. Occasionally, a quotation requirement for extra or credit percentages will directly reveal what the competition is charging for services on this type of work. Such information is helpful for future bidding.

Of course, open bidding also has disadvantages. In times of stringency, public work is often the only type available. At any time, prerequisites for qualification are not strict and allow most contractors in business to bid if they so desire. A shortage of other work will allow them little alternative. The result is extreme competition in numbers and types of competitors in times of shortage of work—and also at most other times. This situation, in turn, forces low prices and little overage for the general contractor and his subcontractors. There is a consequent use of the lowest quality of material and workmanship which the specification and supervision will permit. Because of this, some contractors are not interested in this type of competitive bidding.

Also, because of their political vulnerability and since they are under perpetual scrutiny, the jurisdictional authorities must be impersonal and inflexible. There is often refusal to certify completion because of some picayune reason, motivated by fear of political retaliation. This condition leads to a tie-up of construction funds and a long-lasting legal responsibility. And for every payment, there is a large volume of forms to be made out and red tape to comply with, leading to high overhead and needless aggravation.

There is always a price to pay for lack of imagination and effort, such as this matter of going after work which is available to all and which is a matter of public knowledge.

6-5 *Special Types of Bidding*

In addition to the standard types of bidding previously described, the contractor may be asked to formulate a bid to meet a specific requirement of an individual buyer. This request will generally be on a closed basis and limited to a few contractors who have certain qualifications of particular interest to the buyer or who have impressed him with their worth. Such specialized bidding requests should be carefully evaluated by the contractor under existing conditions to determine if and how the price is affected.

It is not always true that such bidding is limited to those with whom the buyer has had previous successful experience. Others may be allowed to compete if they sell their organization properly to the buyer. Of course, it is easier to revive a previously successful contact than to bring a new one to the contract stage.

A. *The Negotiated Bid*

The term *negotiated bid* is misleading because most bids are negotiated. Actually, this type of bid involves a choice by the buyer of which of several contractors to use, based on factors additional to and overriding price. Such factors may be friendship, reputation, specialization, or appreciation of previous good work. The worth of the organization is sold, rather than the price of the job. This type of work is sought because the profit, while not guaranteed, is usually better than normal. (The limitation of the number of competitors always allows a better price.) The contractual terms may also be better than normal.

B. *The Upset-price Bid*

Here, the buyer is trying to protect himself. He wishes to give out a contract which will not amount to more than a definite maximum amount even though something will possibly vary. In effect, he asks the contractor to take an insurance risk. To get the job, the contractor becomes, in effect, a self-insurer. This is not an advantageous contract for either party and is not often encountered.

C. *The Cost-plus and Unit-price Bids*

For these two types of bids, there is a mutual problem handled in a different contractual manner. The volume of a particular class of work, or the work itself, cannot be outlined before the job is actually done. (For example, conditions must be exposed to be met.) Here, the buyer tries to keep down his cost (1) by limiting the overhead and profit allowed on the actual developed cost or (2) by limiting the monetary amount allowed for each of the units involved. Which of these methods is used will generally depend on the designer's judgment.

Sometimes the buyer, having faith in the honesty and capability of the contractors with whom he is dealing, may not consider it necessary to take the time and expend the energy to obtain a complete advance cost estimate. He will then ask only for the percentage or the fixed fee that will be added to the actual developed cost, without asking for a fixed price. For the contractor there is no loss possible, and this is a very advantageous form of contract. It is not common. But like every man-made instrument, this type of contract also has its problems. There is no money motivation to keep costs down, and thereby the buyer may become dissatisfied with what develops.

6-6   *Factors in Choosing Which Jobs to Bid*

From the practical standpoint of running a business, there are other job variations which further influence the choice of work for which to aim.

A. *Size*

Jobs can be classified as large or small, according to size. The size may be measured in area covered, volume enclosed, height, weight, amount of material to be moved, number of units to be constructed, total money to be expended, or any other measure of value.

The size of the job is important. The larger the job, compared with the average size of work in the vicinity, the fewer will be the number of firms figuring such work—and, of course, the less the competition. The percentage of estimating cost in terms of the total job cost decreases with increased size. Among other items, estimating takeoff time remains about the same for a large as for a small job. (The number of items remains about the same.) But in estimating, a large job is more apt to warrant the use of improved methods and machinery (and their prior investigation) than a small job. Because of their necessitous overhead, some large organizations can take only large jobs.

Adversely, the larger the job, the greater will be the risk. In terms of capital and credit availability, labor productivity, and general business safety, there is a limitation on the size and number and location of such larger jobs which should be bid for. Having a larger number of small jobs will tend to decrease the effects of such construction contingencies as inclement weather, labor rate changes, delivery and payment delays, and errors of omission and commission. Keymen will be more constantly needed and will justify steady employment. Some organizations should take jobs only up to a certain size.

A small job may also be advantageous as a means of getting some share of the construction business of a company in a continuously changing industry, such as a steel mill, a medical-supply producer, or an oil refinery. The work at any one time may be small and unprofitable, yet it may go right to the seat of authority and may provide invaluable contacts and reputation for later, more profitable eventualities. It is a form of advertising.

B. *Care, Attention Required*

Jobs should be of a type that is profitable for the organization which is considering estimating them. Small family groups with little formal education yet with considerable associated intelligence and skill may do well on jobs requiring individual attention. They can make money on masonry or carpentry alterations when overhead and work rules would make excessive the costs of larger organizations. The installation of a new elevator and shaft in an old but valuable walk-up building is a case in point. This type of job would be of worth to a small organization.

C. *Profit Advantage*

Some jobs can be classified as being conducive to obtaining profits beyond normal expectations.

Several jobs concentrated in one locality offer inherent advantages. Good local subcontractors are known because they are already working in the locality. Additional plans and specifications may easily be made available to them for examination in their own locality. There is a very distinct possibility of obtaining lower bids, reflecting knowledge of local labor conditions and availability and direct foremanship by the subcontractor, which leads to increased efficiency and better workmanship.

For the work which the contractor may do himself, local labor relations would improve with the possibility of shifting good workmen from one job to another in the same district. Such grading up of quality labor leads to better productivity. There is a saving of equipment, running expense, maintenance, and trucking.

There is a time-saving and much improved coverage of supervision and management. Quantity purchases of material lead to price discounts and to prompt deliveries for a valued account.

Of course, there are always some jobs on which, for various reasons, a contractor may anticipate a favorable reception from the buyer. Such specific instances will naturally receive individual consideration.

D. *Continuity of Employment*

Jobs offering consistency to the employment of labor give advantages. A single large job requires a considerable time lapse for the development of various phases. This may entail present labor layoffs and loss of key personnel or the carrying of payroll wastefully. A succession of smaller structures will tend to repeat oftener those phases which use steady employees, who then earn their pay more productively.

A further advantage may occur in the wording of laws controlling construction. The Social Security Act previously noted in Section 2-5E will serve as an instance. Taxes are figured not only as a deduction from the wage of the worker but also as a maximum yearly contribution from the contractor acting as an employer. Once this maximum amount has been reached, no further deduction and contribution are required of the contractor until the next fiscal year. Yet all estimating includes a continuous deduction for every employee for every job (reflecting the concept of a changeable labor supply). If continuity of employment allows the maximum yearly contribution to be reached, the balance stays with the contractor as a distinct accrual to his job return. It does not have to be contributed because the law says only a maximum must be contributed.

E. *Labor Conditions*

The employment of labor also means the employment of the same type of labor. There can be no competition between union and nonunion labor, either in hourly wages or in working conditions. Union labor, like every one, is not perfect, but in attempting to make social progress, it benefits everyone associated with the construction business. Nonunion labor is uncohesive and powerless to set wages and working conditions. There can be no bid price comparison. There can be no job mingling of union and nonunion labor, leading to conflict between diverse modes of thought—with a resultant loss to the contractor, who suffers if there is a conflict. Similarity of labor use by competitors and by job associates must, therefore, be investigated and made sure of before a job is figured.

Also, when a general contractor does his own work, the cost of union labor is greater than that of nonunion labor. His own estimated costs will be higher on a union basis. Work rules differ in every location. A simple example might be the stripping of wood forms and the removal of nails. In some locations union carpenters, at a skilled, higher rate of pay, would have to be hired to oppose nonunion laborers at a lower rate of pay. Production costs would then be higher.

Another source of loss might be jurisdictional disputes. This type of dispute occurs between union locals of differing trades, each of which claims the right to have only their own membership occupy the payroll position. There are additional wages inuring to the membership of a local organization which can secure additional work privileges of this nature. Such disputes are settled by the delegates and the membership to their own satisfaction and generally with the enforced concurrence of the general contractors. Should the local unions be unable to reach an agreement, executive union machinery exists to adjudicate any dispute and come to a binding decision. Unfortunately, this procedure takes time, and should such a dispute occur, the general contractor affected by this trade would be caught in the middle and would unavoidably lose if wages went up. (The jurisdictional dispute will remain a prolific source of loss to any contractor until new methods or materials are adjudicated.)

F. *Subcontracting*

In some jobs, the reaction and bid of the subcontractor can be of vital importance. Depending on the individual project, the major part of the general contractor's estimate may be composed of subcontract bids. If the contractor can be assured of obtaining low subbids from reliable subcontractors, he will have a good chance of getting profitable work. When a job is obtained, it is necessary to nourish the subbidders with work so that they can stay in business, keep estimating, and continue to submit good bids. From this purely selfish standpoint, "bid shopping" (the act of trying to peddle a subbid for a lower price than that originally quoted and used in obtaining a work contract) is unbusinesslike and shortsighted. It may obtain a lower bid than was originally estimated and, ostensibly, a better profit, but the action has antagonized the subbidder and has warned him that the next bid to this general contractor had better be higher to allow for future cutting. Such higher prices from subbidders are not conducive to getting future work.

G. *Integrity of Buyer*

Jobs must offer a reasonable assurance that a price tender will be treated by the buyer fairly and without prior decision having been made. Through salesmen, subcontractors, and other industry sources of information, it is readily possible to discover how a purchaser is rated in the trade. A sharp buyer is usual and need not be considered unethical. An unfair buyer (such as one having a predetermined contractor) is a hazard to all using the existing manner of conducting business to obtain work. This type of buyer should not have his job estimated. A very descriptive phrase covers this situation: "Mixing with dirt, one becomes dirty."

Some buyers are not deliberately unfair but are not apt to be impressed by a bidder who does not belong to their golf or bridge club, is not a college alumnus, or is not on the same board of directors. If the contractor cannot meet the requirements of such a customer, it is an exercise in futility to attempt to get his work.

Estimating costs money. Why do it with the odds against success?

H. *Financial Solvency*

Jobs must be considered from a financial viewpoint. Advance information on contractual financing terms is generally part of the request to bid or can be obtained. Such information clarifies payments, retainage percentages, assurance against unwarranted delays in approval of payment—in short, any cause for depletion of working capital. This is particularly important when a contractor does his own work and must meet a weekly payroll—with no excuses.

In many cases, the ability to furnish a construction bond with the quotation is a requisite of the invitation to bid. Before issuing the bond, any insurance company will investigate and insist on a statement of present financial worth regardless of past favorable experience, and especially if there has been no previous experience.

Also, taking trade discounts for prompt payment of material invoices is a very important factor in continuing to do business and, of course, is dependent on ready cash. On some jobs it may constitute the margin between profit and loss. Keeping a fixed minimum of working capital on hand is vital.

Contractual terms vary from job to job, but they always must be examined carefully as to their influence upon a bid. Should there be any question about wording or intent, a legal opinion should be obtained.

I. *Financial Safety*

Jobs must be considered from a credit standpoint as to how business safety is involved. An apartment house, a nursing home, or any other structure may be motivated either conservatively or speculatively. Before bidding a job, the contractor must know a considerable amount about the backers of a job and how the job is being financed. If such information is hard to obtain, that paucity of knowledge is already a bad sign. The primary purpose of being in business is to establish and maintain a livelihood—not to jeopardize that business by taking unnecessary chances, particularly for others.

This is another reason why the cultivation of trade news sources is of importance. Much information generally exists on most topics (including individuals), and the lack of knowledge in itself may be a sign to be questioned. The contractor need have no hesitation in asking about the financing of any work which appears questionable in any manner. He is a disinterested individual taking a business risk for a transient return, and he must, above all, be interested in getting paid. If credit information is not made freely available to him and is not satisfactory in every way, he should definitely avoid commitment.

A great deal of hard work is required to make up for one loss.

J. *Competition*

Jobs must be considered in terms of the competition to be encountered. This competition may affect the pricing to such an extent that it may not be desirable to go after a job.

The greater the number of competitors, the lower will be the contract price. Because of plan and specification similarity, the construction cost will be comparable for all. Therefore, any decrease in price below a certain point can come only out of profit.

The type of competition also influences bidding. The contractor who prices every takeoff correctly to make an assured and reasonable profit is a customary business rival. But the type who prices low simply to ob-

tain a job—and to wring out a profit later by skimping on the workmanship and materials—is not rational or predictable. Many firms will not
figure a job against certain companies.

Particularly is this problem noticeable in work involving civil or gov-
ernmental supervision and approval of payments. Such work customarily
involves considerably more overhead in requisite red tape than does the
normal industrial job. Provided the overhead costs involved can be obtained, there is no problem. But when the competition will not permit
such proper inclusion, production and overhead allowances will be
dangerously low. Figuring such work to make money is a questionable
practice.

6-7   *The Aim of Bidding*

In the above discussion, the many items which must be considered before
a job is even bid were noted. A firm which follows a policy of bidding
every job available to it only depresses prices for itself and for others.
From a profit standpoint, such a procedure hurts everyone, including the
firm itself.

To obtain a larger proportion of the work bid and to get profitable
work must be the aim. This goal can be reached in more intelligent ways
than by meeting price competition on anything and everything. Consider,
for example, the policy adopted by the highly competitive yet successful
chain stores: cut costs in buying and elsewhere, compete on prices when
necessary, offer some type of "come-on" to bring the customer into the
store and then try to sell something else with an excellent markup, and
above all, on average, sell to make a profit.

One of the methods of getting additional work is to engage in more
services. Jobs require financing and realty work, architectural and engineering work, construction, equipment, and supplies. On some jobs the
builder performs all functions for the buyer, and when the key to the
lock is given to the purchaser, the latter receives a finished building in
operating order. The savings to the purchaser in overhead, time, financing, detail responsibility, and responsibility for supervision of construction and design more than pay for the contractor's overall increase of
profit margin. Such completeness also places additional emphasis on
ability, honesty, reliability, and finances. There is always a danger, of
course, and that is the antagonism of other members of the business
community.

Every function which is combined with others preempts a source of
work from the market and removes a source of construction business. The
builder whose organization handles financing, realty, design, and the
construction for which it was originally organized has taken over work

which others did previously. From an economic view, this action may be justified. It does not, however, make friends among many who were a former source of construction inquiries. The financial setup must afford enough strength to offset considerable opposition.

Other methods of gaining a benefit from some particular knowledge or other asset will occur to every individual. All require weighing the advantages and disadvantages involved.

7

APPLICATION
OF SALES PLANNING

Knowledge of the principles of getting work does help in planning successfully. Work itself, however, will not be obtained without the application of intelligent *and consistent* effort. *That effort must not moderate* with the attainment of a contract and start again only with the approach of a need for additional work. Because eventually work becomes scarce, contacts have to be maintained when times are good and business easy to come by. There never should be an obnoxious and independent attitude conferred by the happy accident of having work. The entrance door should be open at all times.

7-1   *The Development of Business*

Opportunities arise in the construction field as elsewhere. Possibilities of work follow as a result of new laws enacted by governing bodies, the relocation of highways, the installation of a sanitary sewer, or some local zoning change. General news, such as a yearly profit statement of an industrial company, may also be of interest if a profitable capital-investment side effect can be foreseen. Occasionally, a political subdivision, such as a state, will publish a so-called "economic review," listing new industries moving into a specific location.

Such provocative news items, however, do require time, circumstances, and cultivation to come to fruition. The day-in and day-out normal construction business develops otherwise.

7-2   *Finding Out Where the Jobs Are*

Generally job information develops as the solution of a previous problem specifically detailed by architects, engineers, or other designers for a client—and in blueprint and specification form specifically prepared to obtain quotations. This information, however, is not broadcast freely. In many cases it has to be unearthed, and the opportunity to bid must then be obtained. Leads may come in various ways, as in the following examples:

A. A contractor receives an unsolicited request to bid from a designer or other buyer. Usually this comes to one who has been actively in construction for some time and has built up a good reputation.

B. A contractor solicits possible initiators of work. He may circularize, personally visit, send individual letters, or otherwise contact local manufacturing plants, municipalities, home owners, or other potential buyers in whatever field he serves. Of course, this list of originators includes architects, engineers, and other designers.

C. A contractor obtains bidding possibilities from other sources of trade news. These include bidding services, periodicals, material dealers, real estate salesmen, and other friendly business associates. Also included are daily newspapers, chambers of commerce or other local service organizations publicizing new industries and facilities to be available, and other similar services of use to all. But when news becomes public property, it becomes subject to employment by others. It has also been available previously. When the public disclosure is made, it may already be too late in point of bid development to contact an unpledged prospective customer or to meet an unmet need. Even when the job is still available, there may be excessive competition. Therefore, it is advisable to work up business before news becomes public knowledge.

To further this objective, it becomes necessary to consider why men build. Motivations for construction are shown on the checklist (Figure 7-1). Throughout this text, wherever such summaries are given, they are suggestive rather than all-inclusive. Additional causative influences will occur to the individual in a particular business, and he will benefit most by also thinking for himself.

---

1. Construction is required in a special or a present location.

   (a) There is a necessity to expand in a fixed location.

2. Specialized requirements and facilities are needed.

3. There is an opportunity to make a greater profit in construction than elsewhere.

   (a) Tax and inheritance laws allow savings.

4. Disaster damage must be repaired.

   (a) Abandoned projects must be finished.

5. New facilities and changing conditions afford opportunity.

6. Depreciation and obsolescence must be corrected.

7. Administrative structures are to be built.

   (a) Municipal buildings, such as schools, courthouses.

   (b) Public-purpose structures, such as hospitals, churches, for sewage districts, port authorities.

   (c) Prestige, memorial, political, or other social.

8. Build or rebuild to take advantage of changes in directives such as zoning, occupancy, or permitted use.

   (a) Altering present structures for occupancy or new uses.

   (b) Erecting taxpayers to carry landholding expenses.

9. Build where speculation is a factor.

10. Contract construction for others on a lease or other basis.

11. Form or join groups for profit.

12. Construct for other and highly individual uses.

---

figure 7-1. Motivations for construction.

7-3   *Sources of Construction Work*

A. Construction may be required in a special or a present location. This is particularly true of stores and other industrial establishments of considerable capital investment which may have to expand in a fixed location. This necessity may be due to existing transportation facilities, established shopping districts and reputation, zoning requirements, machinery or other foundations, and similar existing and limiting factors. When the requirements of growth necessitate increased space or additional facilities, the already developed value of existing trade and improvements makes a location change almost unthinkable. Such industries are almost compelled to alter or add to their existing investment and expand in the same or an adjoining location.

Incidentally, alteration work of this nature is not always pursued aggressively because it requires knowledge and close attention to detail. For this reason, it offers an excellent opportunity to make a better-than-average profit.

B. Specialized facilities may be needed. Many companies are unable to obtain rental requirements on the open market. A cold-storage warehouse may require insulated walls, the ability to carry heavy loads, a railroad spur connection, and accessibility to a commercial airport. A chemical plant may have to be located in a district zoned to allow odors and the disposition of fluid industrial wastes and may have to be free of adjoining fire hazards. An automobile salesroom may require showroom and office space in front, a service station with a lot of storage space and easy access in the rear, and special ventilation to take fumes directly from operating automobile engines being repaired to a special exhaust system and stack.

C. There may be an opportunity to make a greater profit in construction than elsewhere. Laws are occasionally passed to foster a particular type of construction to meet a need. Such legislation generally also makes financing available, and this situation helps make the proposition attractive. In times of stringency, many bank institutions holding defaulted mortgages may have to take over obsolete buildings. To modernize such holdings and get them out of the bank's portfolio, institutional financing must be made available even though money is generally unavailable.

Government financing is available for many large-scale projects. And at any time the construction and sale of a structure may afford long-term cash advantages which are profitable from a tax angle. Or rental of shelter, office space, or space for industrial use may offer an attractive investment.

D. Disaster damage must be repaired. Fire, flood, storm, or other calamaties result in repair or replacement of present installations and sometimes in new work. In many cases, owners of damaged property must get advance cost estimates for the negotiation of insurance settlements. There is an inside track created here to the owner's attention, resulting often in the possibility of estimating work with little competition from others.

This category includes abandoned projects which must be finished by others, such as for the bonding company or other creditors. Such repossession may entail redesign or refinancing to obtain completion and has many legal intricacies. This type of business, because it is out of the ordinary, can be most worthwhile.

E. New facilities and changing conditions afford opportunity. The installation of a new storm sewer (for water only) will permit the drainage of old basements and the design of new ones. The installation of a sanitary sewer (for disposal of waste material) may foretell new zoning and land use—with probable local construction activity.

A new transit route may open up an extensive area for development. Not only speculators but also well-financed investors are attracted. The subsequent regrading will precede new curbs and paving, power and gas requirements, supermarkets and taxpayers, places of worship and schools.

F. Depreciation and obsolescence must be corrected. Depreciation, of course, is a lessening of value due to use, age, defective construction, or some similar cause. Roofs leak; plumbing pipes do not run off quickly or do not run off at all; sidewalks and parking areas settle, bulge, or crack dangerously.

Obsolescence is also a lessening of value but is due to a change in design, material, application, use, or other variation which makes usable articles become archaic because of social change. The incorporation of such modern ideas as decreased ornamentation, increased light and power services, air conditioning, or improved vertical transportation will often renew the earning power of well-located real estate.

Such changes involve complementary requirements and lead to other sources of business.

G. Administrative structures have to be built. A municipal building involves functionalism, aesthetics, and construction for exceptionally long usefulness. As with a school, courthouse, and even a municipal garage, such a building is designed for prestige and as a memorial of the past. The result is accomplished at a cost which is considerably greater than the cost per cubic foot of a similar commercial structure. Acceptable results are obtained through care in design and specification and through public bidding, as heretofore described. The market is large, diverse, and relatively free of unfair influences, but it is unduly competitive. Undoubtedly, such work is sometimes profitable and must be considered.

H. Advantage may be taken of changes in zoning, occupancy, or permitted use. For example, a neighborhood of private dwellings becomes a business district, including apartment buildings. Every property owner who has not already made a substantial reinvestment in the future is a prospect for a construction change.

This variation includes necessitous temporary construction. Occasionally a piece of property may be held back because of caution or because it cannot be developed to its full use at the time. The owner, nevertheless, is a prospective customer. To pay taxes and other carrying charges, a small store building or other structure might be indicated. Some construction may be involved at this time, with more to come at a later date.

Existing zoning might permit other uses which are both feasible and profitable. An alert builder can suggest an additional profit possibility in the same land ownership to merit a new construction job. It is true that some of this missionary work turns out to be fruitless. This is a business risk which can be successful, however, and pay off profitably.

I. Speculation may be a factor. There are always those who will attempt to exploit others to make money. Because they are generally egoists, with faith in their own ability, a knowledge of the law for their self-protection, and a complete disregard for the welfare of others, they are a danger to the legitimate business community. Yet because of their risk taking in initiating projects, there is always considerably more construction activity in their presence than would appear without them. It is hard to recognize them because they may be apparently well financed and operating within the law. Yet a consistency in diverting funds from those who merit them is a probable sign (although only one) of involvement with such an individual (see Section 12-7).

Here, the contractor must beware. One job resulting in loss of working capital can offset many jobs with some percentage of profit obtained on the cost of doing work. The speculative builder may take refuge behind his own contract terms. For example, he may have arranged a construction loan with payment to be made after the plumbing fixtures are installed—which involves, in turn, his payment to various subcontractors. This time arrives, the loan is consummated and paid, but the deserved subcontract invoices are not paid in full by him. Trouble may be anticipated.

Occasionally a contractor may figure on stopping work until he gets his money or on protecting himself in other ways. There is no sure protection against a knowledgeable, hard, and shrewd individual whose actions are always in advance of the reactions of his contractors. The safest policy is strict preexamination of reputation and credits and noninvolvement in any job which is a possible source for suspicion.

J. When complete contract building to service the needs of others becomes a method of doing business, additional manpower is required. The process of creating and maintaining entire projects requires corollary functions. These include site location and acquisition, planning, financing, construction, equipment, and furnishing. This type of contractual arrangement allows one firm to be responsible for everything from a lease to the electric light bulbs. There are relatively few firms capable of such service, and competition is considerably decreased.

Note again, however, that the contractor must build up a continuously active and specialized management and sales force (requiring invested capital) even if he uses the adjacent real estate office, the local bank, and his own hardware-supply house as assistants. He must use time and money actively to promote inquiries. This has become part of his business. But such service offers advantages. When a prospective buyer is also an owner and his organization is limited in size and the particular experience needed, he will welcome competent assistance. For these reasons, his work is easier to obtain and more profitable.

There is a danger in the planning function. Should the contractor occasionally try to do his own design work, he runs the risk of competing with and antagonizing the architects and engineers who are his good friends and a source of the majority of the work which he does. Some contractors handle such situations by stating that professional associates will be employed for such work. This device obviates the need of establishing an architectural department and pays off in good relations.

K. Forming trade groups may initiate work. Although the contractor generally builds for others, he is in a most advantageous position to be his own beneficiary. Ownership of structures, in whole or in part, affords a steady yearly income and fosters financial stability. If inflation continues its slow rise and the long-term face value of money continues to decrease in actual buying power, there is no better hedge to retain what one has made and saved than the ownership of something of real and income-producing value. The currency income should go up as the money value goes down.

A number of costs can be eliminated or reduced. If his own business associates and subcontractors cohere under his leadership, the contractor can obtain participation in plans, financing, subtrade construction, operation, and sales. Some contractors have purchased sites for industrial parks with a real estate agent as one of the partners (and, of course, the latter also acts as renting agent, with an added incentive to do well). Others have cut initial cash required by having subcontractors install various trades needed as their investment. Wherever an opportunity exists, a trade group can take advantage of it.

7-4   *Using Information Sources*

To get his share of the competitive work of the marketplace, the contractor must make use of the existing sources of information. Customary origins of news are given in Figure 7-2. News, however, means fresh news. When a number of competitors have already received plans and specifications to figure, there will be no more plan sets available. Even if the buyer wants to get another bid, the field is already overcrowded and the plans from the designer are limited in number and identity. Also, time is required for estimating and obtaining subbids. Usually a closing date is set for receiving bids which permits a time period that is just barely adequate for formulating a careful quotation. Therefore, sources must be contacted constantly to obtain plans and specifications even when one has work. To leave until the last possible minute the obtaining

1. Architects, engineers, surveyors

2. Owners, buyers, and prospective investors

3. Real estate news, indications, business relations

4. Insurance (salvage, casualty, bonding, fire, and other)

5. Public agency (federal, state, county, municipal, special authorities, and purchasing, building, engineering departments)

6. Trade services, newspapers, periodicals, special function (reports and services)

7. Industrial (earning reports, purchasing inquiries)

8. Public service and other localized companies having industrial development departments

9. Financial institutions (to salvage loans, mortgages or other foreclosures)

10. Religious (diocesan, individual, regional)

11. Personal (friends, business acquaintances, contacts)

12. Previous clients

13. Material supply and equipment companies

14. Miscellaneous local service organizations such as chambers of commerce

15. Advertising (requests for bids)

16. Initiating projects

figure 7-2. Some sources of information.

of work to estimate, or anything which will be needed for that estimate, means failure to get that item when it is required or to allow sufficient time for accuracy.

The contractor must not put too much faith in present business relationships. Even when there is an adequate supply of work on hand, there is no assurance that such an auspicious state of affairs will continue. Relationships and conditions change, as when the sons of a founder move into control and bring their own friends with them. Any organization dealt with today will have others in charge at some later time.

Also, competition is always present and always trying to get business. It should not be underestimated, even when excellent relationships exist. In comparing propositions offered to him, a business acquaintance and present client, even a most friendly one, must think first of the interests of his firm and of himself. In so doing, if the proposition offered to him by the competition has merit, even if he has not asked for it, he will consider it.

Of course, this policy of continuous bidding may overload an organization with work which it has figured to do with its own forces. If it is now compelled to sublet, with a consequent loss of profit, this change will affect the worth of the job. Also, financially there may be an overload and actual monetary stringency. Lack of adequate planning and supervision may cause a loss. Delivery promises are jeopardized, and clients may be antagonized.

At such time of plenty, the quotation should be arbitrarily increased in price to take care of any possible increased costs. If the work is obtained, the money has also been obtained to buy relief by allowing a margin for contingencies. If the bid is a little high, at least a competitive quotation has been submitted to keep the contractor in a reliable contact position. (Work opportunities occur regularly with the same people, and their goodwill must be maintained.) Incidentally, if volume of work prevents a contractor from using his own estimator for an additional makeup, it is possible to use a subcontractor specializing in quantity takeoffs. This procedure carries the added insurance of competent checking and is well worthwhile to keep the firm on the active bidding list. Subcontract quantity takeoffs have the disadvantage of not always giving the understanding which will allow minimum pricing.

Attractive work should always be sought.

7-5 *Going After Work*

After the contractor has decided what work to go after, he has to convince the buyer of his ability to do the job. Due to other prior satisfactory relations or to a lack of previous information regarding the contractor, the buyer will probably require convincing. Therefore, the contractor should assemble and have printed on separate letterheads of the firm such credit information as will be basicly representative (Figures 7-3 and 7-4). This format permits mailing the information or leaving it after a personal call, and it can be added to should something pertinent appear. (Brought up to date every year, it is also good advertising to go out with any mail to others who might also be prospects for work.)

Upon closer inspection, the prospective job may have drawbacks. The specification may be obviously set up to favor the buyer, with prohibitive contingencies and exorbitant retainers. Or the contractor's experience may indicate to him that the design requires revision; a refrigerator-room floor, for example, has been placed on unventilated concrete slabs without provision for heaving. The contractor would like to have the bidding changed to become more favorable in certain respects. Normally this attitude would lead to antagonism and loss of work. But in the

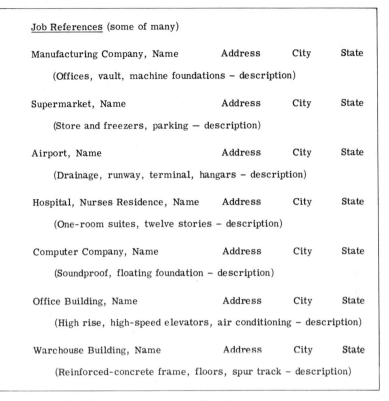

figure 7-3. Qualification summary, job references.

construction business, the buyer and contractor often influence each other.

It is true that the buyer sets the rules under which he will accept offers to do work. Unquestionably, he has the power of the purse. But the buyer can get the advantage he is seeking only if he can get a number of competitive bids for comparison. Not only must these be comparable bidders known to the buyer for good workmanship and good repute, but one of them must be willing for some reason to take the work below the price of the competition. Note specifically that the experienced buyer recognizes a limitation in the number of those with whom he can deal. He realizes that being in his own type of business, he is not a builder and cannot afford to antagonize those whom he needs. He will therefore be amenable to reason.

The contractor, for his part, does not wish to antagonize any prospective customer. Yet the contractor is preparing to spend money in making up a quotation and is entitled to consideration. He can always direct that

Financial References (some of many)

First State Bank	Address	City	State
	Attn: Name		Title
	Phone number		

National Craftsman Bank	Address	City	State
	Attn: Name		Title
	Phone number		

Masonry supply company	Address	City	State
	Attn: Name		Title
	Phone number		

Carpentry & Trim Mill	Address	City	State
	Attn: Name		Title
	Phone number		

Readymix Concrete company	Address	City	State
	Attn: Name		Title
	Phone number		

Plumbing & Heating supply company	Address	City	State
	Attn: Name		Title
	Phone number		

figure 7-4. Qualification summary, financial references.

time, effort, and money toward some other work in which he has a better chance to make money. The contractor's attitude will also be flexible.

7-6   *Follow-up*

There is, thus, a necessity for the contractor to contact the buyer directly (affording the additional benefit of getting to know each other). This communication requires the preplanned use by the contractor of some method of follow-up so as consistently to develop approved sources and contacts. The procedure may entail the use of the telephone, the mail, industrial directories, friends or business acquaintances, or any conceivable method of obtaining personal information. There are not many jobs which an organization cares to or can go after. Each factual one, therefore, is worthy of whatever effort is necessary to obtain the appropriate contacts—including noteworthy details, such as correct spelling of names and titles, actual location, and other information.

In using the telephone, one procedure is to ask for the secretary of the head of the buyer's firm. Confide your purpose to her, ask her assistance, get her name and record it, and address her personally as an individual of importance—which she is. You need her cooperation and the information which she can give. Attention to every foreseeable small detail is one essential for success in selling single units of very considerable money value. (Other information methods require other devices, but all require personal action.) Such action means finding the correct person. It is a waste of time and effort to see someone without authority. Deal with the right person from the start.

7-7   Letter Writing

After such preliminary intelligence has been obtained, the use of a form-paragraph book is indicated (Figure 7-5). Provided a conscious effort is made in advance to personalize every letter, the forms will not be too impersonal and are advantageous time-savers. Numbered paragraphs (for the stenographer) are made out ahead of time for reiterative situations. Such paragraphs should be formulated way before any deadline, affording an improvement in language, spelling, and effectiveness, and with due regard to emphasizing the bidder's strong points. Of course, an individual paragraph may be added concerning anything that warrants special attention. Of importance is the mental reminder offered of what should be included. Paragraphs, in turn, can be further subdivided into topics for easy use, such as introductions, descriptions, proposals, references, endings.

The form-paragraph book, like a computer, works on the principle of mechanically using prearranged material to save time, but it is much less expensive.

Correspondence is one of the articles of concrete evidence by which the conversant buyer can judge the respective suitability of close competitors. A logical and clear approach suggests that the same trend of mind will be used in solving the problems of construction. Every communication from the contractor to the buyer not only is a record but must be thought of also as the carrier of a sales impression. Each letter must impress the buyer as being a good letter. A clear block setup with generous margins and spacing will add to legibility and appearance. Such items are developed in letter-writing texts.

Referring again to the form-paragraph book shown in Figure 7-5:

Paragraph 1. The date is an important point of reference for all future action.

Paragraph 2. Personalization is conferred, and a buyer's ego amplified, by using his name and title.

Paragraph 3. The subject to be discussed requires close attention. It affects the body of the communication. Much unnecessary wordiness

---

(1)   Date

(2)   Name   Address   Town   State

        Attention   Zip Code

(3)   Re:

(4)   (a) Dear Sir: (b) Gentlemen: (c) Dear Madam:

(5)   (a) Confirming our conversation with_____

        (b) We ask to be placed on your bidders list for the above work.

(6)   Responsible and yet competitive bids are necessary for your require-ments. You will get such quotations from us. Our responsibility can be verified from the enclosed qualifications, and the photo postcard is representa-tive of the structures we build. Our pricing passes on to you the savings effected by grouping in one area our purchases of labor and material.

(7)   We do our own concrete work, masonry, and carpentry so as to have these key trades under our direct control for workmanship and time of comple-tion. You are assured that you are associated with an existing organization which can fulfill your future expansion requests directly without the necessity of subletting your work to others.

(8)   In addition to other locations, we have successfully finished a structure in your immediate vicinity for_____. We are familiar with the unusual ground and water conditions. At your request, we have asked Mr._____(Title) to tell you his exact experience with our organization and to show you our workmanship.

(9)   (Other distinctive paragraphs)

(10) Kindly advise us if you are contemplating new or alteration work of any nature. Our experience in fulfilling the diverse requirements of others indicates that we can be of help to you.

---

figure 7-5. Form-letter paragraphs.

can be eliminated at this point by using this section as an expository reference.

Paragraph 4. The purchasing function varies with the company. The sex of the buyer is not always indicated by the name and is one of the items of information to be requested. Some companies may also require that communications to purchasing be sent in a special manner or to the firm.

Paragraph 5. Combine *a* and *b* if at all possible. Otherwise, outline in this first paragraph what you want. (One of the principles of effective letter writing is to emphasize this aim in different words as many times as it can be said in a new way.)

Paragraph 6. This is an example of a paragraph to attract the buyer's attention to the benefits accruing to his company by using the organization of the writer. He has to be induced by such a paragraph to read this one of many letters in its entirety.

Paragraph 7. This paragraph is a follow-up of paragraph 6, calling attention to additional advantages offered at no additional cost but with better workmanship. A target of superiority has been set up, indicating that the buyer should look into this factor as against the work of competitors. What a firm does is important.

Paragraph 8. A reference paragraph further personalizes the letter by inserting mention of a similar job or location. Wherever a personal reference is mentioned, permission must be obtained first. This courteous approach is correct and flattering to a former client and also affords an opportunity to ask if more construction is contemplated. Occasionally another lead develops.

Paragraph 9. As a reminder that some individual treatment may be possible and requisite, this paragraph is provided.

Paragraph 10. Here is a reiteration of the aim of paragraph 5. The last paragraph of the letter has strength conferred by position and should clearly restate the message to be acted on.

Every letter must be brief yet informative and individual and must include the conscious use of sales principles. A prospective buyer will surely read your message only once. That is when you may be a source of benefit to him. At that time your message must be as good as you can make it.

Such letters, when addressed to circularize a mailing list of a specialized industry, may uncover unusual and unforeseen sources of business. In particular, architects and engineers from out of the locality who possess unusual capabilities or associations with some particular local company should be contacted. Their names are not generally indicated anywhere, and prospective local bidders will be of interest to them.

The mailing-list letters, when individually addressed, tend to get to the right party with no officious interference, as might be the case with other means of communication. Due to the broadcast nature of the mailing, there is a wide field of possible motivations covered, which increases the possibility of obtaining replies.

7-8   *The Qualification Summary*

In the form-letter wording of paragraph 6 above, mention is made of a qualification summary. This is typed or printed as a separate enclosure in order to keep the main letter reasonably short (and to minimize the typing burden on the office staff). Considerable additional information can be given in this manner for the buyer to assimilate if he is interested. For such qualifications, Figures 7-3 and 7-4 show types of forms which can be changed as soon as there is favorable new information. New jobs and new references offer opportunity again to circularize prospective buyers. It is this constant circularization and reiterative impact which produces results. Needless to say, such forms should be carefully worked over. There should be a minimum of verbiage and a maximum of clearly presented facts.

Such assurances carry weight with buyers. Particularly when a firm has no printed brochure, some printed matter should exist which can be filed with a prospective customer. Purchasing agents, particularly, are habituated to receiving this type of information, which they can compare as they assemble bids.

Some qualifications required for public bidding may have to be made out in a special way. These should be done as wanted, and copies attached to the quote copy for future need.

7-9   *Graphic Aids*

In the form-letter wording of paragraph 6 (Figure 7-5) is a reference to a photocard illustration. A picture is better than a great many words. Buyers do not look in classified telephone directories or periodical advertisements for the names of construction organizations. They are interested in receiving pictures and short descriptions of work similar to what their present knowledge indicates are their own future requirements. They file such information to build up future sources of obtaining their own budget figures and such other information as is necessary to meet management requests. There is no better source of cost information than a contractor who has just finished similar work. There is no better advertising for a construction firm than its own work. A reproduction of a job photograph together with a short description of its features (and an approximate cost indication in an accompanying letter) is a good advertisement for any direct-mail campaign.

The use of attention-getting devices is also helpful. Figure 7-6 shows an advertising postcard made from a black-and-white photograph; a colored photograph may be used for extra attention value. The brief

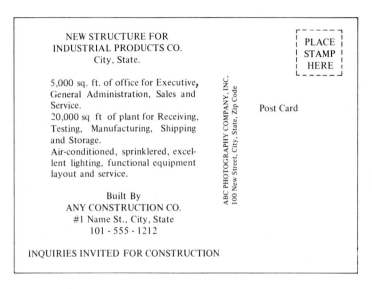

NEW STRUCTURE FOR
INDUSTRIAL PRODUCTS CO.
City, State.

5,000 sq. ft. of office for Executive, General Administration, Sales and Service.
20,000 sq ft of plant for Receiving, Testing, Manufacturing, Shipping and Storage.
Air-conditioned, sprinklered, excellent lighting, functional equipment layout and service.

Built By
ANY CONSTRUCTION CO.
#1 Name St., City, State
101 - 555 - 1212

INQUIRIES INVITED FOR CONSTRUCTION

ABC PHOTOGRAPHY COMPANY, INC.
100 New Street, City, State, Zip Code

Post Card

PLACE
STAMP
HERE

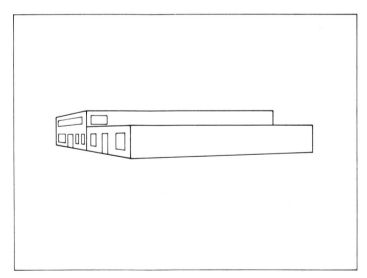

figure 7-6. Photo postcard advertising.

message about an actual new job will be noticed, read, kept, and applied. It may be mailed out alone at a minimum of office labor, time, and expense, or it can be enclosed with a business letter going out of the office.

If the organization has done considerable newsworthy construction and has the wherewithal to do a good job, it should make out a printed brochure to represent the firm in the best possible light. The makeup of such a massive advertising effort is warranted only by actual jobs successfully completed and by an organization that is capable of doing more work. Considerable professional printing know-how is involved, from text and illustrations to paper and format. The making and utilization of the brochure are a job for a competent advertising agency. The product is an expensive sales tool and has to be put to use upon being achieved.

There is no one best method of pursuing business. The results are what count.

7-10 *More Follow-up*

A sales letter alone rarely leads to permission to estimate except with an out-of-town firm. Every buyer is subject to many influences intended to get other competitors on a bidding list for a worthwhile job. Consistent personal follow-up is necessary to confirm information, secure prequalification when required, and above all, get results. A follow-up form is shown in Figure 7-7. It should be clipped up prominently in front of the person entrusted with this vital business task as a daily reminder.

In types of business having a number of leads to follow, it may be advisable to transcribe this information to 3 × 5 inch index cards. Each card is punched to fit on a rod-type clipboard and is placed in chronological order on the rack so that the bid due dates turn up in rotation. This method conserves office manpower by allowing those jobs which are most pressing in point of time to be followed up first. This is particularly useful for a subcontractor receiving request postcards for various jobs which are to be bid on differing dates. The postcards themselves can then be punched, clipped to the rack in order of due dates, and attended to in that order.

The form the follow-up may take is the telephone call, personal visit, use of favorable influence, or whatever seems best suited to get on that particular bidding list. Frequently the buyer has so many requests to allow bidding that he must limit his list to that number which he can adequately handle. He actually does not know whom to choose.

His decision will be human and therefore not always logical or just. He may choose on the basis of reputation, financial stability, acquaintanceship, other influence of some nature, type of work, or equipment to

(Date)

Office Building – (5 stories, floor area 10,000 sq ft)

Owner	Address	City	State	Telephone
Architect	Address	City	State	Telephone

Carried forward from (date). Spoke to Mr._____ (Owner's representative).

Financing not arranged. Phone again on (Date).

Factory and Office – (20,000 sq ft, 90% factory, 10% office)

Owner	Address	City	State	Telephone
Architect	Address	City	State	Telephone
Original Report		Date	Source	

(Date) Spoke to_____(Architect).

Plans not ready. Phone again (Date).

Administration Building – (Board of Education)

Architect	Address	City	State	Telephone
Original Report		Date	Source	

(Date) Spoke to Miss_____(Secy. of architect).

Public proposal to be published (Date).

Auto Freight Terminal – (35,000 sq ft, 1 story)

Owner	Address	City	State	Telephone
Architect	Address	City	State	Telephone
Engineer	Address	City	State	Telephone
Original Report		Date	Source	

(Date) Spoke to Mr._____(Local district manager for owner). Many requests. May not get on bidders list. Write home office at

Address	City	State	Attn: Mr.

(Date) Visited Mr _____(Vice-pres. for owner, local hotel). Nice interview. Got special requirements. Will receive plans and specifications by mail about (Date). Thereafter will receive phone call from Engineer to visit site with other competitors.

figure 7-7. Prospect follow-up.

be used. He may be guided by any of many reasons. He must be *personally* swayed in making his choice.

Again, note that in addition to previously mentioned sources, a wide acquaintance and good relationships give news and entrée in many places. Whether the source is a knowledgeable subcontractor or a golf-course friend, the information and assistance are where you find them. The indicated course of action is a constant yet flexible follow-up to obtain for bidding a series of jobs with profit potential.

8

SUBCONTRACTING
POLICY DETERMINATION

When a satisfactory plan and specification are on hand for estimating, a contractor must decide what work he will do with his own forces, material, and equipment and what work he will sublet to others (thereby becoming a general contractor). The choice will change the manner of takeoff and the pricing, the cost of the final quotation, the quality of workmanship, and even the future relations with the buyer. The decision will depend on what is most advantageous for the contractor.

8-1 *The Role of Subcontracting in Construction Work*

A contractor may do all the work contracted for with labor under his control and in his pay, with material which he purchases, and with equipment in accordance with his designed method of installation. He has direct control.

On the other hand, a contractor can give out to others any percentage and any type of the work contracted for if he believes that the benefits will outweigh the losses to him—and there are benefits and losses in subcontracting.

106

In becoming a general contractor, there is chiefly a loss of direct control over time, workmanship, and material. There are offsetting gains in financing, delivery, meeting payroll, and other items.

The amount of subcontracting varies from giving out very little to giving out every trade; in the latter case, the contractor becomes a broker of construction service. He is known as a general contractor regardless of the percentage of work which he handles himself, because he accepts responsibility for a large part of completion.

When a buyer gives out a trade contract directly, that is, does not include it in the contractual agreement of the general contractor, such a contract is known as a *prime contract*, as differentiated from any other contract.

Subcontracting is a recognized function of construction because of the many valuable business purposes it serves.

8-2 *Policy Determination*

The choice of subcontract trades to use will vary from job to job according to changes in design. Therefore, the bidding documents are studied and may result in a different invitation list to required subbidders for each successive job. Of course, these invitations to bid presuppose that the general contractor has resolved the question of using union or non-union labor on the job, discussed in Chapter 2. As the two classes of labor are totally incompatible and noncompetitive, the general contractor will have to use one or the other. He therefore must be assured:

1. That the classification of labor used by any subbidder will match that of any other, including that of the general contractor, and will not clash on the job.

2. That any contractor is protected by whoever is taking the bidding, so that he will compete only against users of the same class of labor. There can otherwise be no comparison of bids.

Many influences bear upon any policy determination. It becomes necessary to contrast separately the advantages and disadvantages involved. Sometimes one series of factors will prevail. At another time and place, other elements will predominate.

8-3 *Advantages of Self-work*

There are advantages to a contractor in doing his own work.

A. *Profit*

The contractor is entitled to, and gets, an overage on work which he does with his own forces. This amount is more than the override which competition will allow him to charge on the work of others. He therefore has

ST-13

To be completed by purchaser and given to and retained by vendor. Read instructions on back of this certificate.

State of New Jersey

DIVISION OF TAXATION

SALES TAX BUREAU

CERTIFICATE OF AUTHORITY NUMBER

CONTRACTOR'S EXEMPT PURCHASE CERTIFICATE

TO _____
           (Name of Vendor)

_____
           (Address of Vendor)

_____

The materials, supplies, or services purchased by the undersigned are for exclusive use in erecting structures, or building on, or otherwise improving, altering or repairing real property of the exempt organization named below.

THIS BID OR CONTRACT COVERS WORK TO BE PERFORMED FOR:

Name of Exempt Organization: _____

Exempt Organization Number: _____

Address: _____

ADDRESS OR LOCATION OF BID OR CONTRACT WORK SITE:

_____

_____

I certify that all information on this Certificate is correct.

_____
        (Name of Contractor)

By: _____
        (Signature and Title of owner, partner, or officer of corporation)

_____
        (Business address of Contractor)

_____

Date: _____

See INSTRUCTIONS on other side.

figure 8-1a. Contractor's exempt purchase certificate (front).

an opportunity to make a greater percentage on the value of this particular trade than he could obtain if a subcontractor were used.

Also, everyone procures labor and material from about the same sources, particularly when limited by a specification. This situation makes material costs similar. The contractor doing his own work, however, does get the benefit of trade material discounts, which are worthwhile. Occasionally such discounts make the difference between profit and loss.

Instead of similar costs, however, the actual total cost may be less. Some locations having a sales tax may exempt certain types of structures (such as churches) or (for gasoline taxes) certain types of use (such as for erection use where highways are not traveled on). After applying for registration and obtaining a temporary certificate of authority, contracting organizations may file exempt purchase certificates with every suitable job (Figure 8-1 *a* and *b*). If approved, this will save the tax for this job. Or if gasoline taxes are involved, the local procedure will govern. The saving is reflected in the quoted price.

ST-13

INSTRUCTIONS TO VENDORS CONCERNING EXEMPT PURCHASE CERTIFICATE

You may accept this certificate as a basis for exempting sales to the purchaser providing:

a. The Certificate of Authority Number, showing that the purchaser is a registered vendor, is entered on the form.

b. The purchaser has entered all other information required and checked the appropriate items.

All sales which are not supported by a properly executed exemption certificate shall be deemed retail sales and the burden of proving the sale is not at retail is upon you as the vendor.

————————————————

Reproduction of form — Private reproduction of this form may be made without prior permission from the Sales Tax Bureau.

---

figure 8-1b. Contractor's exempt purchase certificate (back).

Any saving adds to any other and is worth obtaining. As in the case of any tax, the authority wants only what is legally called for, no more and no less.

B. *Workmanship and Material*

By doing his own work, the contractor may get a better job. He directly controls the actions of the journeymen in his own pay and rarely lowers the standards upon which his business is based. But when a subcontractor has taken a contract at a questionable price, he may tend to skimp. In such a case, the contractor will definitely suffer, as he is responsible to the buyer for this and future work. Workmanship and material must meet specification and inspection requirements.

C. *Erection*

The contractor doing his own work can take immediate cognizance and action reflecting the progress of other trades, weather conditions, contractual requirements, material and equipment deliveries, and similar conditions. The general contractor can usually afford to rent the most modern equipment, best suited to the job being estimated (rather than having a subbidder use what is previously owned, which may be ineffective).

The general contractor's control of the overall time of erection is vastly improved when he uses his own labor. Almost needless to say, a saving in erection time impresses and helps the buyer, cuts overhead for both job and office, and sometimes earns a bonus.

D. *Bidding*

The contractor who figures his own costs is reasonably sure of obtaining a correct figure for an important part of the quotation makeup. Cases occasionally are discovered in which quotations from the same subcontractor are higher to one general contractor than to another. This situation may be because of previous relationships, area influences, credit circumstances, or some other factor. The contractor's own estimating or the comparison of his own and other bids acts as a check on such actions, to minimize the results of collusion or errors by others.

E. *Negotiation*

A working contractor gets a good understanding of job details and the money value placed on individual minor phases. As opportunities arise, he may suggest material and other cost changes which may sway the letting of a contract in his direction.

Also in such negotiations, a contractor who does his own work is considered as less of a broker and more of a permanently organized and solidly established businessman. He can be relied on to have his own organization should repairs, replacements, or additions become necessary. When a general contractor grows to a certain size, however, he may tend to take only large work and then actually subcontract everything. Here is where the smaller organization has a valid selling point.

F. *Sales*

There is a further advantage in doing the work of a key trade. Many large companies maintain engineering departments that design and give out their own special work. Procuring some of this work for his own firm acts to put a contractor in an inside position, where he can learn to know individuals, the lines of authority, and the sources of future business. His work is directly visible and will act as "on-the-spot advertising," supplementing his own attention to further strengthen personal contacts. When larger and more profitable work is contemplated by an owner or buyer, the contractor has already established his competence, reliability, and workmanship to business associates who have become friends.

G. *Diversification*

Occasionally a job will come along in which one trade alone is desirable business in itself. Perhaps the total proposition is so large as to be beyond the financial and manpower capabilities of a small general contractor, or small work may be welcome for some other reason. (Work may be required to keep keymen employed during a slack period, or the financial condition of the firm may make it advisable to obtain smaller contracts so as to spread the risks.)

8-4 *Advantages of Subcontracting*

There are also advantages to the contractor, however, in awarding the work of certain specialized trades to subcontractors. This is recognized by the architects and engineers who make up the plans and specifications for the jobs. Sizable plans are usually divided by the designer into architectural, foundation, structural, specialty, and mechanical sets (plumbing, heating and ventilating, sprinkler, and electric). In all cases, the specifications are indexed and written as separate trade sections for easy takeoff and estimating, indicating the value of subcontracting.

A. *Delivery and Coordination*

In cases such as structural-steel frame or a requirement for high-speed elevators, a very considerable lead time is required—for drafting, approvals, acquisition of material, and then the further necessity of getting specially fabricated equipment. These, therefore, would be among the first trades to be contracted for. The subcontractor has the necessary specialists and special equipment. Other trades, such as roofing or tile, require skilled journeymen or are used infrequently and never considered as anything but a subcontract. All trades, however, have influence in establishing finished detail drawings and fabrication time, upon which all subsequent progress is predicated.

B. *Supply and Fabrication*

Certain trades entail the scarcity factor in material and machines. There are always times when material shipments are delayed or prices go up. The subcontractor carries some material in storage at all times and acts as a buffer in regard to price changes and delays in deliveries.

Specifications frequently compel action which will use subcontractors. Cases in which columns have to be milled off square with the shaft or girder beams have to be cambered (given the shape of a bow for added stiffness) in the length are illustrations. The requirement for special machinery forces the use of a subcontractor who has or can get the use of such equipment. As another example, a heavy granite facing is needed which is not a stock material but has to be cut to size in a quarry and then finished on special machines. Not every firm has the facilities and equipment required. Sources and resources must be examined so that contracts are given only to those who can ensure delivery.

C. *Cost*

Particularly on smaller jobs, the general contractor may get workmanlike production at lower cost by subcontracting than with his own forces. In any special-trade subcontract, the estimable production habits of steady employees doing one type of work only do give a relatively low labor cost. The subcontractor can buy for several jobs at one time, obtaining the benefit of quantity discounts. He has specialized equipment and tools for his trade. His overhead is usually less than that of the general contractor. He knows where to go and whom to see should he require additional or emergency labor, material, or equipment. In addition, when several subcontractors of one trade are vying for the same job, the general contractor has in his favor the "competitive price factor."

D. *Workmanship*

Excellent work can be obtained from a subcontractor who maintains constant employment of specialists. Otherwise a workmanlike job with passable material may be anticipated. Although subcontractors will naturally try to make as much as possible on any contract, it will not be to the extent of jeopardizing future entrée and work for present clients.

E. *Contractual Information*

The subcontractor's bids offer immediate definite information about how prices will run. Far in advance of starting a new job, the general contractor will know the financial tendency—whether it is going to be necessary to concentrate every effort to avoid a loss or whether he can anticipate a normal profit and can concentrate on improving that profit.

F. *Working Capital*

The subcontractor gives assistance by directly paying his own labor, material, and equipment bills and later invoicing the general contractor. Thus he expands the scope of the working capital of the latter. This procedure can be of considerable help when there are delays involved in such factors as weather, deliveries, labor conditions, and payments.

G. *Credit*

Should a completion bond be required by the contract and should the bondable credit limit of the general contractor be inadequate, the subcontractor may be of help. When the subcontractor uses his own credit to obtain his own completion bond, he thereby guarantees completion of his own work. This will decrease the amount of the bond required of the general contractor.

H. *Estimating*

The subcontractor may also save time and expense for the general contractor in estimating a job. Some plans and specifications are received with a minimum of time available for bidding. The general contractor rarely has a surplus of estimators sitting around waiting for plans to come in. Usually there are just about enough, as determined by experience, to handle an average number of proposals. Any conservation of estimating time is therefore advantageous. Subcontract takeoffs are relied on to eliminate the general contractor's having to make takeoffs in these particular trades. A comparison of the bids of several subcontractors will give a check of their correctness. Of course, when it is essential and otherwise unavailable, the general contractor can always buy the takeoff from a subcontractor who specializes in making independent takeoffs for the particular trade.

This subbid situation permits more jobs to reach the quotation stage in a given period of time with the same estimating manpower used by the general contractor. From this procedure follows the percentage possibility that he will obtain more work with less overhead.

Also, there is sometimes a possibility that a subtrade can be bought cheaper if a general contractor figures the work differently than as laid out by the specification writer. As an example, the same specified trade section may include both the structural-steel framework of a building and the miscellaneous iron required (such as steel stairs, pipe rails, and gratings).

The specification writer has correctly considered that the same type of contractor will give a price for each of the two subdivisions of the same class of work. Yet there is a considerable difference in machinery and shop investment, type of expert workman needed, and volume of business required for the investment. As a result, the structural shop may give out the miscellaneous work to a specialist in that type of business, or vice versa. Depending on the detail of the specific job, it might pay the general contractor to take two separate subbids to make up the complete trade.

There are also occasions when subbidders may suggest methods of cutting costs, to the benefit of all, by some stratagem possibly not known to the designer. For example, to meet insurance requirements a specification called for a ceiling fire rating, which is customarily attained by using a construction of fireproof plaster on a wire-lath base. The plaster subbidder suggested fire-rated ceilings of preformed panels hung directly from the floor joist above, at a much lower cost. This change was approved by the designer, with the benefits split between buyer and general contractor. The subbidder got himself a job.

I. *Personal Relations*

An understanding and thoughtful policy with subcontractors is of considerable importance. Subcontractors know and receive requests to bid from many of those who are competing for the same job and can advise a well-liked general contractor about the competition he will meet. Such information can be of great help in making up a bid.

Also, when time is limited and a quotation for a certain trade is lacking, a friendly subcontractor will arrange to make an immediate takeoff and submit a bid at once so that the general contractor can complete his own summation. There must be an understanding that there is a mutuality of interest and a resultant helpfulness in getting work. The general contractor and the subcontractor should be able to rely on each other.

8-5 *Objections to Subcontracting*

Of course, there are also disadvantages for a general contractor in hiring a subcontractor. Due to keen competition among subcontractors, there exist many "sharp" business tactics to offset price. As a result, constant care and understanding are of primary importance, although there are other factors to be considered.

A. When the bid of one subcontractor is competing with that of another for the hurried (deadline-time makeup) attention of a general contractor's estimator and *must seem low yet not actually be low*, the device commonly used is that of "exclusion and inclusion." This is a stratagem of offering a subbid that appears to be close to what is wanted but varies from the specification in some respect, apparently because of the subbidder's particular manner of doing business.

For example, one bid may eliminate in the proposal wording items of temporary light, power, and heat (called for in the specifications), requiring them to be furnished by the general contractor. The next competitor may offer material made by his company but not specified—and therefore requiring the problematical approval of the architect in order to be used. A third competitor may call for shop delivery, no field erection, and no field painting. The subcontractor who includes all the specified or actually necessary items will be higher in bid total price than any of the three previous bidders, yet upon analysis all the quotations are about the same in final work value.

The general contractor is obligated to pay for any item required by the specifications, even though that item has been omitted in the subbid. Therefore, in using any bid the general contractor's estimator must figure the worth of the omitted items and add them into his own bid. Someone has to pay for them, as they will definitely be required. In addition, when approval of a substituted material cannot be obtained, what happens? Who pays for the increased price of using the material originally specified, and how much? These are only a few of the reasons that evasive bidding tactics must be guarded against.

B. When there is delay in receiving subbids which are needed to complete summaries, the on-time completion of a whole quotation is threatened. Unfortunately, in many cases this delay is occasioned by the actions of a few brazen general contractors who will shop around prior to completing an estimate in an endeavor to get better subbids and, thereby, a lower overall quotation. In so doing, they hurt everyone else. To forestall this harmful comparison, certain subbidders will consciously delay giving out any quotations at all until the last possible moment. Such action, of course, is self-defeating, even though defensive in nature. Unless a general contractor can give a complete bid to the buyer before the set closing time, all prior efforts of everyone are wasted. It is obligatory upon all in the business to publicize the provable actions of bid shoppers and refuse to do further business with them. Subbids must be received ahead of the final makeup time to be of use.

Occasionally delay is caused by the fact that a subcontractor will, in turn, have subordinate subcontractors and they cause delay. For example, a ventilating subcontractor might use a local vent-duct fabricator to save cost. The local man does not only his own shopwork but also his own estimating. Time is lost. Here the delay is unintentional, but the results are just as serious.

Also, subcontractors receive requests to bid on many different jobs and from a number of companies. For good and sufficient reasons, they may decide to bid on one job and not on another. As a result, the general contractor may obtain an inadequate number of bids, or even none, on a particular trade. When this situation occurs and the trade is a specialty which cannot be adequately estimated by the general contractor, a last-minute scramble ensues to get in hand this trade quotation from someone.

When such subbids are not received, the unfortunate result is that the general contractor's bid is in jeopardy. If the subbid is truly vital in content and price and cannot be safely "guesstimated," no bid can be given to the buyer. The effect of this is to give the contractor a reputation among architects and engineers for being unreliable. They have possibly recommended the general contractor to the buyer in a small and closed list, and the lack of a bid submission has cast them also in a bad light. For this reason, whenever subcontracting is resorted to, someone must be appointed to continuously follow up all subbidders long before the due date to ensure that all required trades have submitted bids. There is thus an added supervisory cost for subbid estimating.

C. Subbid figures may be deliberately too high or too low. A subbidder figuring high may wish to allow a spread for negotiation should the general contractor be awarded the job. Or there may be an intent to favor a particular firm by giving them a lower price and all others a higher price. A subbidder figuring low occasionally does so because he needs work and wants to make sure that he gets it from whoever is awarded the job.

However, a bid which is obviously too low in comparison with other subbids for this trade may indicate a serious subbid takeoff error. And even though a general contractor's livelihood depends on low bids from others, a situation such as this presents dangers. There is always the temptation to use the low price because some unscrupulous competitor, who also received it, will take a chance and use it. But when a general contractor does obtain work because of using such a low subbid, the trade in question must be bought at that price. If the subbidder takes the work and gives a poor job, the general contractor loses reputation and often the time and money to make good the poor results. If the subbidder refuses to enter into a contract, then the general contractor has the problem of executing this special work within the quoted price incorporated in his accepted bid. If he cannot do this, there will be a loss on such an item.

From a purely selfish viewpoint, there is one sure way out. The subbidder must be warned in advance to check his bid, and such a warning will, of course, get immediate attention. He should be notified emphatically that should he discover an error in his bid, *all* general contractors to whom he has issued that bid should be notified immediately of the increased price required. This will rescind the low bid and place all competitors back on the same subbid status. Should the subbidder hold his price after being given an opportunity to check his takeoff, that is the bid which, for his own reasons, he wishes to use.

Such consideration may tend to convince perennial late bidders that this general contractor's firm is one for whom it pays to put in bids early. It is only with advance knowledge and time to check that discrepancies can be corrected or verified.

D. Coordination is most important on a construction job in which many trades are involved and all are interdependent. In obtaining the other benefits of subcontracting, a general contractor loses control of material delivery, equipment use and supply, and labor supply and functioning. The subcontractor now controls these functions. Of course, for future good relations the subcontractor would rather act so as to please his general contractor than not to do so. The necessity of business survival, however, is a very potent force. The subcontractor in the final analysis will construct his contractual part of a job in accordance with his self-interest. Should the subcontractor hold back on labor employed or material delivered to a job because he is short of working capital, because he feels that the general contractor's credit is poor and payments slow, or for any other reason, the result is damage to coordination.

The one consistent method of getting action is to advance money on request to the subcontractor, even if he does not yet deserve a payment. When money is in short supply for the general contractor, the situation can be rugged for both of them. Yet unfortunately, in this relationship, the responsibility for adequate financing rests with the general contractor. The latter must be prepared to meet this contingency.

E. The local law should also be considered. In most localities anyone expending toil, using equipment, or incorporating material in a structure is entitled to a lien against the property for the claimed worth of his bill. A subcontractor, however, may not have paid his hired help or material or equipment bills before invoicing a general contractor. The latter, therefore, must exercise business caution in dealing with others, not only when making payments but at all times. He must obtain a written document releasing liens or take any other necessary action as called for by his contract, by his legal advisor, and by sensible caution. Of course, a lien should not be filed at all if there is any honorable way to avoid it. A lien can be a very ominous credit indication to other businessmen. The credit relations of general contractor and subcontractor are of vital importance.

F. The use of subcontractors develops an overhead cost which must be included in the estimate makeup. The cost of subbids is not only their summation; there is an additional percentage which must be added to account for administrative supervision and other overhead. In the office, subbids must be obtained from various suppliers and installers, shop drawings processed, approvals obtained (including insurance), installations coordinated and arranged, payments approved and paid, and completion requirements taken care of (punch lists). On the job, subcontractors' coordination meetings must be arranged and cooperation attained; work arrangements, including dates, storage locations, plans, and installations, must be made; and supervision, including interpretation and enforcement of plans and specifications, must be provided.

8-6 *Special Cases*

From the foregoing discussion it is evident that the self-interest of the general contractor is the predominant factor in the choice between doing his own work and giving it out. Because of the many factors involved and because circumstances and jobs vary, policy should be reviewed at the beginning of every new estimate. As an instance, a general contractor may do really good carpentry work as part of his usual business of building individualistic homes. Yet when conditions change, he may be forced to figure a public housing project, including a very considerable number of duplicate apartment units of wood construction. This type of job does not warrant and will not pay for the highest type of carpentry work. On such a job, a knowledgeable carpentry subcontractor has specialists for every small operation. These journeymen know what is required, have special tools, and produce as much as possible in a manner to just pass inspection. In this case the subcontractor will have a very definite price advantage over the contractor's own organization.

The determination of what work to do with one's own forces and what to give out is a prerequisite of estimating.

8-7 *Contracting Practices*

In customary practice, excluding heavy construction, the subcontract work makes up a large percentage of the money value of the bid makeup. The subcontractors' bids, therefore, carry a great deal of influence in the general contractor's final quotation—and, therefore, in his chances of getting any particular job. This situation leads to constant effort on the part of the general contractor to get the lowest possible subbid price for every subcontract trade. And if the general contractor gets the job, he endeavors to buy still better. He will always try to get a larger profit percentage than he originally figured to obtain. His quoted price to the owner may have been cut down during negotiations. The subbidder's price possibly is in excess of what it should be and can also be reduced.

Due to human error, certain items of the general contract may have been left out or incorrectly figured, and the cost will have to be compensated for.

Compulsive economic forces induce general-contractor excesses. This is particularly noticeable in purchasing. Using an obviously unfair price of one competitor to hammer down the quotation of another is far too common. Some *sub rosa* agreements will be entered into whereby, if a general contractor gets a job because of a low bid given to him by a particular subcontractor, the latter will also automatically get the job. This is regardless of the fact that a number of bids for the same trade are worthy of consideration.

Worst of all, from an ethical point of view, a few general contractors will disregard their manifest obligation to do business with those sub-bidders who helped get the contract with their effort and reasonable bid. Such general contractors, in attempting to get lower bids from others after having been awarded a job, defeat their own purpose.

They lose respect, tactical freedom to negotiate (whereby the low bidder of the *sub rosa* agreement may not be the low bidder after all the subbids are received), and future opportunity to deal with reputable subcontractors. This denial of opportunity comes about again through the pervasive power of the so-called "grapevine." It is indeed surprising how correctly and quickly trade sources know exactly what has happened and is happening. The discredited organization can continue to exist only so long as its reputation is not known to all and some unaware companies remain with whom to do business.

Unfortunately, *bid shopping*, as it is called is uniformly condemned but surreptitiously condoned. Bid depositories have been established to take all subbids in advance of submission and record them for the benefit of the particular industry. Human nature and necessity have prevented this device from succeeding. When such a device is not in use, individual bidders will occasionally submit bids late so that knowledge of their estimate cannot be used to force down the price of someone else. This procedure hurts everyone because without subbids many general contractors could not bid at all, mistakes are prevalent under last-minute pressure, and coverage of the subbid market is inadequate. All these factors lead to the wrong price.

The subcontractor who is inadequately financed is particularly vulnerable to sharp practices after a job is awarded to him. He will naturally look for assistance to the general contractor for whom he is working and with whom his assets are. Should that party be trying to make money in any way possible, including from his own subcontractor's agreed-upon price, the latter may be told that the general contractor has not received his own money due and has no available cash (which is false). He may be told further, however, that the general contractor can borrow from the bank or others and will charge the subcontractor with the interest which, in turn, must be paid on the loan. Naturally, if the subcontractor needs cash, he will pay the interest charge for money to which he would be rightfully entitled in some short period of time. Should he learn that he has been lied to, his remedy is to not bid again or to bid high—and neither of these is a particularly satisfactory method of retaliation.

Again, however, the protective grapevine works against the discreditable individual or organization. Informed subbidders will bid high, and the general contractor will not be able to submit a competitive bid. Eventually, these so-called "smart tactics" will be harmful to the perpetrator. Unfortunately, he has first hurt others. The entire industry must police itself by freely giving information.

8-8   *That Selfish Best Policy*

There is only one best policy for the general contractor to use after determining with what trades to deal: Treat all subbidders and subcontractors honestly and decently without predetermined favorites or sharp practices. Read the specification, study the plans, and prepare to buy the subcontract with knowledge of what is required. Local bidders may help attain lower subbid prices by the productivity of local labor and a knowledge of local personalities and material sources. But these factors are not always present. If necessary, deal with a subcontractor who may be located at a distance from the job but has some compensating advantage.

Use imagination and effort in making up every subbidders' list. And when work is given out and a job is under way, be prepared to help the subbidder to work efficiently. Thereafter, pay promptly—in advance, if necessary. The reputation of a general contractor and his good relationships with subcontractors are his best insurance for getting excellent subbids in the future.

9

TAKEOFF, PRELIMINARY

The quantity takeoff of a job is the preparation for making and later using a special sales instrument, the quotation. It is built anew for every job. To have the greatest possibility of success, this tool must be put together with the sales requirements of the particular job investigated, estimated, and priced. And it should be set up in a manner which will make it easy to use.

The details are important. The takeoff is used not only for pricing and the quotation but also in negotiating, office procedure, and construction.

9-1 *Preliminary Requirements*

The takeoff of any particular plan and specification is not a matter of routine. There are individual differences and requirements in every case. Depending on what is shown or specified, there may be material and quantity variations, a bid bond, added insurance, reference documents, prequalification requirements, or similar divergences. The form, time, and place of the bid closing are also of importance in that additional time must be allowed between actual takeoff and the closing of subbids for makeup of the estimate, transcription to a quotation, and delivery.

To attain correctness, all estimating is subject to the urgent practical necessity that the estimator be subject to as few distractions and time losses as possible. Close attention to plans and specifications is necessary to observe, understand, record, and price (as modified by site conditions)—and then to make up an inclusive quotation with no errors of omission or commission.

The work is crucial for sales since it involves an influential written quotation. A set completion date is fixed for all competitors, and this must be met to retain status and to get an opportunity to bid. There are few extensions of time, and for the most part, these are because of late changes by the designer. Such extensions are thus only a possibility and are out of the control of the bidder.

This avoidance of distraction does not mean isolating the estimator but, rather, allowing him privacy from unwanted interruptions. The office layout necessary to accomplish this result is as essential a part of the preliminary setup as the site examination. Office machines for mechanical valuation and arithmetic add accuracy and multiply time saving.

9-2   *The Request to Quote*

The work starts with an invitation to bid or, frequently, with something originated by the seller. This may be a request from a source, such as an owner, architect, engineer, or past client, or a favorable answer to an inquiry. Whatever the source or however it is obtained, the information in such a request is of importance in the subsequent makeup of the take-off and quotation. Figure 9-1 illustrates a typical invitation to bid. This document, or information of a similar nature, becomes the start of the material to be acquired and filed to make up a particular estimate.

Each request is always just a little different from what has been done before and should be carefully read, understood, and summarized for use. If a lump sum is required, an alternate is to be added, a unit price is to be included, or any variation is called for, the purpose of this inquiry must be answered. It is to get a series of competitive prices to the same questions for comparison. The buyer is serious, impatient of lack of clarity, and unfortunately, willing to take advantage of error.

Therefore, the objectives of the takeoff lead to an exact and competent quotation for the buyer. Such aims must be split into the various subdivisions required, and when these subdivisions can best be figured separately, *the takeoff must be set up to get such information.* In some cases, the buyer may include a form to be filled out. Here, the actual manner of takeoff may have to be varied from that usual with the bidder to comply with the request.

OWNER CORPORATION
Street
City, State, Zip Code
Telephone

Any Construction Co.
Street
City, State, Zip Code

Re: Type of Structure
Address, City, State

Gentlemen:

You are hereby invited to submit a bid for the construction of the above building on (_____) at (_____) in this office. Bidding documents will be available at this office from 9 A. M. on (_____).

We will require a deposit of (_____) per set, the same to be returned within one month from receipt of the bids, and further provided a bid has been submitted, and that plans and specifications are unmarked and in usable condition. Additional sets may be bought at cost, and are not returnable.

If any questions arise as to the intent of the plans or specifications or in connection with the project itself, please refer them in writing to this office at least seven days prior to the date of bid opening. Such enquiry will be answered in writing to all bidders.

Note that the steel contract has been given out to expedite delivery, but the general contractor will assume this contract as part of his supervision and quotation. Full details are in each bidding document set.

Kindly notify us immediately of your desire to quote.

Very truly yours,

OWNER CORPORATION

(by) Person in charge

figure 9-1. Invitation to bid.

The request to quote may raise other questions. For example, a three-story wall-bearing office building may be required in a limited number of weeks. Practically, each tier of steel can be erected only after the floor below is completed to carry it. Will the time delays involved in this operation allow punctual completion of the building? Or steel is to be supplied from the rolling mills, which have unalterable schedules of size rollings. Would the buyer welcome an alternative bid that would save delivery time by purchasing the correct sizes immediately from steel warehouse stock but at an increased price? Of course, trade coordination would also have to be checked for other timing requirements. This type of question, however, would afford an opportunity to open direct contact immediately with the buyer in a favorable atmosphere for future negotiations. Prospective jobs should be viewed to get an understanding of their sales possibilities and requirements.

9-3   *The Bid Coordinator*

A member of the organization, not necessarily the estimator, should be assigned to very definite duties in connection with inquiries. He must first note the requests received to determine if the best interests of the firm will be furthered in going after the work entailed. Either the invitation itself gives the requisite information, or actual further inquiry and examination are made. In any event, a request to bid should be answered promptly, *yes* or *no*. If the action is *no*, some courteous reason for the refusal should be given and a request should be made for future consideration. This keeps the door open in a limited market. If the action is *yes*, the personal contact necessary for selling is initiated.

Should it be decided to figure a job and should this involve only a few trades, one plan and specification may be adequate (and usually this is all that is furnished). If, however, many subcontracts are involved, it is almost obligatory for the coordinator to obtain two complete sets of plans and specifications. Even when only the first set carries a returnable deposit and the second set must be paid for, the overhead cost saved (and the chance of error diminished) far outweighs this small business expense.

One set may then be used continuously by the estimator for the general contractor without the loss of concentration and time consumed in constantly giving up working documents to visiting subbidders. The other set may be placed in a separate estimating room reserved for subbidders and apart from the main office. The layout of this room is important.

9-4   *The Subbidders' Room*

Outsiders should be able to enter this room directly from the entrance lobby without the necessity of passing the receptionist. There should be no time lost by the visiting estimator in getting to see the bidding documents. He, too, is earning a living, and his feelings about delay and the consequent cost to his firm must be considered. Most important, however, there need be no reason for anyone to come into the main office to divert and delay employees—and possibly pick up information which is not his business. For the strictly necessary reason of asking a question in connection with what he is working on, the subbidder may always ask the receptionist to send out someone to help him. That someone can be the coordinator or anyone else—even the general contractor's estimator, if necessary.

Selfishly, there is a good reason for the representative of the general contractor, at his option, to be in contact with and on good terms with the representatives of his subbidders. They move from office to office and carry trade news, particularly because they, too, want to establish a personal relationship and this is one way to do it. When other sources are unavailable, they know who is figuring (and this is important in pricing). They know when a buyer is being unethical in privately extending a published due date so as to get the bid of others (and who those others are). They can obtain quick action, not only in getting estimates but in servicing an actual job. They are a considerable part of the grapevine of trade news. Glass in the dividing wall of the estimating room is, therefore, necessary to determine if anyone is there and if they should be spoken to.

9-5 *The Quantity-takeoff Process*

Because at this point the actual setting down of the takeoff material starts, it becomes necessary to consider the mechanics of the process. The takeoff must be made legibly and clearly, with future utilization by others in mind. Large ruled legal-size sheets (8½ × 14 inches) offer a stock size for which manila folders and metal files are made, afford considerable working space per sheet, are easily distinguished from other office stationery, and are not readily mislaid.

Although such sheets can be printed in any specialized manner which a company considers advisable, stock columnar pads can be purchased in most stationery stores as needed, and they have proven adequate and satisfactory. Not only are these forms relatively inexpensive and readily obtainable, but they are flexible in use. As illustrated in Figure 9-2, such columnar sheets come with lines already ruled and numbered. They can be used for referencing, have space for names and computations, and are available with various numbers of columns, as required. Figures 9 3 and 10-2 show a multiple width of the stock size that may be used as a work sheet and yet be folded to fit into the same estimating folder as the other estimating sheets. (Such multiple-width sizes are 17 × 14, 25½ × 14 and 34 × 14 inches; each may be folded into the single-sheet size of 8½ × 14 inches, which they supplement.)

The two-column sheet (Figure 9-2) is used for typing or generally by a subcontractor doing only one class of work. It gives separate columns for the two items of labor and material and allows the greatest space for computation. A need for additional columns is developed because various overall percentages must be added to various totals for certain types of takeoff.

As an example, a three-column sheet will be used by a general contractor doing some of his own work and also some subcontracting. He will need separate total columns for his own material and labor and also

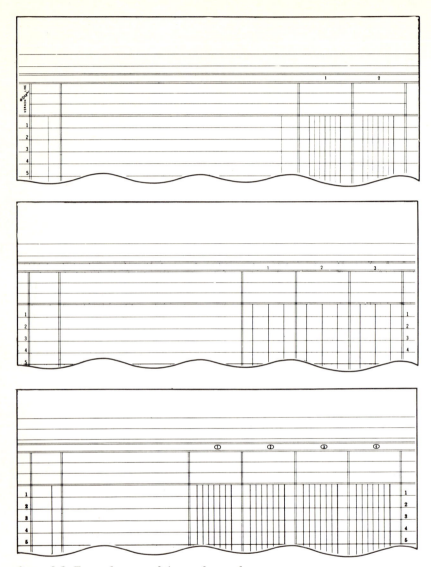

figure 9-2. Two-, three-, and four-column sheets.

a column for his subcontractors. The reason for this is clear. His material summation will require the addition of a definite sales tax percentage. His labor summation will require the addition of an entirely different percentage to cover the fringe benefits, insurance payments, and other items to be added to wages. His subcontract summation will require a still different profit percentage to be added to the work of others, against that

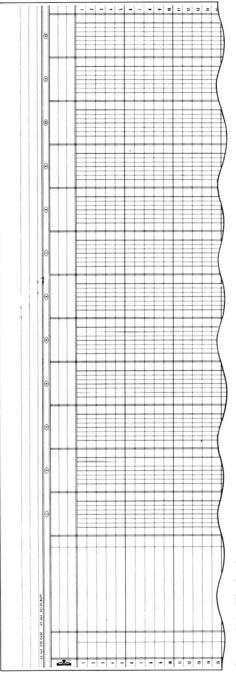

figure 9-3. Work sheet.

127

to which he would be entitled for doing his own work. He must keep separate the various classes of work in making the takeoff.

A four-column sheet might be advantageous to a steel erector who must enter certain costly specialty items to obtain a correct estimate— such as the actual number of field connections to be made along with every differing beam size taken off. Here the decrease in computation space left on the sheet due to the increase in column space is not important. Erection-estimate computations for this trade subdivision do not require much space. If they did, a separate work sheet would solve the problem.

As soon as a decision is made to estimate a particular job, a tabbed manila file folder should be started and an entry made on a follow-up clipboard for the use of the coordinator. Each of these should carry the job name, a quotation number, a due date, and any other pertinent information.

The manila folder should be large enough to hold legal-size estimating paper and all other correspondence without folding. All estimate documentation of any nature should be filed *and locked* in legal-size fire-resistant steel file cabinets every night. These estimate sheets are an invaluable part of a going business. If bills are lost, the creditors will undoubtedly send new ones. The loss of estimate material, however, involves the loss of time, thought, and labor. Often such documents cannot be replaced before the due date of the bid.

9-6   Conserving the Estimator's Time

There are several nontechnical functions involved in every takeoff which can be handled by others at a considerable saving in time for the estimator. The actual construction contracts received by a firm always represent only a small percentage of the number of jobs bid; the greater the number of estimates completed and quoted, the more opportunity there is of getting a contract. Although when manpower is limited the estimator will necessarily have to do some of the following work, the policy setup should always allow a coordinator or someone else on the staff to do it when possible. Should this result in some item which is not clear to the estimator, he can always telephone for clarification at a considerable saving in his own time and effort.

9-7   Preliminary Estimate Items

Certain items, such as those listed below, are routine and must be done for any and every estimate passing through an office. Anything which cuts down takeoff time helps to increase the number of finished quotations going out to seek work. Therefore, the use of takeoff help is emphasized.

A. It is necessary to make sure that all instructions, plans, specifications, addenda, and modifications have been received. These items should be checked against the letter of transmittal, against any subsequent communications, and with the sender before the quotation is completed.

B. A summary cover sheet (Figure 9-4), which becomes the first page of the estimate, should be made out. This should incorporate the invitation to bid, and subsequent information should be added to it as received. It thus becomes a guide to the later requirements of the contractor's purchasing agent. Certain items for present use, such as bonds or insurance certificates, require time to obtain yet must be submitted with the quotation. (They must be ordered at once, and the order followed through until received.) Occasionally the buyer himself will give out certain subbids prior to giving out the general contract. Yet he may also give instructions that an allowed cost and the responsibility for and coordination of such trades be included in the overall job quotation. In such circumstances the buyer is assigning a subcontractor to any subsequent general contractor. The general contractor, nevertheless, is always completely responsible. This, and any other instruction or circumstance which will affect the bid and the work, should be written out and emphasized.

Although there are many instances in which no fixed form of estimate submission is required, there are others in which a form is to be followed so that all bids read the same to the buyer for ease in comparison of the prices. Such a form may affect the manner of takeoff so as to obtain certain information in a certain way. When necessary, this need should also be noted.

C. A subbidders' notification list (including material suppliers, if necessary) must be made up, and notification cards requesting bids should be mailed out immediately. This is done by either the estimator or the coordinator. As all jobs and trades vary with the work to be done, the list used for any preceding estimate is not necessarily correct, even though many trades will be needed again. Also, merely referring to the index of trades, which may be part of the specification, is not satisfactory. Due to unavoidable lack of practical knowledge of every vocation, a specification writer may include in a craft an item which that trade does not supply and install and which it will exclude from its subbid. Of course, this will leave something missing and needed when assembling the final prices. Also, sometimes a complete item or trade is omitted in making up a specification, although it is clearly shown on the plans. There is usually a clause in the specification holding the general contractor responsible for such contingencies. The coordinator or estimator must pick up such lapses.

```
                                                    Estimate Sheet #1

  (1) JOB NAME                          Estimator's Initials    Date
      ADDRESS           CITY      STATE    ZIP CODE

   (2) Architect   Address      Zip Code   Code (4) Telephone #
             Person in charge   Secretary

 1    Engineer (Same info as above)
 2
 3    Owner    (Same info as above)
 4
 5 (3)  Request to Bid Requirements
 6       (a) Due date & time
 7       (b) Location
 8       (c) Bid quotation form
 9       (d) Added expense items – Bid bond     (To be included in quotation)  Date
10                          – Insurance & limits                    Requested
11       (e) Completion date & penalty (Figured as insurance premium )
12       (f) Other inclusions required (Reference letters, completion bond)
13
14
15 (4)  Bidding Documents – Architects Identifying Job No. & No. of Dwgs.
16          (Further detailed data for necessitous use)
17          Plan #A-1 Site ; Date
18                A-2 Plan-Bsmnt & first floor ; Date
19                A-3 Plan-Second floor & roof ; Revised date
20                A-4 Details ; Revised date
21                A-5 Elevations; Dated
22                A-6 Sections & finish schedules ; Date
23                B-1 Boring diagram ; Date  (Based on survey of_____)
24                P-1 Plumbing layout ; Revised date
25                H-1 Heating, ventilating & air conditioning; Revised date
26                E-1 Electric layout ; Dated
27
28          Specifications ; Dated (No. of pages )
29          Addendum & identifying number & date ( No. of pages)
30
31
32 (5)  Alternate Requirements as Indicated on Plans & Specifications
33          (a)_____
34          (b)_____
35          (c) Bidding document indications (Example - B1, Boring diagram   Water interference)
36
37 (6)  Alternate Possibilities for Sales Negotiations
38          (To be entered during estimating process as developed)
39
40
41 (7)  Site Survey Report
42
43
44
45
46
47
```

figure 9-4. Cover sheet.

130

Also, occasionally, local or seasonal factors or supplementary information require additional subbids not noted anywhere on the bidding documents (such as a wintertime price for heating ready-mix concrete or the cost of installing, maintaining, and removing a well-point installation to take care of a high water-table level shown on a boring diagram). The party in charge must have adequate construction experience to spot such items, get complete subbid coverage, and keep his firm out of trouble. Complete understanding and thorough assimilation of information are necessary before even starting.

Trades and subbidders are the subject matter of a separate card-file makeup. As shown in Figure 9-5, individual listings are compiled on a series of 3×5 inch numbered cards for all categories and companies which are frequently used or which call and ask to be listed. The individual card entries include trade, name of company, street number for notification, telephone number for follow-up, names of firm members and other essential people, such as the estimator and the secretary, trade name of any specialty handled, and the card subcontractor account number for quick identification in making up the mailing list with a minimum of written instructions to subordinates. Only when the card file does not list a trade adequately should it be necessary to refer to sources such as classified directories, local material suppliers, or architects' samples showrooms for further information.

The reason for this procedure is simply good business practice. A general contractor has the obligation of affording his usual subbidders the opportunity to quote on anything they may be interested in. This courtesy is due them regardless of their location in reference to the job site. They have quoted previously, and their efforts, possibly without return at that time, are worthy of recognition.

Of course, the general contractor also has an obligation to himself. During negotiation, as a means of getting acquainted, he may ask a buyer whether the latter wishes to recommend a deserving subcontractor —on the distinct basis that there will later be no compulsion to award the job to that party should the general contractor get the job (and should the recommended subbidder not be low or otherwise preferable). Also, trucking expense and local labor conditions are important pricing factors and may enter into the choice of subbidders, as indeed are many other considerations.

Making up the list promptly is necessary in order to get out the notices. General conditions, subbidders, and summary tabulations are made, as shown in Figures 9-6 to 9-8. After writing a stock request to bid, subbid-request postcards (Figure 9-9) are printed, possibly using a small mimeograph machine, and mailed out to the subbidders on the list. Individual postcards can be written on when a trade requires special

DOORS – ROLLING STEEL	P. 1
① Atlas Door Co., # Street, City, State	
Ch. Attley, Mabel Goodkind	101-123-1234
Rep. – Steel Shutter Co.	
② Franklin Shutter Co., Hgwy # & Street, City, State	
Jos. Franklin	104-376-2467
③ Kinnel Mfg. Co., # Avenue, City, State,	
Ed. Riley, Mrs. Riley	112-411-1432

RESILIENT FLOORS (& also see Carpeting)	P. 2
④ Union Flooring Co., # Street, City, State	
Bill Saxon	101-Mu 8-1205
also handles Edgemont Carpeting	

STRUCTURAL STEEL (& Misc. Iron)	P. 3
⑦ Fenner Fabricators, # Street, City, State	
Bob Bowen, Ed Kaltenbrue (Shop Supt.)	101-872-8860
Gary Pilder (Engr. Dept.)	
⑧ Evan England & Son, R.F.D. #1, City, State	
Bob England,	104-743-7700
(Small Shop - Max 16" Punch)	

figure 9-5. Subcontractors' listings.

			Material	Labor	Subcontract
1 (1)		*General Conditions*			
2	(a)	Surveys - Site Location & in Position			
3	(b)	Supervision			
4	(c)	Job misc. labor, timekeeper, watchman, or others			
5	(d)	Trailers (office, architect, trade & storage)			
6	(e)	Telephones, (office & pay)			
7	(f)	Toilets (chemical or sewer system)			
8	(g)	Electric light & power (plus maintenance labor)			
9	(h)	Meters, (Domestic water & sprinkler), temp. water			
10	(i)	Pumping. (Diaphragm, centrifugal, or well point)			
11	(j)	Monthly Rentals (Estimated)			
12	(k)	Premium time (Estimated)			
13	(l)	Contingencies (Rain, cold, other delays)			
14	(o)	Penalties (Cost figured as insurance premium)			
15	(p)	Heating, Fuel & labor for trailers, forms;			
16		Protection (Salt hay, pliofilm, paper)			
17	(q)	Demolition & clean site			
18	(r)	Permits, fees, Service charges			
19	(s)	Special provisions; Architect, Engineer expense			
20	(t)	Remove rubbish & clean structure & site			
21	(u)	Added expense items at request to bid (Premiums, Bond, etc.)			
22	(v)	Misc. (Scaffolding, protection, etc.)			
23	(w)	Other variations			
24					
25					
26					
27 (2)		*Architectural index plus estimator's purchase items.*			
28		Section - (For this job only)			
29	1.	Excavation, Fill, Grade & Tamp			
30		By general contractor			
31		Work sheets, Cols. 1,2,3 Fig. 10-2 Total			
32					
33	2.	Bituminous Paving			
34		Subbidders list Fig. 9-5			
35		Comparison, best bidder			
36					
37	2-A	Stall Lining			
38		Subbidders list Fig. 9-5			
39		Comparison, best bidder			
40					
41	3.	Concrete			
42		By general contractor			
43		Work sheets, Cols. 4-12 incl. Fig. 10-2			
44					
45					
46					
47					

Estimate Sheet #2 — (1) JOB NAME — Estimator's Initials — Date

figure 9-6. General conditions and miscellaneous items.

Estimate sheet #3

(1) JOB NAME   Estimator's Initials   Date

Architect Index#	Date Out SUBBIDDERS Trade & Names, Phone Numbers—	Subbids	Low Bidder	Alternates Inclusions Exclusions
1	E. Electrical			
2	① Name			
3	⑤ –do–			
4	⑥ –do–			
5	⑪ –do–			
6				
7				
8 Not indexed–	Fencing			
9	② Name			
10	③ –do–			
11	④ –do–			
12	⑦ –do–			
13				
14				
15	8. Overhead Doors (steel)			
16	③ Name			
17	⑤ –do–			
18	⑧ –do–			
19	⑨ –do–			
20				
21				
22	15. Piling			
23	① Name			
24	② –do–			
25	③ –do–			
26	⑤ –do–			
27				
28				
29	7. Structural Steel (& Misc. Iron)			
30	⑥ Name			
31	⑦ –do–			
32	⑧ –do–			
33	⑨ –do–			
34				
35				
36	Plus Other Required Trades			
37	and Alternate Computations			
38				
39				
40				
42	Note– Card list names (and respective numbers)			
41	will vary with job, location, additional			
43	bidders, compliance with specifications			
44				
45				
46				
47				

figure 9-7. Subbids.

JOB NAME	SUMMATION	Estimate Sheet # 4
		Estimator's Initials Date

			Material	Labor	Subbid
		Carried Forward			
1	4.	Mason (Gate house only)			
2		By general contractor			
3		Work sheet for this section			
4		;			
5	5.	Standard Steel Building & Misc. Iron			
6		Subcontractors bidders list, Fig. 9-5			
7		Comparison, best bidder			
8					
9	⊗ 6	Carpentry			
10		By general contractor			
11		Work sheets for section			
12		Recap. sheet for above			
13	Ⓓ 6-5.	Millwork (Delivered only)			
14		Subcontractors bidders list, Fig. 9-5			
15		Comparison, best bidder			
16					
17	⊗ 6-7.	Hollow Metal (Frames & doors delivered only)			
18		Subcontractors bidders list, Fig. 9-5			
19		Comparison, best bidder			
20					
21	Ⓓ 6-10.	Hardware (Delivered only)			
22		Allowance (Specification) Amount			
23					
24					
25					
26					
27	E-	Electric			
28		Subcontractors bidders list			
29		(Loan plan, return) Comparison, best bidder			
30		Transmittal sheet			
31					
32	P,	H & A.C. - Plumbing, Heating & Air Conditioning			
33		(Loan plan, return) comparison, best bidder			
34		Transmittal sheet			
35					
36	Sp	Sprinkler			
37		(loan plan, return) comparison, best bidder			
38		Transmittal sheet			
39					
40					
41			(+) Sales tax %	(+) Overage %	(+) Overhead %
42					
43			(+) Profit %	(+) Profit %	(+) Profit %
44					
45		Total Estimate →			
46		Actual Quote →			
47	⊗	Erection to be in carpentry			

figure 9-8. Subbids summary.

```
┌─────────────────────────────────────────────────────────────┐
│   YOU ARE INVITED TO BID ON WORK IN YOUR LINE FOR:            │
│                                                               │
│      PROJECT:                                                 │
│                                                               │
│      LOCATION:                                                │
│                                                               │
│      ARCHITECT:                                               │
│                                                               │
│   BIDS DUE TO US:          (Date)                             │
│                                                               │
│   PLANS AND SPECIFICATIONS MAY BE SEEN AT:                    │
│                                                               │
│                     ANY CONSTRUCTION COMPANY                  │
│                     1 Name Street, City, State                │
│   Telephone:                                                  │
│   Note and Quote: Addenda, unit prices, alternate.            │
│                                                               │
└─────────────────────────────────────────────────────────────┘
```

figure 9-9. Subbid-request postcard.

attention for additional prices (certain bid requirements call for extra information from subbidders). Subbidders can always be added to the list by sending out additional requests to bid or by telephoning during the takeoff period.

D. During the takeoff, occasionally a plan or specification error will be discovered which must be brought to the attention of the designer and of visiting subbidders so that all takeoffs will be correct and the same. A dimension, a quantity, or a notation may be in error. Or the specification may be divided into two separate and nonreferring parts which should be furnished by the same trade (such as the plate glass and the metal setting making up a storefront). Sometimes an addendum will be received from the architect or engineer on a date in the bidding period when many of the subbidders have already completed their takeoffs.

In every such case, the change will have to be called to the attention of every possible subbidder. Here is where the necessity of a clearly recorded subbidders' list becomes evident. The general contractor, by trade custom and often by specification, is responsible for necessary changes. Of course, unreasonably late addenda are legitimately subject to a request for an extension of bidding time. But in any case, an additional written modification will be sent out as a matter of record, requesting notification in writing that the final bid conforms with all such revisions.

E. The so-called "mechanical" trades—plumbing, heating, and electrical work—are often so extensive that they cannot be taken off in a general contractor's plan room in a few hours, especially with interruptions, lack of reference and communication, and sometimes the necessity of also getting sub-subcontractors to figure subdivisions of the trade. If now two sets of plans, as previously mentioned, are on hand, they can be taken apart and limited portions loaned, with photocopies of the requisite specification included, to the specialized trades in need of the documents for estimating.

In this connection, *no* material of any nature should ever go out of a general contractor's office without being accompanied by a letter of transmittal in duplicate (Figure 9-10) so as to provide a record for filing. This can be most valuable as a record to *anyone* in the organization for getting back bids and contract documents, many of which have to be returned to the buyer for deposit returns. Of course, letters of transmittal are also used for other purposes of immediate bidding communication; in such cases, a carbon copy under a ball-point original will bear witness and record as to the passage and content of information. (For an important job, subcontractors often take out plans and specifications themselves or use the plan-room facilities of reporting organizations.)

9-8   *Follow-up during Bidding*

As a matter of self-convenience, a subbidder may physically turn over possession of all bid-request cards with due dates and other information to his own trade estimator for follow-up and bid takeoff. There is, thus, considerable opportunity for delay before the request is acted on, subject to the workload schedule of an employee. There are many reasons for requiring that every requested subbid be telephoned in as soon as possible and that it be confirmed in writing. It is necessary to know:

1. Which of the subbidders on the request list will respond with a bid
2. That on the date set to make up the bid, there will be a subbid on record, even if only a telephone figure with no written confirmation
3. That such bids as are received are in enough detail to be readily compared with others

Follow-up is essential. Again, note that exclusions and inclusions may always be present. Their comparison places a different worth upon the value of a bid than first indicated.

9-9   *Telephoned Information*

As subbidders telephone in and various office members take messages for the estimator, there is the ever-present possibility of not getting all the necessary information or of mislaying scraps of paper on which the messages are written. These messages are a vital part of the takeoff record and must be correct, complete, and permanent. The estimator, as well, should clearly write down all information he receives so that he will not have to trust to memory and others will not have to depend on his physical presence for factual information. Everything should be written down.

LETTER OF TRANSMITTAL
This is a letter – Please file

ANY CONSTRUCTION CO. , #1 Name St. , City, State, Zip Code
Telephone

To _____   Date _____

_____   Job _____

_____   _____

Attn. of _____

WE ARE SENDING: Herewith _____   Under separate cover _____

For Estimating _____   Approval _____

Distribution _____   Other _____

No. of Copies: Dwgs.:   Description:

Kindly return _____ copies; Corrected _____; Approved _____

Other comment:

WHEN ESTIMATING, PLEASE RETURN PLANS AND SPECS AS SOON AS
POSSIBLE

ANY CONSTRUCTION CO.

by _____

figure 9-10. Letter of transmittal.

An estimating essential, therefore, is a telephone-bid receipt form (Figure 9-11) printed or mimeographed on standard letter-size paper for filing. The outline of the form allows anyone in the office to take the basic information. Should this be incomplete for any particular estimate or questionable in any respect, the estimator can always make a return call for clarification. The telephone is an excellent tool and should be used.

Should subbids come in slowly, the bid form allows the coordinator or estimator to ask anyone available in the office (even of no technical training) to follow up the trades for quotations. This procedure can save a great deal of time and aggravation in locating, among many, the few who may be figuring a particular job. When one subbidder has a diversified business and submits a quotation that includes bids for several different trades, this form permits the office help to make up separate bids for each trade for easy comparison with other like trades.

As subbids come in and are compiled for future use, the necessity of comparing them with others of the same trade can be met by using a simple filing system. Each subbid, as received, is marked at the top in colored pencil with the index number which the architect is using for the job and trade being figured. Of course, such symbols and numbers will vary with different designers and jobs, but this filing system is intended to conform to the architect's specification for one job at a time, that is, the job being figured. All subbids with the same architect's index number are then filed together for safety and accessibility in the job folder until they can be compared.

9-10 *Site Examination*

Once the subbid list is taken care of, and particularly when the mechanical trades have plans and specifications, a site examination should be arranged for immediately. Generally one or several of the subbidders will be confronted with their own problems of supply, access, delivery, or other variable and will wish also to inspect the site. The presence of a representative of the architect or buyer may seem advisable, and a one-time visit attended by all parties will bring up interrelated questions and will save time for all. Time should be allowed for a later visit if required.

A. The first step is to telephone primary subbidders asking if they wish to send a representative on some tentatively set date. In a new job there are problems for everyone regarding the nearest sources (or lack of them) for utilities, transportation, access, or similar items. All such problems can be circumvented, but generally at additional estimating cost. For alterations, there are existing material to be matched, working conditions and locations to be coped with, additional alterations required in

TELEPHONE BID FORM

Archts. Index No. _____

ANY CONSTRUCTION CO., #1 Name Street, City, State, Zip Code

BID FROM: (Company)   Date

Address   Trade

Telephone   (File)

Person calling

FOR: (Job)

Location

PRICE: _____   (Furnish)

(Deliver)

(Erect)

As per plans and specs: Yes____ No ____ Any addenda included _____

If NO,
INCLUDED:

EXCLUDED:

VARIATION:

ASK FOR CONFIRMATION:

figure 9-11. Telephone bid form.

order to do what is shown on the plans, and present facilities to be connected into. (This is a very small list of possibilities.)

After the visit has been tentatively arranged with the subbidders it must be definitely set up with the architect and, when necessary, the buyer. Even though an apparently complete location and plot plan have been included in the invitation, finding the exact site may be a problem. Reference points may be missing or hidden, roads not marked, or routes to the exact site not existent. And in the case of an alteration job, time of inspection may be determined by some regular commercial daily process, by the necessity of guidance, or by permission to inspect adjacent structures.

The inspection visit affords an opportunity to make personal contact with someone who may be of influence and possibly to obtain a benefit at a later time. A particularly worthwhile representative is a production supervisor for the owner. Such men often have meritorious ideas which may not have been incorporated into the plans but which offer excellent negotiation possibilities. The aim of all this preparatory work is to sell a job. The ideas of subordinates are important.

When directions have been given and date and time determined, all arrangements involving others should be made by telephone and confirmed by mail.

B. Due to the variety of conditions which may exist or be required, it is not practical to make up a general checklist. A memorandum and suggestion list should be prepared by the estimator for every job. It is possible for any individual to form a guide of his own, with specific relation to his own business. Some of the many items to be looked for are discussed below.

1. *Accessibility.*   Is the job location on a site attainable from an existing road, or does access have to be built? If an alteration is wanted, how does a contractor get men and material into the existing structure, and how far is it from where supplies must be unloaded to the work site? If the location is on an upper floor, are there existing freight elevators and what are the restrictions on maximum allowable load and time of use? (It may pay to consider some other means and location of hoisting under the direct control of the contractor, even if an additional cut, patch, and maintenance expense is involved.)

2. *Obstructions.*   Occasionally there will be rock outcrops on one part of a site and not on another (and not shown on the plan). Particularly when the site involves the reuse of a former industrial complex (or even a former farm building), hidden obstacles to construction are almost certain to be encountered. Old reinforced concrete machine footings may be exposed in new excavating, as may be live water mains under considerable pressure or old cesspools. Such items will require possible

handwork and considerable supervision, as against less expensive, machine operations.

3. *Contingencies.* Conditions inherent to that particular site should be noted. There may be groundwater, requiring pumping, or an absence of construction water supply, requiring trucking to the site. Material of delivery roads may mean rock ballast for heavy loads or additional cater-pillar-drive machines for tractive power to avoid delivery tie-up. Exposed power lines on a right-of-way may cross the property and be dangerously low for steel crane erection. In city work, an adjoining building may require underpinning or the neighborhood may necessitate hiring watchmen for crime protection. It is just not possible to see every condition or foresee every contingency. An allowance should be noted.

There are rare conditions which do appear, however, which should not be treated as those which are to be expected. Whenever the property itself or adjacent property of any nature may be damaged by the contemplated work, and if the condition has not been covered in the design and specification, that condition should be immediately, and unobtrusively, called to the attention of the designer in a questioning manner. He may or may not be aware of the situation. (For a contractor, there is no profit in being mixed up with future problems and possible litigation, particularly when one is not being paid for such assumption of responsibility.) There is a great deal of goodwill involved in the timely and proper disclosure of an unforeseen condition. At this time, if the situation warrants, the specification can yet be amended. The use of an extra order may later be warranted and necessary, but care should be taken to avoid the appearance of unfair tactics.

4. *Site Clearing.* Although the architectural plans will probably indicate in outline what is to be removed, the location, the nature of the site, and the demolition involved are only a few of the items affecting the cost. If the coverage is underbrush or small trees which can be pushed down by a heavy bulldozer in clearing the site, one cost will ensue. If large tree trunks must be sawed down and the roots removed, another cost will be called for. Demolition of present structures may be extensive and suggest subcontracting or may possibly be done at lesser cost by the contractor's own forces. Alterations are particularly difficult to estimate. Walls or floors may require support. Old brick may have to be closely matched, as may carpentry windows and trim dating back to a previous generation. The variations in cost are limitless.

5. *Facilities Available.* Public utilities and particularly power sources may or may not be available. In the latter case, portable generators must be rented and operated to energize electrical tools. The absence of sanitary sewers and the cost of installing temporary facilities may indicate the advisability of renting portable chemical toilets for the duration of

the job. The nearest freight terminal for deliveries may be located miles from the site, and special purchasing and delivery arrangements may be required. Local service inadequacies may also involve the furnishing and maintaining of shelter and commissary facilities as part of the bid. All these possibilities affect the makeup of the proposal.

6. *Existing Operations to Be Maintained.* A chemical plant dissolving metal to form acid will have periods of hazardous activity in the tank room when no work is possible. Of course, this operating condition will affect pricing, yet it may not appear anywhere on the plans and specifications. Or a daily-newspaper printing building requires large stocks of newsprint rolls to be delivered in the morning and distributed in the afternoon. Truck access must be maintained, and temporary detour means must be provided from the present printing room to delivery trucks during plant alteration. In such a situation, the newsplant superintendent is a necessary man to see. Occasionally local contractors, having done work previously, are considered reliable and thoroughly informed as to existing connections and conditions, and their subbid is necessary to take, although not obligatory to use. However it is covered in the specifications, it is necessary to make further inquiries about the conditions to be encountered.

7. *Future Possibilities.* While examining the site, a construction or sales possibility may occur to the searcher. Sometimes plans and specifications are improperly finalized in that existing grades, as shown, do not indicate the necessity for excavating, fill, or grading. The distance required for a utility connection may not be indicated. The terrain itself may suggest a less expensive contractual expedient. Such observations may be important and should be noted.

9-11   *The Written Report*

A site inspection (Figure 9-12) or other written report becomes part of the takeoff documents and should be on the same type of paper. It should show the inspection date, the people present, and all existing information which may be pertinent. The acquisition of special knowledge, or knowledge used to special advantage, will sometimes give a temporary price advantage in figuring a job. A hard-clay steep incline, intended to remain, may not require the anticipated shoring. In the same type of soil, a sewer line driven underground from manhole to manhole is stable, practical, and does not require the customary trench excavating, pumping, sewer-pipe laying, and backfilling. If such cost-saving possibilities are presented to the estimator, he will dispose of them as he is instructed or as he thinks proper.

To this report should be added such office information as will affect

Page

JOB NAME   Estimator   Date

<u>SITE INSPECTION</u>

Met their construction supt., Mr._____. Their job phone_____.

1. New factory, 1 story, to be built adjoining existing structure. All working
    areas for new plan already cleared by others of trees and shrubs. Site
    also leveled off and graded. <u>Not required by us</u> – clearing & grading.
    <u>Not on hand for us</u> – topsoil.

2. Dirt access road swamped through by others from present asphalt county
    road #7 (good condition) to new site. Specification prohibits use of present
    factory road and gate for use of new construction equipment and material.
    <u>Road made into all-weather type by adding:</u> Crushed stone 6" thick, rolled
    and choked with stone dust, and impregnated with one coat of hot road oil;
    approximately 160' long by 20' wide, from present county road to edge of
    new parking lot now specified – to be paved.

3. Fence marked on site plan to be relocated by us has already been reset by
    others. <u>Not required by us</u> – New fence.

4. Their construction supt., Mr._____, informed me that original
    structure construction met heavy ground-water condition. Original
    construction required to use well points operating 24 hours per day to trench
    and lay necessary sanitary sewer to existing sewer in middle of county
    road #7. Soil clay with little absorption, and surface water presently
    showing. <u>Add if required:</u> well-point system for trenching below grade.

5. Obtained names and addresses of previous subcontractors.
        Electric: Contractor A, address
        Masonry: Contractor B, address
        Plumbing and Heating: Contractor C, address

6. Obtained information new steel being negotiated by buyer for owner but not
    yet given out.

7. Present factory face brick to be matched: hard burned common red brick.

8. Nearest construction water and power in present building. Not noted in
    specification. <u>To be noted in our quote</u> – furnished by owner.

Submitted by

figure 9-12. Site inspection.

pricing. Wage negotiations under way, indicating a possible rate increase during the course of a job, should be brought to the attention of the estimator. A foreseeable material-price increase may have been brought to the attention of the office purchasing agent by his suppliers and should also be noted for the estimator. Subbidders will point out special conditions requiring rectification (such as inadequate water pressure and volume, relatively high sewer elevation with only gravity drainage shown on plans, or improper design to meet the local code).

During the process of completing the quotation, the estimator will discover, in addition to such items as noted above, other sales possibilities for correction or improvement, to carry forward to negotiation. (It may not be advisable to develop such items until the status of personal contact is reached. Many suggestions have been adopted by buyers with no benefit to the initiating party.)

9-12 *Site Reexamination*

Plans are sometimes developed over considerable periods of time. Approvals are not immediately obtained, money requires appropriating, plans and specifications and other requirements are changed. Should there be a lapse of time between inspection and completion of estimating and quoting, the original report should definitely be checked. The site may have been cleared or drained, roads and parking areas installed, or additional utilities furnished. The original plans may not have been changed, but such details may have—and they involve the job and the profit. They are worth checking.

10

TAKEOFF, FACTUAL AND SUMMARY

The basic determinant in obtaining a quotation is accuracy. When all the parts are included and extended in their correct quantities, a reasonable estimate for doing a job should result. Errors, however, are made by everyone. Because of the size, number, and complexity of construction units, anything wrong can be seriously wrong. The principal effort in making a takeoff is, therefore, to eliminate mistakes by emphasizing correct procedure and exact notation.

Space and clarity cut down mistakes, and estimating paper is of little expense compared with that involved in even one error. Every estimate should be legible, with full notations, illustrative sketches, and considerable space allowed for clarity and corrections, and time should be taken for a self-check of every item. As items are taken off, they should be individually checked for understanding and correctness. As items are extended, they should be habitually completed mentally again, in round figures, so as to verify the number of digits.

Time must be taken for an independent check after the quantity survey is finished. The summary must be correct. Business safety depends on it.

10-1   *Optional Takeoff Methods*

The actual takeoff is a most important management tool because one document accomplishes several necessary functions. These ends are attained by knowing what will be required and preparing the takeoff in a form to get such results. This so-called "quantity survey" can be made either directly by the contractor's organization or by a specialist who performs this work as a business. There are advantages and disadvantages in each method.

A. For the contractor doing estimating with his own staff, some advantages might be better pricing due to the contractor's special knowledge, a takeoff in a form to take advantage of his firm's ability in certain lines, a saving in overhead cost. A disadvantage might be a time delay when, due to limited manpower, an experienced estimator is unavailable at a time of many inquiries.

B. For the contractor giving out the estimating to others, an advantage might be getting a takeoff known to be complete, checked, on time, and legible. Some disadvantages might be a higher job estimating cost, a summation form not in precisely the manner preferred by the contractor, a removal from the office of necessary plans and specifications just when other trade subbidders are coming in. There may well be an uncertain cost attained because an estimator is familiar only with his own manner of taking off a trade (which is not always the same for everyone). For example, in estimating masonry work, the openings in a wall can be figured and taken out of the total wall area because that amount of wall material will not be used. Or the estimator may just as correctly figure the equivalent of replacing half the masonry units to compensate for the additional cost of setting the side jambs for the openings. The unit price for one method of takeoff would necessarily be different from the unit price of the other, yet both would give the same result when correctly used. The estimator using a purchased quantity survey, however, must play safe and assume a takeoff giving the greatest possible quantity at the greatest possible unit cost. If a variation can occur, it probably will.

At any one time, expediency is the determining factor. Under normal circumstances the contractor tends to do his own work. In this way, his organization learns to know the prospective job and can properly price it.

10-2   *Necessary Functions of the Takeoff*

A. Primarily, the takeoff provides a method of determining the erected cost of a certain plan and specification so that an offer for doing the completed job can be made. The procedure is to break down complex work items (with differing materials) into simple units. These parts are then susceptible of individual cost determination and later summarization. To the totals are added general items which are made the responsibility of the general contractor by the wording of the specification. Such items might be enclosure fencing, safety barricades, and cleaning up—which all cost money but are not in the province of individual trades.

B. Another use of the takeoff is as a record of what was actually figured. Plans and specifications may change during the period of time between the date of issue and the bid closing date. A notice of amendment to the original plan and a revised plan, when necessary, are sent to every contractor who is recorded with the architect or engineer for this particular project. (See Figure 10-1 for an architect's drawing with a typical revision notation.) As the ethical behavior of these designers is above question, their actions are depended on by all as being strictly impartial and as giving the same information to all. But—have all competitors received or figured on the same thing? This question is of importance to the buyer. With the quotation price, he wants to know if all changes have been included as sent out by the designer. Thus, every

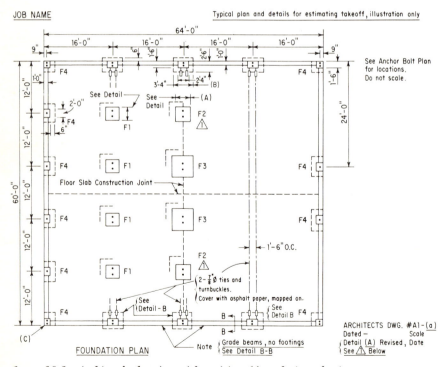

figure 10-1. Architect's drawing with revision (foundation plan).

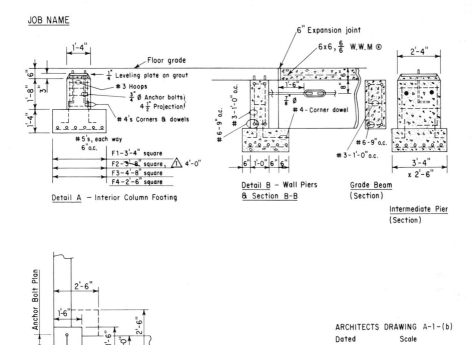

figure 10-1 (Contd.). Architect's drawing with revision (details for foundation plan).

takeoff must record dates and details corresponding not only to the original bidding documents but also to any modifications, such as addenda, which are to be included. A record of changes is incorporated in every bid as protection for both sides.

C. Also involved are possible construction changes to be made at a later time. These potential changes should be handled in a manner so as not to antagonize but to be helpful in obtaining personal contact for later use. A bid or a revision is only a phase in getting a job. Sales contacts must be worked up in advance toward that aim.

Any addendum received from architect or engineer prior to whatever due date is finally set also has to be estimated. The base bid will then be changed as necessary.

D. It is hoped that this quotation will be used in selling. It will be only another sales step, to be followed up by an appointment to negotiate. One of the buying tactics used in a comparison of bids is to ask competitors to isolate certain items of work and price their elimination.

A further tactic is to modify some detail during negotiation and ask for a change of quotation. There are, of course, many other contrivances of the buyer.

But they all lead to the necessity of being able quickly to find a definite item in the takeoff. Every item must, therefore, be in a form so as to be easily separable in both quantity and pricing. It is obvious that fully noted, complete, and clear individual takeoff details are a necessity for later negotiating. It is also clear that the method of doing work, such as hand digging versus machine digging, must be indicated, because it makes a difference in pricing.

E. Another sales step is the development of suggestions for later use. These are not the corrections discussed in subsection C above but rather are suggestions which will be made by the seller to the buyer at the appropriate time as additional motivations toward a contract award or as offering an additional source of profit if the job is obtained. They may involve changes of plan, arrangement, material, or anything which experience and judgment may advise. The proposals are evolved during the takeoff period, clearly marked and recorded—but not necessarily expanded —to obtain a cost. Should there be actual later negotiations, such possibilities can be explored. And when the buyer shows interest is the time to price and quote. A little delay in negotiation is sometimes worthwhile.

Usually the original bidding documents for the general contractor will also call for alternates, or additions and deductions to the price of the base bid. Such alternate prices give the buyer leeway. They are a necessary part of the takeoff and should be priced separately from the quotation in accordance with the bid request.

F. A further function of the takeoff is to provide for contingency items which are not included as required by the bidding documents but which do occur. They must be estimated separately from the main bid and clearly noted for reasons of competition. Otherwise, unfortunately, such an allowance added to the base bid may not be thought necessary and may not be included by a competitor. The result may be the barring of a higher bidder from future negotiations for a reason of which the buyer is not aware.

For example, the boring diagram or examination of the site shows groundwater above the level of the bottom of the construction. This condition may indicate the expensive necessity of a well-point installation, with its accompanying maintenance labor. Unless asked for, if this is added to the base bid as a construction necessity, the total price might throw the bid out of contention. But if such items are priced separately and quoted separately with qualifying wording, such as, "If this contingency occurs, add the following amount to the base bid," there can be no doubt but that the contingency was foreseen and that the price for it is not in the base bid. The buyer is put on notice that the problem exists and that he should include it in his dealings with other bidders.

G. Another most important function of the takeoff is its use after a job is obtained. The documentation serves as a purchasing guide, in which the aim is to use the makeup computation subtotals as *maximums* which can be bettered. This takeoff includes not only the material, labor, and equipment of the general contractor but also the subbids (from whose file the prospective subcontractors will be interviewed). The saving in time and outlay can be appreciable.

The takeoff also serves as a labor and material cost control, in which the material purchasing and production costs attained on the actual work are immediately compared to the amount presupposed in figuring the job. Should an adverse relationship appear during the course of construction, it can be considered at once. Savings are possible only before or at the actual time of erection.

The takeoff also indicates the method of erection figured, the equipment used, and the time required for superintendence. Possibly the costs involved can be bettered.

10-3   Takeoff Background

The assumption is made that anyone employed in the construction business has or can obtain an adequate knowledge of plan reading. Therefore, a simple plan (Figure 10-1) is given as a readily understood example for takeoff examination. The work involved is the installation of reinforced concrete.

This is a trade which may be done either by a general contractor or for him by a subcontractor. In either case, the general contractor will probably make his own takeoff even though he can save time and expense by getting subbids. He will make his own estimate as a basis for understanding and pricing his own quotation. Should he get the job, he can later decide if it is advisable to give out the work as a subcontract. In this case, the contractor becomes a buyer, and it is his business to "sell the subcontract." Based on his own takeoff, he offers a price to the subcontractor and bargains up to what he must pay. Along the way he attempts to convince the subcontractor that the latter's own estimate is overpriced—hence the reference to "selling" in the trade expression above.

The process of making a takeoff requires considerable study and practice and is the subject of many books. Thorough training is essential and is best realized through actual experience. The mechanics of setting up this procedure vary from office to office and are influenced by individual aims and experience. The method hereafter described is but one of many. At some time or other, however, an understanding of how to make a takeoff is required of everyone and for any trade. The details vary, but basically the procedure is the same. Because concrete placement is easily understood and yet involves considerable detail, it will be used as an example in discussion of takeoff procedure.

10-4 *Takeoff Procedure*

A trade is not one operation complete in itself but a series of discontinuous actions which are put together. When material cost is relatively fixed, installation efficiency is the determining factor in getting work. Also, differing types of work, in various locations and of diverse structural sizes and components, will give differing costs.

A. It is possible to group various operations and computations provided the same series of actions is involved in putting work together. The advantages of grouping include saving of estimating time and constant reminders to reiterate necessary actions. The work sheet (Figure 10-2) illustrates this measure.

The kinds of work and the locations involved are:

1. Footings	Interior
2. Piers	Interior
3. Footings	Exterior
4. Piers and grade beams	Exterior
5. Floor slabs	With topping integral

The types of action for each of the above are:

Excavation.   Machine, hand, or subdivisions such as tamping or insulation

Form building.   Including construction and expansion joints, anchorbolt spreaders, and other carpentry

Reinforcing.   Rods, welded wire mesh, or accessories such as hoop forms, stirrups, and other specialties

Concrete in place.   Including transportation, screeding, applying integral surfacing, setting supplementary leveling plates

In any individual case, there will be more, fewer, or different items, depending on plans and specifications. On the work sheet, the takeoffs and extensions are separately made and identified so that the subdivisions can be used as completed and wanted—and at that time they may be clearly marked with colored pencil to indicate where they were transferred.

B. In preparing to set up the work sheet for any estimating takeoff, it is necessary to provide an adequate number of subdivisions in every classification to allow for differences in pricing. Certain work, even if in the same general classification, will not be done for the same price as other items.

For example, detail *A* in Figure 10-1 indicates certain isolated interior column footings and piers. Here the concrete will probably be poured by hand, after being moved in buggies from a ready-mix concrete supply truck outside the building line to the interior location, where forms and reinforcing are in place. The footings of the exterior walls and later the wall itself, however, can be poured in place by a chute direct from an immediately accessible location for the ready-mix truck on the outside of the form location. Of course, there is a very considerable variation of labor cost for every cubic yard of concrete placed in the two locations in such differing manners.

The cost differential will customarily be recognized and taken care of by separating the takeoff items, as shown on the work sheet. Then different unit prices are applied as required. However, this is not always possible. Situations frequently occur which require the use of considerable manpower to obtain very little measurable physical result. Or a unit-price extension may be inadvisable for some other reason, such as the necessity of estimating something new about which little is known.

In such a case, recourse is had to a stratagem. The particular work item is taken off by a further breakdown into a manpower hourly cost, material, and equipment basis—just as if it were a separate small job all by itself. On the work-sheet example (Figure 10-2), note that subdivisions 3a1 and 4a1 or 2d1 and 4d1 are set up for this type of pricing and figuring. Only strictly normal takeoffs are subject to the application of unit prices, as previously noted. The estimator must have or must be guided into a knowledge of construction practice.

The above example demonstrates that for future profit every prospective job must first be studied before being estimated and the work implications must be understood. It also demonstrates that in actual practice not all jobs are big ones. Small problems occur often and are as important to note and solve as the big, showy examples given in some estimating texts.

The work-sheet setup must be clear, legible, completely marked for reference, including necessary cross-references, and arranged so that it can be continued by others. Sickness and accident do occur, and someone with the requisite technical training should be able to take over and benefit from previous work. He can do this only if the takeoff text indicates what has been done and what is not yet taken off or figured. Full notes, sketches, and cross-references should be completed every day for every successive estimate sheet. Consecutive sheet-positioning numbers are thus essential as a matter of record and also to ensure against omitting takeoff material when making up summaries (Figure 10-3).

Such attention to detail is never a waste of time. Verifying the correct transposition of figures from plan to work sheet, proving all calculations

JOB NAME _____   WORK SHEET

	(a)	(b)	(c)	(d)
	1 2 3	4 5 6	7 8 9	10 11

For details see Fig 10-1

(1) Interior Pier Footings
Detail 9/4 (see Fig 10-1)
Note for backfill, Line-11.
Use dimension 2'-0" greater
than footing size. Allows
for Construction clearance

(1a) Excavation - Machine (Incl piers)
F1 - 4 x 50' x 50' x 3.6' = 360 c.F
F2 - 2 x 56' x 56' x 3.6 = 225 c.F
F3 - 2 x 4.67' x 6.7' x 3.6' = 316
                          8
                90 1 cF = 33 2/3 cs

(1a) Trim - Hand, Allow 1 Lab - 4 hr

(1b) Forms
F1 - 4 Pcs x 12.0 x 1.34' = 65 S.F
F2 - 2   x 14.67' x 1.34' = 40
F3 - 2   x 18.67' x 1.84' = 50
                             155 S.F
F2 - ⚠ Small addition, not included

(1c) Reinforcing & Dowels
F1 - 4 x 2 x 6 #5 (105#) x 30' = 151 lb
F2 - 2 x 2 x 6 #5   x 3.67' = 92
F3 - 2 x 2 x 6 #5   x 4.67' = 118
Dowels - 8 x 4 x 4 (67#) x 15' = 22
Dowels - ⚠ Small addition, not included   383 lb

(1d) Concrete
F1 - 4 x 3.0 x 30 x 1.34' = 47 c.F
F2 - 2 x 3.67 x 3.67 x 1.34' = 36
F3 - 2 x 4.67 x 4.67 x 1.34' = 52
                            141 cF → 6 cY
F2 - ⚠ Small addition, not included

(2) Interior Piers
Detail A/4

(2a) Excavation (none)

(2a1) Backfill & Tamp (Incl strip)
All footings - 8 x 2.0' x 2.0 x 1.34' = 43 cF
All piers use average dimension
4 x 5.0' : 20'
2 x 5'.67 : 17' = 46 1/3 = 5.75' Avg
2 x 6.67' : 14
8 x 5.75 x 5.75 x 1.67' = 442 cF
485 cF + 50 cF = 535 cF Total → 20 cY

(2b) Forms - 8 x 5 3/4 x 6.7' = 74 S.F

(2b1) 8 Anchor Bolt Spreaders

(2c) Reinforcing
Corners - 8 x 4 x 4 (67#) x 15' = 33 lb
Hoops - 8 x 3 x 3 (.31#) x 4 x 3' = 40
                                  73 lb

(2d) Concrete
8 x 1.5 w x 3 x 1.6 T = 24 cF → 1 cY

(2d1) Set 8 Pcs Leveling Plates

Add 10% extra for tamping —

154

(3) Exterior (Buttress & Walls) Footings Only Detail B, C/4	(3a) Excavation - Machine Corners - 4 - 4.5' × 4.5' × 4.5' = 367 Intermediates - 12 × 5.33' × 5.5' × 4.5' = 1580 Cross Ties - 4 × 55.0' × 2.5' × 1.25' = 690 2737 C.F. = 101 C.Y. → (3a1) Trim - Hand; Allow 1 Lab. - 8 hr.	(3b) Forms Corners - 4 Pcs. 10.0' × 1.34' = 54 S.F. Intermediates - 12 × 14.67' × 1.34' = 236 290 S.F.	(3c) Reinforcing (Corners & Inter. Fig Same) Mats - 16 × 2 × #5 (1.05#) × 3.5' Avg = 118 lb Dowels - 16 × 6 × #4 (.67#) × 1.5' = 97	(3d) Concrete Corners 4 × 2.5' × 2.5' × 1.34' = 34 C.F. Intermediates - 12 × 3.34 × 2'-6" × 1.34' = 115 Total C.F. = { 6 C.Y. Allow
Computations for Excavation (4) Exterior (Buttresses & Walls) Piers & Grade Beams Line {18, 19, 20} 4 Pcs. 16.0'(−) {(4.5' + 5.33')/2 = 7.17'} = 8.83' net 2 Pcs. 12.0'(−) {(4.5' + 4.0')/2 = 6.5'} = 5.5' " 2 Pcs. 24.0'(−) 6.5' = 17.5' " 4 Pcs. 16.0'(−) {5.33' = × 2 = 5.33'} = 10.67' " 4 Pcs. 12.0'(−) {4.0/2 × 2 = 4.0'} = 8.0' " 16 Grade Beams	(4a) Excavation - Machine - Grade Beams) Next to corner - 4 × 8.83' × 3.0' × 3.17' = 336 2 × 5.5' × 3.0' × 3.17' = 105 2 × 17.5' × 3.0' × 3.17' = 333 Intermediates - 4 × 10.67' × 3.0' × 3.17 = 405 4 × 8.0' × 3.0' × 3.17 = 305 1484 C.F. = 55 C.Y. (4a1) Trim - Hand; Allow 1 Lab. - 4 hr. (4a-2) Backfill & Tamp (Incl. Strip) (Neglect buttress for figuring outs) All footings - 16 × 2.0' × 2.0' × 1.34' = 86 C.F. All exterior walls - 252' × 1.5' × 3.17' = 1200 All interior walls - 248' × 3.5' × 2.67 = 2320	(4b) Forms ((Complete Over footing) Perim - Exter.; 248.0' × 3.17' = 786 S.F. Inter.; 246.0' × 3.17' = 780 Add - Cor. Buttress; 4 × 1' × 3.17' = 13 Inter " ; 6 × 3.34' × 2.67' = 54 6 × 2.0' × 2.67' = 32 1665 S.F. (4b1) 10 Anchor Bolt Spreaders (4b2) Set 6 Pair Tie Anchors	4(c) Reinforcing Grade Beams, perim. + lap 4 × #4 (.67#) × 252.0' = 675 Piers (Allowed Cor. Buttr. Reinf. Not Shown) Vert. - 10 × 6 × #4 (.67#) × 3.0' = 120 Hoops - 10 × 3 × #3 (.38#) × 5.0' = 60 855 lb →	(4d) Concrete Piers, (Cor.) 4 × 1.5' × 1.5' × 2.67' = 24 CF ((Cols.) 6 × 2.34' × 1.5' × 2.67' = 56 (Interm.) 6 × 2.0 × 1.5' × 2.67 = 48 (Grade Beams) 16.0'(−) {(1.6 + 2.34)/2 = 2.17'} → 4 × 13.83' × 1.0' × 3.17' = 175 CF 16.0'(−) {2.34/2 × 2 = 2.34} → 4 × 13.66' × 1.0' × 3.17' = 173 24.0'(−) {(1.5 + 2.0)/2 = 2.5} → 2 × 21.5' × 1.0' × 3.17' = 136 12.0'(−) {(1.5 + 2.0)/2 = 2.5} → 2 × 9.5' × 1.0' × 3.17' = 61 12.0'(−) {(2'/2 + 2'/2) = 2.0} → 4 × 10.0' × 1.0' × 3.17' = 127 800 C.F. → 30 CY (4d1) Set 16 Pcs. Levelling Plates
Finished elev 6" below grade → Add 10% for tamping	360 C.F. + 3610 C.F. = 3970 C.F. Total = 145 C.Y.	(5b) Forms (Construction Joints) 120 Appox. Lin. Ft. (1" × 6") (5b1) Expansion joint 6" at perim. Detail B/4 → 260 Lin. Ft.	(5c) Reinforcing 6" × 6"; 6/6 W.W.M. 58.0' × 62.0' = 3600 S.F. Lap 10% 360 } → 4000 S.F.	(5d) Concrete 58.0' × 62.0' × (.5') = 1800 C.F. → 67 C.Y. (5d1) Finish - 3600 S.F. (From Reinf. Comp) (5c)
(5) Floor Slab (Integral Finish) Add 5% for waste	(5a) See Line 40, Tamp to finish grade (5a1) Pliofilm - 60' × 64' = 3840 S.F. + 390 = 4230 S.F.			

figure 10-2. Work sheet.

```
                                                        Takeoff sheet # 6

  JOB NAME                SUMMARY                    Initials    Date


   Numbers below from individual computations of work sheet    Section 3, Page 3
   See Fig. 10-2
                        Concrete          Unit Prices  Material  Labor
1     Excavation-Machine
2     1a, 3a, 4a ⟶ 189½ C.Y.
3     1 Day - 1 Back hoe, 1 Truck; 1 Each Engr. } Lab.
                                        Driver
4     Trim - Hand
5     1a1, 3a1 — 1 Laborer 12 hours
6     Forms - stops
7     1b, 3b, (1" x 1'-4")⟶445 Lin. Ft.
8     5b, (1" x -6')⟶120  -do-
9     Built Up
10    2b, 4b, ⟶ 1800 S.F.
11    Anchor Bolt Spreaders
12    2b1, 4b1 ⟶ 18 Units
13    Set tie anchors
14    4b2 ⟶ 6 Pair Units
15    Set expansion Joints
16    5b1 ⟶ 260 Lin. Ft.
17
18    Reinforcing bars
19    1c, 2c, 3c, 4c ⟶1526#  Allow —16.00#
20    Mesh 6x6; 6/6 (Welded Wire)
21    5c ⟶ 4000 S.F.
22
23    Concrete in Place
24    Footings- machine poured
25    1d, 3d ⟶ 15½ C.Y.
26    Walls- machine poured
27    4d ⟶ 30 C.Y.
28    Piers; interior, hand poured
29    2d ⟶ 1 C.Y.
30
31    Backfill & Tamp (Incl. Stripping) to Bottom of Slab
32    2a1, 4a2 ⟶ 165 C.Y.
33    Pliofilm
34    5a1 ⟶ 4400 S.F.
35
36    Floor Slab Concrete, Hand Pour
37    5d ⟶ 67 C.Y.
38    Floor finish
39    5d1 ⟶ 3600 S.F.
40    Misc. allowances
41       Screeds ⟶ 3600 S.F.
42       Liquid hardner & cure ⟶ 3600 S.F.
43                              Total Costs
44    Additional Overages: Material sales taxes         %
45                    Labor Wage insur.prem, Soc. Sec.contr, etc.        %
46    For Masonry                                               %
47 ⟶  Note - Include 20 leveling plates, Fig.5-2; Sect. 2D11 in masonry takeoff
                                                   4D11
```

figure 10-3. **Work-sheet summary.**

(including extensions, additions, and divisions), checking the inclusion of all factors in the completed work takeoff—these may seem a reiteration and a waste of expensive estimating time, but it takes only one serious error to invalidate an estimator's worth to himself and to his firm. He must, therefore, check himself as he proceeds and not depend on the work of others.

He will develop his own methods of improving the correctness of his takeoff technique. These may include making a habit of changing feet and inches to feet and decimals of a foot on the takeoff before making any computation, using a computing machine to eliminate decimal-point errors, or using a convention whereby takeoff dimensions are always entered in the order of length, breadth, and height. (Note that the super-accuracy afforded by machine computation is not always warranted, and mechanical summations are often rounded off.)

10-5   *Additional Takeoff Procedure*

Certain key trades, such as masonry or carpentry, are often done directly by a general contractor because of their influence in controlling time of erection. Until the foundation, frame, floor, shell of the building, roof, and partitions are in place, the balance of the structure cannot be completed. (This, like all generalizations, is not always, but almost always, true.)

Even when trades must be separately figured, however, a work sheet is not always required or even advisable if it uses unnecessary time and space. As shown in Figures 10-4 and 10-5, the takeoff sheets alone may be adequate. This will be the case provided the individual actions set out for analysis are in enough detail so that they can be readily priced in simple units, which in themselves incorporate reiterative items of the same kind of work.

For example, in item 7 of Figure 10-5, where the laying of block wall for any area always includes the same reiterative items, this would be true. (This unit price includes the cost of labor and material for building the scaffold and transporting block and mortar to the location and rental charges for equipment used, such as mortar mixers and tubs.) Thus in this case, since the unit price will be on the basis of a cost in place per block, all that is necessary is the number of blocks required for this phase of the job. The procedure for the simple computation to obtain a cost is discussed in Chapter 11.

Because the pricing of the job is a later phase of the estimating procedure which is established by the estimating data, information must be included with the takeoff material for this function. As part of each item, therefore, certain variables which affect pricing will be prominently

JOB NAME   Initials   Date

			Section 4, Page 1
	SECTION 4 - MASONRY	Material	Labor
1	Specification Requirements		
2	Face Brick - as noted - Running bond and stack bond, cavity ties		
3	Allowance - $60/M		
4	Wire Reinforcing - Every 2nd course, as detailed		
5	Backup Block - Waylite, parge cavity face		
6	Tool exposed joints as noted		
7 Detail			
8 ①	(2) Manholes		
9 A/₁	(Footing by others) Use stock manhole - ⌈30" inside top dia.		
10	From stock list - 2×#1×12 Pcs. = 24 Pcs. ⌉⌊48" inside bottom dia.		
11	2×#2×12 Pcs. = 24 "		
12	2×#3×10 Pcs. = 20 " ⌉ Blocks		
13	2×8 Barrel ×12 = 192 " ⌋		
14 2	30"∅ Grating and frames set in bituminous paving		
15			
16 ②	(1) Meter Vault		
17	21'×4'×(8"Block) = 84 S.F. 100 Pcs.		
18 1	Hatchway door and frame set in top arch		
19			
20 ③	Face brick (From Details B,C,G/4) Including Brick Parapet		
21	⌈North Elev. - 78'×27' high = 2110 S.F. ⌐		
22	Outs - Windows - 29.37'× 24.5' = 720 S.F. ⌐		
23	Sign recess - 5.5'× 5.5' = 30		
24	Spandrel stucco - 78'×2.25' = 170		
25	(-) 920 → 1190 S.F.⌐		
26			
27	⌈East Elev. - 65'×26.15' = 1700 S.F. ⌐		
28	Outs - Windows - 29.37'×20.5' = 600 S.F.↓		
29	Spandrel stucco - 65'×2.25' = 140		
30	Main door detail -16.75'×23.5' = 390		
31	(-) 1130 → 570 S.F.⌐		
32	(+) 1760 S.F. @ 6.8 brick/S.F. → 12 M (+3% Waste) → 12¼ M brick		
33			
34 ④	Face brick - Ornamental Reveals → Include Reinforcing		
35	Details indicate number of courses ⌉ 89		
36 D,E/4	8 - Windows × 240 brick = 192 pcs. brick 17 12		
37	28 96		
38	1- Entrance detail → 300 pcs. (Incl. waste) 240 96 51		
39	2220 pcs. 32 275		
40	Allow 2 Masons, 1 Laborer → 14 days		
41			
42 ⑤	Exterior Scaffolding (Including Entire Perim)		
43	300 Lin Ft. × 25' = 7500 S.F. ———→		
44			
45			
46	Note - Detail A/₁ means detail A, drawing 1		
47	Note - These details to be purchased and to be built in		

figure 10-4. Masonry takeoff.

JOB NAME

				Section 4, Page 2
	Section 4 - MASONRY			
		Carried Forward from P.7	_____	_____
1 ⑥	½" Portland Cement Stucco - Exterior			
2 See page	Spandrel 143' x 2.25	= 325 S.F.		
3 4-1, lines 20-30	Window panels, N.elev. 29.37'x24.5' = 720 S.F.			
4	E.elev. 29.37'x20.5' = 600 S.F. / 1645 S.F.			
5	Outs - 8 windows x 3.34'x20.5' = (-) 545 (Approx.)			
6	1100 S.F. → 123 S.Y.			
7				
8 ⑦	Block ——— Use 8"x18" Face, Lightweight			
9	(12" Interior Partition inspection area, point			
10	joints 2 faces) - 25.67'x11.' = 282 S.F. (+) 1% = 385 pcs.			
11	No doors out			
12				
13	(12" Exterior S. & W., Point 2 Faces)			
14	143' x 27' = 3860 S.F.			
15	Outs - Windows 6 x 5.5' x 7.5' = 248			
16	No doors out 3612 (+1%) 3650 pcs.			
17				
18	(8") Backup, Point 1 Face			
19 See page	143' x 27' = 3870			
20 4-1 lines 20-30	Outs - Windows - 1320 S.F.			
21	Main door - 390 } } 2160 S.F. 2200 pcs			
22	(-) 1710 S.F. }			
23				
24 ⑧ (a)	Joint Wire Reinforcing (Every 2 courses)			
25	(12") Line 9 - Height - 11' → (8.3 spaces of 16") 9x16' = 144 Lin.Ft.			
26	" 14 " -27' → (20.3 - do -)21x143' = 2980 Lin.Ft.			
27	3200 Lin.Ft.			
28 (Detail) G/4	(b) Use 12" with 8" Backup block to project as tie into face brick			
29	(12") for Line 19, Height - 27', same as line 26 2980 Lin.Ft.			
30	(c) From Concrete Recap. - 20 Leveling plates & grout			
31 ⑨	Parge (½" Stucco, face between backup block and face brick)			
32 from line (16) → 3612 S.F. } 5772 S.F. → 620 S.Y. ——————→				
33	(21) → 2160 S.F. }			
34				
35 ⑩	Wash Down and Clean (Same as Above) 6000 S.F.			
36				
37 ⑪	Set Stone Sills 8 Windows x 3.5' x (1"x6")			
38	6 -do- x 5.5' x (1"x6")			
39				
40 ⑫	Misc. Specification Requirements			
41				
42	Additional Overages: Material sales taxes	%		
43	Labor wage insur. prem., Soc. Sec.,			
44	union welfare fund, and other contributions	_____	%	
45				
46	___	___		
47				

figure 10-5. Final masonry takeoff.

noted. These will include such items as the thickness of a wall, any specific wall height or height location above grade, and any unusual corners or openings to be formed.

Note, as in item 8 (Figure 10-5), which refers to wire reinforcing, that work items which would not normally be included in a unit price will be taken off separately for individual attention anyway. The limited working space provided on the takeoff sheet is, therefore, adequate.

In the short period of time allowed by the request to bid for the over-all makeup, certain subbids may not be received or some additional verification may be required. Therefore, any trade quotation not received may have to be the subject of an individual takeoff. The general manner of the takeoff as affecting every trade should, therefore, be known to the estimator.

10-6   *Reference Books*

The necessity of assembling correct information that will be useful to others in a takeover or in a checking procedure, requires the establishment of a reference office library of useful information. This material should include trade information, such as the commercial size of wallboard to determine wall coverage, the weights and sizes of members customarily kept in stock, as against those which are obtainable but with delayed delivery and at premium prices, and rental charges for the temporary use of some item of equipment required by a particular specification (such as an earth tamper). On architectural plans, the draftsman will usually insert a key to explain the abbreviations he has used and the conventional indications for determining material (such as different markings for masonry or stud partitions)—but not always. Very often the estimator must refer to a standard manual of drafting practice for an interpretation. Occasionally a specification will refer to a standard of work to be done as outlined in a manual of trade practice supplementary to the main specification.

As an example, in Figure 10-1 the sizes of reinforcing parts are given by trade number convention (such as numbers 3, 4, and 5 for ⅜, ½, and ⅝-inch-diameter rods). The material takeoff under work-sheet column lines 7, 8, and 9 (Figure 10-2) correspond to these numbers for each takeoff, with the weight per foot for each number as given in standard steel manuals next to it. Such a manual, of course, must be available in the office. It is necessary to translate the takeoff length into weight because that is the way the material is bought. The weight also gives a measure of the cost of the placement manpower, *which must also be estimated*.

Weights vary as indicated by these trade manuals, which also give meanings and weights for other abbreviations. The slab of Figure 10-1, detail *B*, shows (*a*) 6 × 6 (*b*) 6/6 W.W.M. This means welded wire mesh, (*a*) sized 6 × 6 inches square and (*b*) with each wire to be of No. 6 gauge. (The size of the reinforcing wire running one way is often different, for design purposes, from the size of the wire running perpendicular to it.) The weight of the required wire mesh per square feet for any required size is given, as are the number of square feet of wire per roll, the length and width of the roll, and other ordering information which may be needed.

As a word of caution, some of these manuals are issued for advertising purposes by material manufacturers. Within their scope they are perfectly reliable, but they cover only the types and sizes furnished by the particular manufacturer. It is necessary for the estimator to know whose reference book he is using and whether it completely serves his purpose.

10-7 *Follow-up*

During the entire takeoff time interval, there should be constant follow-up for additional information to be received from others. Now comes the time, prior to final pricing, when it is urgent for all items to be complete. Filed and grouped subbids will be checked against the subcontractors' mailing list. This procedure will determine which trades have an adequate number of received bids and which should be followed up immediately to bring in additional quotations. Every possible subbid should be obtained. Any other necessary inclusion involving a document, such as a bid bond or an insurance certificate, should also either be present or on its way.

Occasionally it is difficult to locate someone who is estimating a required trade on the particular job being figured. As possible suggestions, the specification may give specialty houses that furnish approved items and that may have received requests from erecting firms for prices. Or local jurisdictional departments may have requirements or inspections to be met and may have advance information as to who will figure. Or the person who drew up the specification may have been queried in advance by interested parties and may himself be respectfully requested for information as to who has evidenced interest.

When subbids do come in, they may not completely cover every item in a specification. Sometimes the specification writer has assumed that a particular trade will cover some item and this presumption happens not to be correct. In such a case, no one in that particular trade may have submitted a subbid for the item because no one handles it. The general contractor then receives no bid covering this specification requirement. To catch omissions, all quotes should be read as soon as they come in. When a complete bid is not included, the missing price must be obtained.

In many cases the specification, also, will make an overall cost allowance (for certain trades) subject to a recomputation later when the job is actually bought and done. When a particular trade, such as hardware, is subject to a wide variation of styles, finishes, and construction, this maneuver allows a job to be bid at the same material cost by every competitor. Such an allowance saves the bidding time of the general contractor's estimator. The fact that the *installation* of any particular trade is not included with any bidder's list for estimate figures may unfortunately be forgotten in the final makeup, and someone gets a job by omission. Should the job be obtained correctly the necessity still remains of following through on completion of this item. There is the possibility that the designer will buy more heavily than he anticipated, and the general contractor will be entitled to an additional sum of money. Such allowance is important and must be recorded. A credit may also be due.

There are also alternate prices which are to be quoted separately from the base bid and which may or may not be made part of the job as finally contracted for. There may be unit prices for additions or deductions to the base bid if later required during construction. There may be additions or deductions authorized by the designer during the bidding period but not included in the original documents. Any items of this nature must be separately recorded, computed, and summarized for separate pricing. Every figure needed for the quotation or for reference should be included in this instrument.

When the request to estimate asks for certain alternates to the main bid, each alternate should be taken off completely and with care as a separate small job. This procedure not only is a vital safety measure but also is generally useful in the negotiation process. Very frequently, bargaining between buyer and construction seller is a trading affair, with something left in as against something taken out of the final contract. Understandable, explicit details and prices are needed.

In negotiation and for any trade, time of approximate delivery of vital parts is of importance. The delivery of the boiler in the basement, the elevators for hoisting, the roof installation, and the electric fire-alarm control system throughout the building are items which affect job progress. This topic of time is certain to come up in negotiations. It is most material. A tentative progress schedule, therefore, is neccessary to figure out the approximate job running time, including deliveries and equipment, and the time for which overhead will be required.

10-8   *Summarization*

Upon completion of these items, it becomes necessary to make up a series of summary sheets for whoever will do the pricing for the firm. Regardless of whether this pricing process is part of the estimator's job and is kept separate for checking or is a function reserved by the management to ensure control, the complete summary itself should be made out by the estimator (Figure 10-6). Up to this point, he is the member of the company who knows the most about this prospective job, and he should be best able to outline those items which have cost significance and, therefore, should be included.

If the inclusion of any item is questionable in the bidding documents, the estimator can make up a completely separate takeoff. The price for this item, when formulated, can be kept apart from other items for individual treatment.

10-9   *Takeoff Tools*

Certain specialized equipment and tools which have been developed to aid in drafting also expedite the making of a takeoff. They are stock items and may be purchased as needed from architectural supply houses or from office-equipment dealers.

A. On the comparative scales shown in Figure 10-7, customarily there is printed material which can be used for estimating. This is available in pads of tracing paper and is used to give line and scale to sketches required for site or takeoff work. The cross sections vary, such as eight, ten, or more divisions to the inch, or are in metric divisions, such as millimeters. This arrangement allows their use for many purposes.

B. On this same figure, the development of the much-used scale rule is outlined. The lower part of line *a* is 6 inches long and is divided into inches and parts of an inch. The upper part is in the metric scale and gives a direct comparison. Line *b* is directly below, and the top illustrates on the left-hand end how each ⅛ inch of the regular scale is arbitrarily called 1 foot. The effect of making up this so-called "⅛ scale" into a useful architectural rule means that the simulation of every foot of length drawn by anyone using this rule is only and actually ⅛ inch long. This compression results in a vast decrease in the size required to represent a structure—and, of course, in the size of the paper on which it must be placed.

As the shrinkage of size with this scale is rather drastic, more detail can be shown using some other reduction scale which is not so extreme. Hence a number of other scales exist and are used when size of structure allows or when larger details are to be shown. For example, the top right-hand end of line *b* compared with the inch scale above indicates how each ¼ inch is arbitrarily called 1 foot. This is made into a draftsman's ¼-scale rule, which gives lengths twice the size of the ⅛ scale. Detail is thus much more visible, although there is still considerable size reduction. The bottom of line *b* shows a comparison of ⅜- and ¾-scale rules with the standard rule as used in measurement.

	From	SUMMARY SHEET	Material	Labor	Subcontract
1	(Fig.4-2)	Page 1 Added expense items, items 3 d,e	——	——	- - - - -
2	(" 4-3)	" 2 No bids			- - - - -
3	(" 4-4)	" 3 Gen'l.Cond. of Subtrades	- - - - -	- - - - -	- - - - -
4	(" 4-5)	" 4 Subtrades	- - - - -	- - - - -	- - - - -
5	(" 5-2)	" 5 No bids, Work sheet	——	——	
6	(" 5-3)	" 6 Concrete recap.	- - - - -	- - - - -	- - - - -
7	(" 5-4)	" 7 Masonry, N.Bid, Carried forward to p.8	——	——	- - - - -
8	(" 5-5)	" 8 Masonry	= = = = =	= = = = =	= = = = =
9		For Self-work, Overages Previously Figured	- - - - -	- - - - -	- - - - -
10		Allow Differing Profits	%	%	%
11		Part totals	- - - - -	- - - - -	- - - - -
12					
13		Complete Total		- - - - -	
14		Actual Quote		- - - - -	

Takeoff Sheet # 9
JOB NAME   Initials Date

Alternate & Unit Prices, Where Necessary

figure 10-6 Final summary.

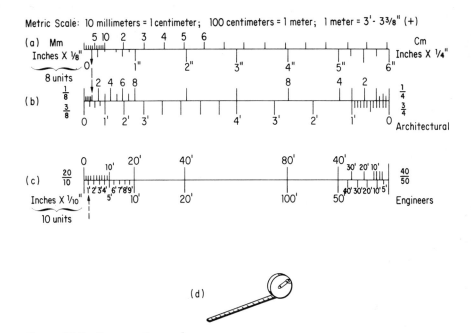

figure 10-7. Comparative scales.

C. If, therefore, a readily portable tape could be marked in units similar to that used by a draftsman in making up a plan, it could be used to read off directly any dimension used in estimating without the necessity for replacing a small fixed scale, finding plan figures, or approximating lengths. Such a flexible steel pocket tape is shown on line *d* (Figure 10-7), printed in ⅛ and ¼ scale on opposite faces (which are the most-used scales). The degree of accuracy obtained in estimating does not warrant exact takeoff dimensions.

Should the draftsman have used a different scale for a particular plan, there are 6-inch-long pocket scales available which are printed on the edges with these unusual scales, thus giving the estimator an easy means of interpretation. Of course, even a 6-foot folding job rule may be used to scale a plan, provided the reduction scale of the particular plan is shown or otherwise learned and the method of scale reduction is understood.

D. Another type of subdivision (known as an *engineer's scale*) is used for some special purposes. Again, the starting point is a system of measurement, such as the foot and inch, but here each inch is divided into parts in multiples of 10. For example, in the lower part of line *c* (Figure 10-7), each tenth of an inch has arbitrarily been called a foot; the scale is therefore called a No. 10. This, again, is an arbitrary trade practice to call attention to the different manner in which the foot and inch are subdivided. The estimator must pay particular attention to the scales which are used in making up any particular set of plans. These variations set up an element of danger, in which a takeoff may be assumed to be like every other scale and actually is not.

The derivation of other scales is shown on Figure 10-7, such as a 50th, which would give fifty divisions, or 50 feet, to the inch. Such a scale might be used in drawing plans covering considerable lengths of construction, such as a new sewer system.

E. The kit used by most estimators is then very simple and consists of a few much-used small tools, which are kept together for travel if necessary. In addition to the estimator's ⅛ and ¼ tape and an architect's and engineer's 6-inch rule showing several standard scales, there are several pencils including a colored one, a small manual pencil sharpener, an eraser, and a shield. These can be kept in a moisture-resistant and zippered pocket-size case, sold in any merchandise chain store. An estimating pad and an individual company stock sheet or other special-products manual will, of course, also be necessary to suit the business being done away from the home office.

10-10   *Arithmetic-extension Tools*

The numbers used in estimating include takeoff items; variables, such as assumed production rates, material prices, the cost of weather delays, and other contingencies; assumed overages; and a margin for error. Since actual local trade requirements limit material minimums which may be ordered—and sometimes maximums which can be obtained—it is just not possible to compute too closely. Any estimate taken off in small fractions is, therefore, not believable. Use of judgment is essential.

The custom has arisen of doing extensions with an approximately correct hand calculator, such as the slide rule. The results are quite good enough for most purposes, and its use can be rapidly taught. It has a serious possible error, however, in requiring users who are multiplying or dividing to establish mentally the number of ciphers to be applied to any answer. The answer can be, and always should be, mentally checked. Computing machines are, of course, preferable. They give a correctly ciphered answer even after many successive calculations. If the total is unreasonably accurate, it can be rounded off. The computations are fast and accurate and can be carried out by most office help. Desk-top machines can be obtained to include adding and subtracting functions as well as extending and dividing—all of which are necessary.

The office copying machine has an important part to play in estimating. For example, a subdivision of a specification can be copied and sent to a subbidder who is receiving a loan of part of the plan for estimating. He has then received an exact copy of the bidding documents that affect him, while the original specification stays in the office so that it can be used by others. Copies can also be made of letters and addenda received by the general contractor which must be mailed to all estimators. Also, it is necessary to copy originals of any documents which must be included with the quotation and of which a record should be kept. (Even part of the plan can be photocopied and pasted together if needed.)

11

PRICING

Job quantities should be about the same when competitors make competent takeoffs of the same plans and specifications, using the same type of labor, material, and equipment. Yet almost always there is a difference in the construction quotation amount to the buyer. One of the possible differences, obviously, is in the value set for doing individual quantities of work.

Note particularly that any discussion of differences in pricing must be predicated upon a similarity of takeoff totals by all competitors. There is no question but that pricing does make a difference. The quoted price should not be too high to bar a chance at the job or too low to do the job with a profit. The purpose of pricing correctly is to gain an opportunity to take a prospective job at a price that will ensure a profitable sales contract.

11-1 *Obtaining and Using Facts*

Pricing depends on having facts developed under present conditions. Past accomplishments are not satisfactory unless checked and brought up to date. Also, past records must accord with those that are being physically figured at present or must be modified so that they will be in accord and meaningful. Every going construction company has estimating records of payrolls, production rates, material bills, and equipment-rental invoices. The estimator will have to make sure that his current takeoff items are matched by existing records which are current in date and which consistently apply to the same things. If not, it becomes the immediate duty of the estimator or his designate to formulate or to procure such information.

The need for verification emphasizes that production records are useless unless they include details of how such records were obtained. Included will be dates, daily working hours, rates of pay used, type of machinery involved, dimensional variations, and location of work. Should the required pricing information be unavailable, the takeoff procedure must include immediate action to get facts for completing the unit prices. Telephone calls, postcards, reference to publications and trade services are some additional sources of facts.

In addition to the job folder, there will be other facts on hand. These facts should include indexed, dated, and detailed information concerning the regular business of a company. The material may include current wage scales, labor rule agreements, jurisdictional decisions, material prices, available stock sizes and grades, and other possibly helpful information.

Flexibility must be provided for in making up cost records, material costs, and other necessary items because of the many ways in which work may be specified and designed. Face brick may be backed up with brick, block, or concrete. The joints may be tooled or cut and may be of natural cement, Portland cement, or colored cement. The arrangement of brick may be in ordinary running bond or in some decorative design. The material may be of various degrees of workability.

Flexibility must be looked for in the types of units used. There is no such thing as a universal use of some takeoff unit. For example, a painting subcontractor in figuring the cost of a field coat of paint on a structural steel framework might base his price on a timesaving, shortcut takeoff based on his own experience. He knows about how much it costs per ton of steel frame to do field painting. Therefore, if he can obtain the fabricated amount of tonnage bought by the general contractor from his steel subcontractor, a price on field painting can be submitted with little estimating work. The general contractor might use another basis. In taking off this item of trade with his own estimator, he would probably obtain the surface area to be painted for the average-size beam used in the framework. This is probably the cost unit that he has filed. Note that in each case a different means has been used to arrive successfully at the same figure, which is part of a much larger estimate. Higher and lower quantities will tend to cancel out.

Conversion tables from one unit to another are often necessary and should be made up as required and kept for future use. Above all, the units used should be perceived with an understanding of their significance. They are meaningful figures.

Flexibility of approach is specifically necessary in using subcontract bids for special items. For example, trade-name steel joists may meet the specifications and be lowest in price among competitive joist manufacturers. Yet the fact that they are low-priced and from a reliable and specified bidder does not necessarily make their use in the quotation advisable. Their very specialized manufacture may have disadvantages. Shop drawings, delivery, and erection may be far behind that offered by others. Terms, such as cash on delivery, may be difficult to meet. The limitation of products manufactured may forestall later required changes of design. Should the job be obtained, the necessary purchasing function may be definitely hampered and limited. It is often better to use the next-higher bid of some generalized supplier who offers other purchase advantages.

Previous and new information is transcribed to the job folder. Each item is directed in colored pencil back to the numbered page and line of the takeoff. The same colored pencil marks the number of the takeoff sheet from which the information is obtained. When telephone information is received, it is completely written out on letter-size paper, with names, addresses, delivery dates, prices, and telephone numbers. A written confirmation can be asked for and filed in the same place when received.

Applicable production records will be extended with related conditions. Changes can be made. Further information can be obtained. In those rare cases in which apparently no one has exact information, recourse must be had to a consensus of opinion among qualified individuals to get an assumed rate of production. This method, of course, will be used only for some small and relatively insignificant part of the total takeoff, where too much time spent in working up the estimate is not called for.

All such preparation requires time and is as much a part of the estimate makeup as the takeoff itself. It does afford unit prices to be used at the right time.

Unit prices are not to be used in every case. They are adequate for normal-size items but may not necessarily be correct for smaller-than-normal areas or quantities. For example, a large concrete floor, which would normally be poured at one time, is specified to be done in small areas and in checkerboard construction. This method forms a series of built-in construction joints and small expansion and contraction areas which reduce the possibility of irregular floor cracks. But this type of construction also increases the cost considerably above that of the normal, single-pour method. Additional material and labor are required to make floor stops or expansion joints. Union rules or other criteria may require certain trades, such as ironworkers and carpenters, to be on the job and paid without working—just to be there in case of necessity. Production rates per square foot of surface area will be decreased, and costs will be increased.

When unit prices seem at all questionable, they should be used cautiously. Such work items should be given individual attention on the basis of being handled as day's-work jobs. The developed cost may then be integrated into the main takeoff.

11-2   *Checking*

Before pricing is started, the physical takeoff should be checked by a knowledgeable person who is not the estimator. Every effort should be made to minimize errors.

The inclusion of all the many items shown on a set of plans cannot be checked without making a complete takeoff again. A spot check, however, can be made of those items of considerable value which make up a large percentage of the work. A quick check of prominent features is also pertinent. Errors of omission due to mental strain and interruption of personnel are common. In a firehouse takeoff, all the fire poles were emphasized and carefully taken off but two sets of four-story-high stairs were omitted! Errors of commission also happen. A 200-foot length of interior partition was properly scaled on an estimating tape but was marked down as being 20 feet long.

The specification and other contract documents are prolific sources of errors to be looked for. Contractually, the job consists not only of structural work but also of general conditions and special conditions to be included and therefore necessarily noted on the takeoff. There may be fencing to be built around the plot, access roads to be built to it, or watchmen to be hired for the site during the lengthy period of construction time. Some of these items will not be shown or called for except in one small notation, but they will be required, and such items can be expensive. They must be noted as an integral part of the takeoff. There will also be special considerations to be figured, such as that the buyer will give out the structural-steel framework apart from the general contract.

Thought must be given to what contingency items are possible. Jobs figured in the summertime may require completion schedules involving winter working conditions and possible costs. (Heated ready-mix concrete carries a premium cost, as does the admission of an admixture to speed up setting time at low temperatures. And the establishment of heated working enclosures represents an addition to normal expenditures.) Undoubtedly some contingent costs will be incurred if the job is obtained, and these should be included.

When bonus and penalty clauses are to be included in the contract (as noted in the bidding documents), there is a risk figure to be added to the quoted price. A premium may have to be paid for both labor and material to get an adequate supply of either or both in rush seasons, such as just before school opening or after a strike. If there is a delay for any reason, the penalty will be assessed. The contingency is a calculable risk to be insured against and priced.

Thought should also be given to supplementary contingencies that may have to be included. A construction job may necessitate first constructing housing, then installing a commissary, and then providing laundry facilities or such other operations as are needed.

Some types of expense will undoubtedly be rearranged in the quotation to get that required low bid, but these should definitely be included as additions to the base figure. This is the place and time to make sure that they are included and to determine how they are to be estimated.

11-3   *Cost Changes and Setup*

Companies do have customary prices for doing similar work. But there are many reasons why costs of doing apparently the same work will vary and should be changed in estimating. Location, time, specification, manpower, equipment—all affect production. *Basically, the application of local conditions is what determines how the price is obtained.* A unit price given in a collection of individual cost records or in a textbook is only as good as the specific surrounding facts which produced that cost. If a particular job under consideration varies in any significant respect from the recorded or textbook makeup, the cost will have to be changed. Pricing places a premium on experience.

The estimator will have acquired a knowledge of the physical aspects of the plan and specification, and his presence is advisable during the pricing study and application. The skill and experience of the practical organization should be represented by another qualified member of the construction company to complete a pricing team. (Although one man often does this work, it is far safer to have the judgment of two.)

Groupings of work items of similar nature are instances of how time can be saved. As an example, similar items of work require similar percentages of overhead, such as an overage for a premium on labor payroll for insurance or a percentage on material purchases for sales tax. Therefore, the total amount in any category can be used at one time for just one computation. Such groupings of work items become very simply a summarization in columnar form. The columns are divided into topics which lend themselves to this additional computation, such as labor, material, equipment, scaffolding. The columnar division controls the total sum for the final computation.

11-4   *Labor-cost Influences*

When the primary decision between union and nonunion labor has been made, other items should be considered.

A. *Work Rules*

These may be a verbal matter of custom only, or they may be spelled out in written form (Figure 11-1). They may be direct or may be slanted to some particular purpose, but they should be heeded.

These rules fix the trades and rates to be used in a particular location for work. And the fact that a particular trade at a particular hourly rate is allowed to do certain work in one locality does not indicate that it will be allowed to do the same work elsewhere. In certain jurisdictions, laborers can erect scaffolding for the masons. In other localities, carpenters must do this work. The difference in the wage scale is appreciable.

Work rules affect many other items, such as the hours that constitute a normal working day, when overtime is permitted and what the additional rate is, and when labor is reclassified at a higher rate than normal. Even when a construction firm is supposedly thoroughly familiar with a location from having worked there, there is no reason to assume that the rules and the rates have not changed and will not change again. The only answer is definitely to find out at this time, *before figuring*. Union rules are a matter of public record and may be obtained by a legitimate application to a local union having jurisdiction. Building periodicals publish such rates, as do contractors' associations. Nonunion conditions and rates are variable and are best reviewed through local trade sources. And the fact that all rates may change during the period of job completion should be taken into consideration.

B. *The Production Rate*

Labor production is not to be construed as constant at any time or anywhere or for anything. It varies with pay rates, the weather, the attitude of labor, the materials used, and other factors.

TRADE WORK RULES (Sample)

Rules vary with the trade, the skill required, the danger of the work, and many other factors agreed to in writing by negotiating parties for union labor and employer groups as an employment contract for a definite period of time. Therefore, articles are only representative.

Article 1. RECOGNITION. The Associations (for the employers) recognize the District Council (for the Union) as the sole collective bargaining agent for certain of their employees, upon the representation of the District Council that it represents more than 51% of the employees.

Article 2. AUTHORITY OF EMPLOYERS ASSOCIATIONS. Employers associations act as bargaining agents for their members and represent that they have the requisite authority.

Article 3. UNION SECURITY. Employees presently employed must become Union members before the lapse of 31 days after date of contract or date of later employment. If Union membership is not properly maintained, employee shall be paid off within 48 hours after Union notice.

Article 4. REFERRAL PROCEDURE. Union shall supply all employees except foreman and one journeyman who may be the choice of the employer. Employer may request services of particular Union members, who have been employed within six months previously. Union will maintain Job Referral system using first-in – first-out basis and no discrimination. Employer may reject any applicant referred by Union.

Article 5. STANDARDS OF COMPETENCY. A place on the Referral list is predicated on a high degree of skill and a corresponding quantity and quality of work. Proof to be by apprentice training and requirement to pass an examination given by an examining board, or a minimum of four years of practical experience and an examination (one year to be considered as 1,200 hours of work).

Article 6. PAYMENT OF WAGES. Wages to be received in cash on the job, no later than 2 P.M. Two days backpay per week may be withheld.

Article 7. WORKING HOURS. Seven hours to constitute a days work; 5 days a week; overtime at rate of double time. Work on holidays shall be paid for at overtime rate. Holidays shall include New Year's Day, Washington's Birthday, Memorial Day, Fourth of July, Labor Day, Presidential Election Day, Veterans Day, Thanksgiving Day, and Christmas Day.

Article 8. SANITARY WORKING CONDITIONS. Provide comfort station on the job. Provide sanitary drinking cups and clean water. Provide suitable toolhouse and changeroom with lock and key in possession of shop steward, and heating equipment when required. Employer to be responsible for tools up to $100 in value.

Article 9. PAYMENT ON DISCHARGE. Journeyman or apprentice on discharge shall be given two hours notice or two hours to recondition tools.

Article 10. WAGES. Schedule to be set during term of agreement.

figure 11-1. Sample trade work rules.

Pay rates vary from one locality to another. Men will be paid according to the territory in which they are working rather than the local organization to which they belong. When men go from one locality to another in a payroll period, the bookkeeper will have to split their time in accordance with the controlling territorial rates. Not only must the estimator have or obtain the rates for the particular job location; he should also know if adjoining areas have higher or lower rates. He may have to pay a premium to get men from elsewhere.

Production will change with the type of job done. Occasionally an addition will be made to a structure housing a going business. The present operation will have to be maintained free of interruption during the entire time of the change. If a newspaper plant is involved, the printing-paper rolls must be supplied daily and each published edition must be freely accessible to the delivery trucks for distribution. If a chemical plant is involved with a hazardous reaction at regular time intervals, all work in that location must stop during that period of time. Each case is different and requires study. Individual solutions are costly, and men must be paid while waiting to work.

Production will vary with the practical aspects of running work. A gang of men pouring concrete may work hard and efficiently. Yet if the next ready-mix concrete truck is delayed in arrival and they must wait for it or if they finish ahead of quitting time and cannot be laid off because they work again next morning, there must be a loss of time. How much is to be added to a recorded quantity and rate is a matter of judgment.

C. Plan and Specification Requirements

The location and physical aspects of the work on the site will also cause the manpower requirements to vary. Horizontal and vertical travel; walls which vary in height, thickness, number of openings, number of corners; finishes for floors which may be broomed, smooth, or abrasive—all change the labor cost. And differences in material which affect labor include quality, absorption, texture, weight, and size uniformity.

D. Seasonal Factors

The weather, contrary to public belief, is not the only daily uncertainty in the construction business. The employment situation also varies markedly. There are times of the year when labor of any type becomes hard to get—for example, the fall months, when schools open, when buildings must be enclosed against coming bad weather, and when other buildings must be completed for tenant occupancy. There are also times in any season when a few large jobs all working at the same time in one district soak up all the unemployed personnel in one or several trades.

This condition of scarcity occasionally requires paying a wage premium to get tradesmen. Such men may not even be competent or may not be willing to turn out a fair day's work for the increased pay. But in any event, again costs have gone up.

In the reverse of this condition, sometimes work is scarce and men are readily available. At such times their work attitude is good and reflects the effort applied to hold employment. But the estimator usually figures the worst condition and hopes to be pleasantly surprised.

E. Contractual Influences

A constant factor of importance is the effect of contractual requirements on employment. This is exemplified by the case in which employment guidelines are set forth in the application to bid (which will become part of the contract). The intent might be, for example, to get equal job opportunities for minority groups, but in so doing, the cost of doing the work may be increased over normal and must be checked before the estimate is finalized. The following are possibilities which might increase costs:

1. The differential between the hourly rates of two classes of labor may have been effectively erased by a minimum hourly requirement for all trades. A rate for this particular job is thus set, regardless of what the prevailing rate in the locality may be.

2. A training program may be called for with an obligatory ratio of one trainee to some set number of journeymen on the job. This proviso will naturally increase cost relative to production actually attained.

3. The qualifications of prospective workers may be determined by jurisdictional authorities and not by the worker's own ability.

Further, note that when work is done but not in compliance with the contract, a retroactive pay observance, leading to a loss, may still be enforced. There is a continuing liability.

11-5   Material-cost Influences

Material prices are not fixed. When a contractor does his own work, the material quantities involved can be large and the consequent saving in price or terms of delivery of material can affect a quotation. The establishment of costs in advance of estimating for each of the many items involved, therefore, becomes necessary.

A. Plan and Specification Requirements

The design features of various materials include strength, weight, size, texture, color, permanence, and imperviousness. All these qualities and others are of importance to the architect and engineer. The design is based on these criteria. And the plan and specification are drawn up to be followed explicitly. On the other hand, a designer recognizes that competitive suppliers and materials may afford the same factual assurance which he requires for his design at lower cost or with other advantages which will benefit his client as well as the contractor. The plan and the specification therefore offer some leeway, which will vary with the job. For critical materials, the substitution may be nil or subject to very stringent approval. Substitution of stock material, however, may be freely permitted. Every case is different, and therefore, the bid documents will control because they will become contractually effective.

There is one specification qualification which must be noted. Should the wording unequivocally state that a certain item is required and no substitution is permitted, a warning to be noted on the takeoff has been given. Regardless of how many advantageous bids are received for substitutes, they may not be taken. Only the price of that bidder complying with the specification can be used.

If the price saving is large and worth the trouble, a separate quotation may be given offering a price advantage to the buyer if a particular substitution is permitted. Or an additional price may be asked for something which is to be considered as more advantageous than that which is specified. Sometimes the specification offers a method for submitting alternate proposals. In any event, such situations should be handled with care and as proposed substitutions only.

B. *Market Factors*

In a competitive market, different material manufacturers will offer price differentials, discounts for cash payments, or delivery-time advantages of one as against the other. Such offers must be weighed and evaluated against each other. Often, offers are made which appear to extend a price saving. Actually, there may be a saving by spending more money. For example, a specification merely called for the material for the partitions to be of cinder block. The general contractor, who also was figuring the masonry work, had a choice of two different types of block. The ordinary commercial cinder block, which would have been allowable, was lower in price than the competitive pozzolana (pulverized volcanic rock), which is also a fire-rated block. Offhand, there seemed to be a price saving in using the cinder block. However, the pozzolana block is much more consistently regular in size and finish, is lighter in weight, and looks better in the finished wall. Further, its use would reduce the fire insurance premium for the owner. But the item which swung the deal to the pozzolana-block supplier was the weight per block. The volcanic rock is full of entrained air and is 35 percent lighter than cinder block. The masons produced enough more partition per day not only to make up the price differential but also to make an added profit possible from their labor. The men were less tired at the end of the day than they were when working with the normal-weight block. Just incidentally, the owner benefited at no additional cost by getting a better job.

C. *Seasonal Factors*

The same weather conditions which cause variations in labor costs also bring changes in material prices. In wintertime, all sand, gravel, and water used in ready-mix concrete is heated as a matter of course, and a certain amount additional is charged per yard of concrete furnished. It is not possible to buy any other way, and this additional cost must be figured in the estimate. In the early spring, which is generally a time of unimpaired shipments and plenty, prices will usually be lower than when shortages develop later due to inclement weather and material demand.

D. *Procurement Factors*

The quantity of material delivered on any specific order to any specific job also affects the price. For example, it is apparent that delivery of full truckloads (5 to 9 cubic yards of material) of ready-mix concrete to a job at some one price might be profitable business for a supplier, whereas deliveries of a lesser quantity at the same unit price would be unprofitable. Job quantities do vary, and the superintendent will order only what he needs.

Customarily, then, the supplier will quote more and will charge more for smaller delivered quantities, longer unloading time than some standard, deliveries required at some other than regular working hours and days, or any other special requirement. The quotation cannot be cluttered up with a number of such requirements, which may not even be used. It is necessary, however, to allow some considered price differential to take care of a possible cost overrun.

When subbidders' quotations specify that anchors, supports, space and elevation grounds, openings and recesses, and cover trim are to be furnished and installed by others, such items can be costly to the general contractor. All bids should be checked promptly upon receipt to determine the exact extent of this or any other exception. There may be other costly requirements, such as temporary heat for rooms requiring laying of linoleum in freezing temperatures, free use of hoist or elevator service, free temporary electric power and light. Someone has to pay for these items.

Some bids will refer to trade customs with which the receiver of the bid is assumed to be familiar. For example, a vinyl-tile subbid may refer to a limitation of colors which will be supplied in accordance with some trade designation, such as color range C. In an unobtrusive manner, an omission has been made of certain expensive designs and colors required by the specification but not included in the trade grouping. Should the designer later rightfully insist on getting such designs or colors, the general contractor is nowhere released from his responsibility to furnish them. The subbidder, however, previously declared them out in limiting his original bid.

Whenever wording is not absolutely clear, one *must* ask. The consequences of any bid exceptions, such as references to sales taxes, unloading from trucks, or overtime hours, should all be clearly understood. Constant alertness and thought are necessary to cover contingencies.

Because the variations possible in ordering necessarily affect pricing, a summary of conditions assumed should be added to the takeoff by whoever does the pricing. Should a contract be later awarded to do this particular job, the purchasing agent for the construction company will have a complete record of what was figured.

Occasionally an estimate may be made up in a period when a price increase is expected to occur after the job is awarded. It is not good policy to raise the contractor's base figure. It is better to stay in the running for the job rather than possibly to oust oneself, for the competition may not use this problematical safeguard. The bid can definitely, *in every and any case, bear a time limitation up to which the price will hold*, to be subject to possible change at a later date.

An estimate is always a calculated risk. The calculation should include a provision for a measure of safety against fluctuations caused by the passage of time.

11-6 *Equipment-cost Influences*

During the progress of the takeoff, a necessary course of construction procedure for the major items of work will be developed. When machines are required, details of these will be entered. In one location a diesel-driven crawler crane with a long boom may be needed. At another point a heavy-duty, electrically driven, and automatic sump pump and discharge hose will be required. Yet another design and progress situation will call for a gasoline-motor-driven diamond-blade saw to cut concrete-floor expansion joints.

When a contractor owns equipment, he should still charge for the use of it, even if that charge is low in order to get a competitive bidding advantage. There is always interest to be earned on money invested, maintenance expense to keep machinery in operating condition, replacement expense (such as frayed cables for cranes or split rubber diaphragms for pumps) to keep machinery operating and safe. In addition, there is always the unavailability contingency, which cannot be foreseen

at the time of estimating. Also, the short time of use may be a consideration. It may be necessary to enter the rental market and pay a fee for the
use of the particular machine. The rental fees will have to be ascertained
and included.

And, of course, equipment is not confined to machinery. It includes
articles and supplies necessary for some particular service, such as
scaffold planks, mortar tubs, space heaters with fuel, or a telephone
installation.

The rental cost of the equipment is as much an estimate charge against
the job cost as the labor and material.

11-7   *Subbids*

Occasionally a contractor will do his own work. But generally he will
subcontract individual parts of the work when it appears to benefit him.
The takeoff, of course, will reflect that policy, as discussed in Chapter 8.
When subcontracting is used, all bids should be received before the
makeup date of the estimate.

The money volume of subcontractors may often be the largest part of a
general contract, far exceeding the direct work done by the individual
general contractor. The lowest legitimate subbids which can be given
out under a later subcontract are therefore necessary. The general contractor must be able to set an approximate price on each subtrade to
determine if the bids he is receiving are low, about correct, or high.
Comparison of the bids is not alone adequate, as the present subbid may
be purposely high to allow future price trading or there may be collusion
to give a high price to one contractor while favoring another. Subbids
are so important in the total price that the general contractor, if he is
satisfied that he is correct, may have to discount the prices that he has
received. On the other hand, an error by the subbidder may bring in too
low a price.

The general contractor should be able to estimate other trades. On
specialty trades, such as the pipe trades or similar installations, it is very
difficult, as well as time-consuming, to make a competent takeoff. In such
cases, recourse is made to the practice of the unstudied, yet shrewd,
speculative builder. He figures his plumbing per apartment building as
being worth so much per apartment or his electric work as being worth
so much per lighting fixture. He can count and figure really well and,
surprisingly, often arrives at the correct figure he must spend to get a
subcontractor. The general contractor should be capable of approximating what the largest money-volume trades should amount to.

As a practical matter, this compulsion enforces attention upon the
subbids. The invitation list for any new takeoff has, of course, been made

out as one of the first duties of the estimator. The inquiries are followed up on the list *as to receipt and complete coverage.* When time is lacking and emphasis is to be placed on receiving a bid on time, when an interpretation of the extent or meaning of something may be needed, or when any other questionable subbid matter arises, it should definitely be discussed by telephone.

Occasionally a bid may be received which is low in comparison with other bids or with what could be expected from other knowledge. The general contractor is always tempted to use the price of the low bidder. In an open market, others will have the same bid, and if it is lower than the competition, the price may help someone else to get the job. The fallacy here is that when a contract is awarded, it must be produced. Can the low subbid be bought at the price quoted, or will the low bid be unavailable and have to be purchased at a higher (and underestimated) price?

There is a fair way out of this dilemma, which will take the low bid out of competition if it is incorrect. If the subbidder is advised personally that there appears to be something incorrect in his bid in comparison with others and that he should check and revise his bid *to all* if necessary, the general contractor will get complete and quick attention. The subbidder will examine that estimate with a fine-tooth comb, and if there is anything wrong, all bids will be rescinded or revised. If the subbidder advises that he has checked the bid and will stay with the price and if his reputation is good, the low figure can be used. (Incidentally, the general contractor has made a firm friend.)

When a plan or specification has been changed by the designer in any respect during the takeoff of a job, all trades, even those only remotely affected by the change, should be notified to check their quotations to ensure that the estimate includes the final arrangement or wording required by the designer. A small change sometimes makes a big cost. These changes must be carefully checked and noted in the quotation.

At this point, the allowances established in the specification should be checked. For example, they may not include the work of handling, safeguarding, and installing the hardware, although the designer has briefly specified that such work is to be done. The general contractor, therefore, is entirely responsible for what may be an expensive item, and one not elsewhere noted.

Any item making allowance for material to be later chosen by the designer (such as carpeting) must be carefully examined and estimated for work that will be involved but that is not included in the allowance. It must also be remembered that the allowance itself is a predetermined cost and must be included in the bid makeup with the other subbids.

Subbids are most important. Someone must follow them up. A sufficient number of bids must be received and in hand before they are required. Such quotations should be in writing so that comparisons can be made among them and against all contractual documents. Cases are common in which comparative prices or detailed information are questionable, and time must be allowed for clarification. Whether an adequate number of bids or no bids are received, a figure is necessary and must be worked up. Particular care must be taken with one's own transcriptions from subbid accumulation and comparison sheets to the final estimate-pricing summary sheet. At completion, there should be one final bid for every trade or item required.

11-8   Pricing and Extension

Every summary total is extended before pricing. Then each total is priced by multiplying it by a rate cost for doing the prescribed work, a rental cost for the equipment and time to be used, or a cost for the specified material, all as already in the record, or by a percentage figure for an average. Here the advantages of both knowledge and experience should be used. Regardless of whether the pricing figure to be used has been refigured, newly figured, or assumed, the method and source of makeup should be questioned. If considered advisable, revision should be made and entered, and the reason for any change should be recorded.

The office help, working with office computing machines, should be used in every case involving figures so that they become familiar with the estimate and can perform the calculations with dispatch and accuracy. There are always times when subbids are delayed or estimate events are limited in some other way. Skilled assistants are an asset in finishing up a cost estimate on time.

The final addition of some customary percentage for profit, as in a regular manufacturing business, is *not* possible in the construction business. There is no such thing as a customary percentage. Rather, a management decision must arrive at a percentage figure which adds an amount of money to the estimated job cost that will allow a profit and yet not cause a loss of the job to competition.

The profit percentage may vary in any one job. The general contractor may figure a certain percentage on those few items of work which he does himself and a different, lower overage on the subcontractors' bids.

11-9   Other Factors in Pricing

The management decision on the profit overage to be allowed is an important factor in attaining an estimated figure which is quotable. The quotation must be *low enough* to impress the buyer as being within the range of negotiation so that he will call in that competitor for direct bargaining.

In closed bidding, only by direct contact with a buyer can a contract be obtained. The initial bid, however, must also be high enough to offer a possibility of making a profit. Should negotiation produce a contract, the final price should then permit a profitable job.

For both closed and open bidding, it is self-evident that the final estimated price is *not* set by a seller alone but is determined primarily by the competition.

A. The number of bidders will have great influence in determining the final price. If the number of bidders is high, the price will be much lower than if there were only a few bidders. Generally, advance determination of the number of bidders is possible. Many firms will not even figure a job on which more than a certain number of estimates will be received by the buyer. The odds against getting a job, let alone a profitable one, become higher as the number of competitors increases.

B. The identity of the bidders is of importance. Every construction firm does work to make money. But not every company has the same method of making money or the same need for work at any particular time. Some firms will want to get many jobs at a low profit per job. Others want a few jobs at a good profit for every job. Some have plenty of work to keep their keymen busy. Others have inadequate work to pay their necessary costs of staying in business and must get work to pay the bills. In such a case, monetary profit has been translated into survival and maintenance of a productive establishment, and this explains many an unexpected low bid.

There are several daily services which offer a list of current jobs to be bid and also the bidders of those jobs. In addition, key subcontractors and material men in a particular location, chambers of commerce, the local banks, and many others are very apt to know exactly who is figuring any particular job. This information requires the support of a knowledge of the competitive facts regarding each prospective bidder. How has each competitor bid before? Is their present work on hand adequate or low? Does the firm have any actual competitive experience with this competitor? Trade reports of a firm can and should be obtained if not on hand.

C. A comparison of the money value of one's own work and that of the subcontract work and the amount of profit allowed on each are important. Customarily, the use of a subcontractor and his bid is shared by many competitors, and their overage will depend on their estimate of what they can charge. If, however, the competitors do their own work for some portion of the total, they can customarily get some greater percentage than if they subcontracted this work, again based on their own judgment of what they can get.

D. The costs involved in indeterminate probabilities must be added to the price. These additions are uncertain only in amount. If a union contract-labor rate is to go up in a few months, at the time this particular job will be operating, the additional cost for labor is added to the bid. If the price of ready-mix concrete goes up automatically for heating after a certain fall date and this particular contract will probably start about that date, the question is not whether the bid will be affected but by how much; the additional price for material delivery will have to be assumed and added to the bid. If there will be a transportation strike and heavy permanent equipment can be rented and obtained at the site now, the storage and interest charges that will have to be paid until the equipment can be used are added to the bid. If at all possible, such charges will be kept out of the main bid and included in a supplementary paragraph in order to keep the bid as low as possible.

Other indeterminates are the subbid prices used. Normally, a set of figures from various subbidders within one trade will be reasonably close. The parties doing the pricing will use a figure comparable to what is received but at which they believe the work can be bought. If, however, certain bids seem high to the contractor (through his personal estimate or other means), the possibility exists of later buying this particular subcontract at a considerably better price than received. Because the money value of the subbids is such a high percentage of the total cost, the pricing is of importance. This particular question requires individual consideration.

E. There is usually a difference between bids to a buyer. The difference varies with the job, the specification, the number of bidders, and other factors. But except in a public bidding situation, in which by law the low bidder must be awarded the contract, there is usually no assurance in general bidding that the low bidder will get a job. The objective therefore is to be low enough to get in to see the buyer but not necessarily to be the low bidder. The buyer tends to deal with bidders from low to higher. The possibility of making a profit on private bidding is enhanced by this negotiating factor. A worthwhile risk is to leave extra money in the estimate for negotiation.

F. Weighting of bids may be resorted to if several unit-price alternates are asked for. For example, the interior masonry partitions may only be specified and not detailed, with an allowance to be made in the bid of so much per square foot for partitions if required. For this commercial building, a few large leases are preferable to many small ones, with a consequent possibility that there will be relatively few interior partitions called for later by the owner from whoever gets the contract. The bidder will therefore decide to use his total masonry bid and deduct *a break-even price* for the assumed interior partitions. This will increase the profit percentage on the balance of the work without changing the total. If the unit price does not materialize, the figured profit margin is higher than it would otherwise have been, for there is no necessity for giving a credit.

If any of the work becomes necessary, the profit on that part of the job only will have been lost. The bidder is gambling against his opposition without much cost and with a possibility of gaining a competitive advantage. To the buyer the unit-price part of the bid looks better than that of the competition, even though the totals may be nearly the same.

G. Doing enough work to pay for the overhead before attempting to make a profit is another means of figuring to get a job. No amount of business foresight and ability will enable money to be made until work is done. The objective is to get work which will pay for overhead and allow an opportunity to make a profit. If a volume of construction amounting to X dollars per year is the objective and if the job being estimated amounts to $X/15$ dollars of the total, the percentage figured by the accounting department must be added to the $X/15$-dollar construction cost to get the total business cost. (Note that the accounting department used the business expenses of the previous year and divided that figure by the sum of total business developed in that year to obtain an overhead percentage.) The volume of work actually done will vary from the amount tentatively set, so that this figure will be subject to change.

11-10   *Additional Percentages of Costs*

The summarization of the various costs developed previously now affords an opportunity for time saving in estimating. Referring to Labor-cost Influences (Section 11-4), the labor cost is now no longer *only* payroll but includes costs *added to* payroll. The addition will include an allowance for the premium to be paid for workmen's compensation insurance, which is paid upon total payroll. There will also be benefits which a union acquires as a labor-contract right and which the contractor must add to payroll: vacation privileges, pension payments, hospital funds, and other benefits.

Referring to Material-cost Influences (Section 11-5), the total will now include local sales taxes, necessary express charges, and other special delivery premiums.

Referring to Equipment-cost Influences (Section 11-6), the total will now include the rental, delivery, and pickup charges required by methods and machines actually decided on.

These additional costs are all figured by the accountant as percentages of the basic labor, material, and equipment costs. They are based on similar costs of the previous series of years and will give a close enough approximation of the additional costs to be paid out to make the takeoff pricing and extension reasonably correct. These percentages are applied to as few columnar costs as possible.

11-11   *Direct and Indirect Costs*

There are other general costs which must be accounted for in the takeoff and thereafter transcribed to the permanent records if the job is acquired.

Some cost items will be spread over the whole job rather than charged against any special portion or trade. For example, the salaries of the job superintendent and the timekeeper, the cost of lighting under the sidewalk bridge, and the premium for public liability insurance cannot be charged directly against a specific phase of the work. But they are necessary costs and should be charged against the job. (If the job is obtained, the general contractor is definitely going to have to pay these bills.) These costs are *not* for doing business in general but only for doing this particular job. They should, therefore, be taken off and summarized *as a direct cost of doing only this job,* under what might be called "general conditions."

The indirect cost is another necessary expense, but it cannot be charged directly to a particular job. It is always present as a cost of doing business. Coming under this category are the rental of an office, telephone expenses, stationery bills, and depreciation allowances for owned equipment. The business, and hence each successive job obtained, must pay this so-called "overhead." Overhead is arrived at in an accounting procedure. The total cost of doing business in a particular year is divided by the total business billed out in any particular year. The resultant percentage figure is applied to every takeoff and added to the total price, allowing a cost as developed during the preceding year. The percentage figure may not be exact, but it is close enough to take cognizance of this considerable amount. Any variations can be adjusted in succeeding years.

Particularly note that this indirect percentage for the cost of doing business is added at the end of the total takeoff procedure and before the profit is added. A small error is introduced because the accountant has used a previous *total* yearly invoicing as a base for figuring this percentage, which is then applied on a volume of cost before profit. But there are so many variations possible in pricing that in this case further accuracy is not warranted and the error is disregarded.

There exists here a definite possibility of being able to save from year to year on percentages given to the estimator for use. The compensation insurance premiums, for example, vary from year to year with the experience rating developed for any particular trade by a construction company. If a safety campaign is successfully mounted to decrease the accident rate and reduce the premiums, a saving is definitely evident. Or material-purchasing practices or equipment rentals may be modified to produce savings. In total, the effect will also be to improve the probability of getting work by making lower bids in competition, yet with the same possibility of profit.

11-12 *Adding The Overage*

All the above factors will culminate in a final management decision on the estimate price to be used and the percentage of that price to be added for profit. *This percentage amount is extended and added to the final estimated cost to arrive at the price for the quotation.*

The profit percentage may vary from a few percent to some much higher percentage. It is not necessarily the same for parts of the same job since within a job times and conditions may change. Although this process, in many cases, is developed on an intuitive basis, it is becoming common practice to arrive at a definite profit figure by the application of modern means and methods of calculation. These devices might include the study of competitive sales theory, the use of various types of probability curves, and the awareness and evaluation of risk. Such additional study is urged.

The aim is always the same: to get a job at a profit. Gaining the profit is the culmination of all the other effort.

When the final price is made up, it should be checked for correctness in every way possible. One of the simple checks is on some unit-price basis developed by trade books or periodicals or by one's own business experience in similar categories. A powerhouse cost based on kilowatts of installed capacity, an apartment-house cost based on number of rooms of a similar rent class, a one-story factory structure based on cubic foot of enclosed cost—all represent types of jobs in which costs should be similar. (There should be enough data available to point out anything not normal which would cause costs to vary from the standard. For example, an item which might cause costs to go up would be a requirement for piling, for polished stone facing, or for an air-conditioning installation.) The amount obtained would, of course, be only approximate. The total figure, however, would be approximately correct, so that there would be no fatal decimal-point error.

The correct pricing of a bid is complicated by the variables which must be taken into account. Some of these many variables are examined in detail in management studies published in the last few years. These researches indicate that the construction business is at the breakthrough point regarding trial-and-error procedures of running the business. It is no longer possible to operate successfully only by intuition and hope. It is necessary to understand management procedures and apply developing principles to maintain and improve one's position. A book which the writer recommends is *The Strategy of Contracting for Profit*, by William R. Park, published by Prentice-Hall (also noted in the Bibliography).

11-13 *Bid Comparisons*

Something can be learned from every estimate, provided accurate bid figures can be obtained for competitors. In public bidding, the figures become a matter of public knowledge and are published or can be obtained from the bidding authority. In private bidding, such information may be held confidential, which does not mean that the information is unobtainable. Some trade sources who are intimate with one of the other bidders will undoubtedly know about what the other bid amounted to. After the job is given out and there is no question of disloyalty, they will divulge the information to another friendly associate. A list of competitors in ascending order of bids will afford a basis of comparison.

Thereafter, study of the estimate possibilities of the original takeoff will lead to comments as to where a change in pricing might have been made to get the job. Analysis will assist in formulating judgment on future jobs. Over the course of the fiscal year, has the aim of attaining a certain number of jobs, a certain money volume of work, or a certain percentage of profit been achieved? Are pricing and accounting practices, facts and figures regularly checked to keep up-to-date and competitive? Is the trend of business up or down? Has an actual profit been made, or is the method of keeping books unintentionally misleading? When bid comparisons are made, judgment should improve and the percentage of profitable jobs obtained should increase.

It is obligatory upon every manager of a construction operation periodically to review his own record and his own future. An easy way to get impartial diagnosis and advice is to approach one's bank for a business loan. Adequate financial records must be submitted to justify action. Interpreting such records is part of the banker's business, and he will give impartial advice. In addition, the bank should be given an opportunity to make money and should not be used only for functions, such as the weekly payroll, which are not profitable. Then, when actually needed, the bank is familiar with the situation and the personalities involved, and favorable action is more likely to be considered.

12

THE QUOTATION
AND OTHER LEGALITIES

Every action taken or not taken and every transaction entered into in business have a legal connotation. This fact is not a preventive against action but a caution against carelessness. The contractor should know enough of his business to know his rights and his liabilities and to be assured of legal encouragement for his actions, including negotiation. Very definitely, he should not attempt to be his own lawyer. The field is specialized and time-consuming, requiring constant study to keep current on developments, and the person dealing with the legal aspects of the business operation should be independently unbiased in arriving at conclusions. The contractor should call for guidance as a necessary business expense.

Although the very act of going into business involves certain liabilities, generally the quotation is the document which first brings a contracting organization into legal contact with prospective clients. Prices will be quoted, assertions made, and deliveries promised—subject ostensibly to acceptance or denial. The quotation serves a most necessary function as a sales document. It also sets up obligations.

12-1   *The Quotation*

The written quotation is a firm offer to do work and supply material and equipment at a time and place, subject to certain plans, specifications, and conditions, for a price or other consideration. The amount of the bid and the time involved should be clearly stated, and details should be given to clarify the quotation. Because the buyer places stress upon comparing the monetary amounts of the various bids, emphasis must be placed on the original price quoted to him. The objective is to submit a bid competitive enough to be called into negotiation and yet allowing a good opportunity to make a profit. To maintain a low basic quotation price, the practice is followed of including only those items which are specifically required by the bidding documents.

The quotation, particularly in closed bidding, is also a sales document. Acting toward this use, declaration will be made of the advantages of this particular bidder for the buyer. The buyer will be influenced by time of delivery, suggestions for savings, workmanship, modifications of terms, and other possibilities.

The language used is of utmost importance to both buyer and seller. Every document, no matter how innocuous, should be written and read with care. A ticket for a worthy benefit comes to mind. It said, "Donation $5.00; delicious dinners sold." Actually, the price was only for a ticket of admission, and the cost of the food was extra.

12-2   *Verifying Bid Details*

The invitation to bid should be referred to in making out the quotation. All essential information should be marked down and filed with the job takeoff papers. Every independent document required should be on hand.

A. Prerequisites might include a certified check, a bid bond, a notice of insurance coverage, or credit information. To reiterate, all requirements must be on hand. No possibility should exist of having a bid thrown out because some legal pretext permits such action.

B. The correct date, place, and time set for delivery of the quotation have, of course, been a determining factor in making up prior closing dates for subbidders. But, for example, if the person delivering the final quotation is delayed in traffic or is confronted with a lack of available parking space because the place of delivery is the center of the shopping district, the time for the bid opening may have passed without him. Special arrangements are sometimes necessary. Bids are made up in advance, complete except for the final price. They are then taken to a rented room adjoining the location of the bid opening, and a telephone connection gives such final information as is needed to complete the quotation right there. Then but a few minutes are required to get the quotation to the place of the bid opening. Of course, in some bidding there may be leeway in the time of taking bids, but verification is always essential.

12-3   *Quotation Requirements*

Itemized documents take time to acquire. There are other items and information to obtain, however, besides what is specifically noted. Sales information should be collected and recorded in advance. When a specialty operation, such as a sewage plant or a refrigerator building, is to be built, the full recording of similar work successfully done can be of interest to the buyer. Specialized status can be claimed. Such detailed information should be strengthened with reference permission obtained from the specific client. The aim is to amplify the broad coverage of the qualification sheet by adding specific detail.

Therefore, in every bid and for any construction job, an individualized qualification summary should be made up. This summary will be based on the actual experience record of the firm. It will be made up of work somewhat similar to that which is to be quoted. It will also include other information which may interest a buyer—such as freedom from labor trouble for a period of years, a clear record regarding workmen's liens filed, good workmanship and durability as evidenced by an offer of personal inspection of previous work completed for a considerable period of time. Such information, on a company letterhead apart from the quotation, can be read thoroughly or skimmed over, as circumstances indicate, without obscuring the clarity of or technically invalidating a printed bid. Because of the large money value involved in every job sale, such additional effort is warranted.

12-4   *The Form of the Quotation*

The quotation is a document of importance, serving as the basis of comparison upon which the buyer's efforts are centered. It brings to a focus all preliminary estimating effort and prepares for the competitive negotiation to follow. The wording varies with the individual estimate and the person figuring it, except that in some small proportion of the jobs figured, a bid form will be made up as part of the invitation. This form is to be used by all bidders for ready comparison, with no modification possible upon penalty of disqualification. In this special case of open bidding, a contract will be given directly to the lowest responsible bidder. The contractor cannot make up his own form of bid.

In the closed bid, however, individual wording may change to meet circumstances, but basic applicability is needed in any case. The quotation will be made up in a certain definite form for the specific remembrance of all important functions. The job will not be immediately awarded to the lowest bidder but will be negotiated by the buyer in accordance with what he considers his best interest. The buyer also wants his time conserved. A quotation, therefore, should be readable, understandable, concise, and yet complete. These aims are possible, but they require a knowledge of modern letter writing and the physical makeup which is part of it. Letter-writing skill is part of the direct selling effort required.

Figure 12-1 will be used as a sample quotation to be made up by an individual contractor. Only pertinent paragraphs needed for safety should be used in any one letter. (One should keep the quotation concise.)

Part 1. The all-important date is noted.

Part 2. The name and address, *as noted and sometimes as required on the invitation to bid,* are written out in full, not only for the quotation but also for the enclosing envelope which is part of it. One should get down to personalities immediately. The letter should be addressed to an individual buyer if his name is known. If not, the letter should be addressed to the highest official working at the address where the bid is to be delivered. The president of a company (as an addressee) is in just the right position to be interested in determining that the proper person gets the bid. Certainly the bid will be propitiously introduced. A telephone call will get the right information, title, *and spelling.*

Part 3. Outlined and specified work makes a job meaningful. Therefore, reference to any plans, documents, or samples which will make clear what work the estimate covers is essential. Because clarity is important to the buyer (and this particular information, although essential, is for the record only), the information is carried at the top of the letter, apart from the main body of the proposal.

The information will consist of the name of the project, the name of the company and the site address, and the name of the designer and his address. Thereafter will come the identifying numbers of all plans, bidding documents, and specifications. Particularly if any changes of any nature have been made during the estimating period, acknowledgement of inclusion of the changes in the final bid must be made. (The buyer must know that everyone received and is bidding on the same thing.) Such definite information is necessary for later negotiation.

Part 4. Immediately after the salutation, at the very beginning of the quotation, should come the proposal and the price. This figure will be in both numbers and writing and should be checked for correctness with the final estimates as typed for transmission. It sometimes seems from his reaction that the buyer reads no further than the price and that the

---

QUOTATION (SAMPLE)

1. Date

2. Company
    Address, City, State, Zip Code

    Attn: Mr._____ (Buyer or a high official)

3.   Re: Addition to Equipment Mfg. Plant
                                    Architect: Name and address
                                    Plans: Nos. , inclusive   Dated
                                    Specification pages Nos.   Dated
                                    Including addenda plans Nos.   Dated
                                                addenda spec Nos.   Dated

4. Gentlemen:

    Our quotation for furnishing labor, material, equipment, and other
    necessary facilities to do the work noted above is the sum of_____.

5.   We will commence work within 10 days of signing contract, and will
    complete in 120 maximum working days thereafter (5 days of 7 hours per
    day to constitute a working week). The above quotation will hold good until
    60 calendar days after this date. We will also complete the heating system
    for your use 30 calendar days prior to such other job completion date as
    may be set contractually. To further save time with good workmanship,
    we do our own carpentry, masonry, and concrete work.

6.   Herewith are Alternates as specified:

    (a) Change electric fixtures, type A to type B   Add   Deduct

    (b) Change facing, stone to brick   Add   Deduct

    (c) Add roofing bond   Add

    (d) Add boiler room labeled fire door (4 hours)   Add

7.   We have made the following assumptions:

    (a) We have figured summer working conditions, with no heating
        needed.

    (b) Water and electricity will be furnished by you.

    (c) Demolition and site cleaning will be by others.

8.   The steel contract has been completely omitted in accordance with
    verbal instructions.

9.   Should the repair of the present cracked Equipment Manufacturing
    Plant floor become part of this contract (thereby saving overhead and
    overage), we will submit a price immediately.

10.   We can start work within 5 days of notification from you of award of the
    contract. Kindly advise us when we may further contact you.

11. Enclosures: Sincerely,

    Qualification Summary A   ANY CONSTRUCTION CO.

    Qualification Summary B   per

    Completion Bond

---

figure 12-1. Sample quotation.

beginning of the quotation is the wrong place to put it. He does read further, but only if it is worth his while to do so.

In an endeavor to save time and effort, the buyer limits his future appointments to those competitors who are close enough in quotation price to be able to do some further price adjusting if they so desire. The buyer believes he can protect himself against a bidder who is below standard in any way by including whatever may be necessary in the final contract wording. This may or may not be so. There is intelligence on both sides of a bargaining table. Self-confidence is necessary, but overconfidence is dangerous. In any event, the price is written out first to satisfy the buyer.

Because he sees only those within the limited range of low bidders, the buyer eliminates many excellent bids on which much effort has been expended. This is an economic risk and waste inherent in our competitive system. It is recognized, and it emphasizes the necessity of having a good first price.

Part 5. Time is of influence in establishing price. The two factors are synonymously considered by the buyer. Therefore, a clause is next required specifying the time of start and the time of completion. A clause allowing termination of the effective period of the proposal at the option of the contractor is also a requisite. The buyer must act within the set time if he is at all interested in the quotation, and he cannot use undue delay as a purchasing tactic. The contractor is thus somewhat protected against increases in labor rates, material costs, or other prices. Furthermore, the contractor is presented with an allowable price option which can be used or not, as circumstances dictate.

This is also an important place to influence a buyer. The buyer is not interested in a construction job as such. He wants a serviceable facility. For example, to set machinery, place furniture, and stock stationery, he needs usable occupancy. A clause offering to complete the heating system by a specified time in advance of the balance of the structure would be of value. Also, a buyer might be interested not only in speed of construction but also in reliability of repair and reasonable cost of additions. A contractor who does his own key work instead of having to sublet every trade is of interest. Therefore, this would also be the place to mention that the contractor does his own carpentry, masonry, and concrete work (not only to get uniformly good workmanship at a reasonable cost but to save time). The contractor wants to negotiate for this job and needs talking points. Right here is the place to plant them.

Part 6. Alternates appear throughout many plans and specifications. These are features which the designer asks to have priced as additions or deductions to a base bid. Such items allow variations of construction detail and price which may be helpful. The possible diversity is infinite and ranges from alternate grades of wood to increased or decreased pile lengths as actually installed. The base bid can be contractually modified if it becomes advisable to use an alternate. Of course, all such items are also used by the buyer in negotiation and should, therefore, be advantageously and clearly noted for the future use of the contractor.

In certain cases, design features may be known but their extent cannot be architecturally limited until actual construction takes place. Such features as the amount of topsoil required for preparing a site for seeding might depend on how much good existing soil could be reused after completing all other work. This type of item will be covered by asking for a unit-of-measurement cost, such as a price per cubic yard in place. In such a case, the buyer is necessarily faced with a variable price, using signed delivery tickets to verify the quantity of material delivered, at a predetermined rate. (This small disadvantage to the buyer, however, is far outweighed by the fixed cost of the base job.)

Part 7. In making up a quotation, certain assumptions will have to be made to establish estimating prices. For example, ready-mix concrete, delivered in the same quantity and requiring the same labor, will cost one amount in the summertime and a larger amount in the wintertime, when the cost of heating every mix must be added to the bill. In addition, the working space may have to be enclosed and heated and electric lights positioned and maintained during concrete installation. In this particular case, no one is able to foresee when the job will actually be contracted for and able to proceed. Therefore, a reasonable assumption, which would establish a certain series of costs, is necessary to permit the completion of the estimate. If the buyer believes the clearly noted assumptions will not materialize, he can modify them during negotiations. Should the job be obtained and conditions arise involving a different cost of operation than that estimated, a basis is properly laid for a changed invoice. There might be considerable money involved.

Part 8. Exceptions will occur during the estimating period to the original plans and specifications, which remain, however, as the legal obligation of the job price. Or the bidding documents may ask for work or responsibility which the contractor does not wish to undertake and has not figured or has been unable to figure. If not covered by the addenda noted above, this exception must be recorded. The buyer may be aggrieved if something is omitted. But the contingent cost to the contractor is the important consideration. Liability must be recognized and disclaimed before possibility of loss occurs. For example, something similar to the following may be advisable: "Not responsible for damage to adjoining property due to vibration of pile driving."

Occasionally, although rarely, something unusual may occur preliminary to making up a quotation. A verbal instruction may be given to allow some certain amount in the estimate to do specified additional work for the buyer, or there may be some other understanding affecting price. Such occurrence is also an exception and should be noted in writing.

Part 9. Possible inclusions or revisions will occur to every estimator while he is taking off a job. A relocation of a factory access door will save employee time. Or information contributed by a subbidder, such as the existence of low water pressure in a municipal system, may be pertinent to the design. Or the replacement of steel covering with aluminum may save present and future maintenance painting at small additional present cost. It would seem that this would be a good place to insert a sales message showing individual thought and worth. There is, however, a danger here.

Such suggestions tend to cast aspersions at some small portion of a big job which may otherwise be an excellent design effort. The desire to influence the buyer may make poor friends elsewhere. It would seem better to present such ideas ahead of time to the designer, with the suggestion that they be included as the subject for an addendum if worthwhile. The influence of the designer will then be for the contractor, and he is quite influential.

If there exist legitimate possible price inclusions which would not involve the designer and if such inclusions would help the sales message, here is the place to present them. An example of a thoughtful and non-antagonistic suggestion might be: The contractor can purchase structural steel from warehouse stock rather than buying from the mill as specified —time saving to erection date, two months; additional cost, $_____.

Part 10. The concluding paragraph should be an integral part of the proposal in that it sets a definite date for starting (after contract agreement). There should also be a definite appointment requested.

Part 11. To ensure that any required supplementary documents are enclosed with the quotation, they are copied as listed in the requirement to bid. A physical check will then confirm their presence and eliminate any possibility of omissions which might becloud an estimate. The use of an extension to the text, headed "Enclosures," will not unduly enlarge the main letter.

12-5   *Letter Presentations*

Any and every letter which goes out of the office represents the construction company to the receiver. In the case of the buyer, who sizes up the competitors by means of small differences, there is an indication of worth in a good letter. Therefore, letters are important. Felicitous phrases should be placed in the form-paragraph book (Figure 7-5) for reuse.

A. The logic of the development should make for easy reading. The principles of newspaper writing should be followed. Items of first importance to the reader should be first in the text, to be followed by items of constantly lesser importance.

B. The clarity of reading should be notable. This is fostered by short words, short sentences, single ideas in each sentence.

C. Conciseness automatically tends to follow such a policy, although completeness of expression should be carefully checked.

D. The modernity of the language used is important in achieving acceptance by the reader. Styles in letter writing change. Phrases that were formerly considered part of every letter are no longer used. If they are used, the letter becomes outdated. The firm using such correspondence suffers by comparison with others using more modern styles. The tone should be personal and modern.

E. Spelling and punctuation should be correct. A mistake indicates lack of education or carelessness.

12-6 *Credit, Basis of Contracting*

There is a universal use of credit in arranging for estimating, quoting, and contracting. Individual payments are large, and job erection time is lengthy—both conditions militate against the use of cash. The construction contract is a written agreement evidencing trust between contracting parties. The documentation outlines the sales agreement. The items may include the plans, specifications, or other references making up the job; the times of start and completion; bonus or penalty clauses; terms of payment and other special agreements. But before estimating, in many cases, and certainly before quoting, negotiating, and entering into a contract, credit should be checked. This evidence of current worth and faith is necessary for every transaction, regardless of the reputation or assumed worth of the opposite party. Time and conditions change, and present information is vital for survival. Only one job of slow pay or no pay can offset much other hard and profitable work.

A. There are advantages in credit sales. Cash does not change hands and is not immediately required. Payments may be made as work progresses and with values fixed in advance. A steady volume of consecutive jobs may be set up, affording continuity of work for keymen. Probable purchasing in advantageous quantities may be anticipated. Possible dishonesty in the office or on the job is minimized. (Every employee should make a record of every transaction and every transfer.) There is an opportunity to grade up, that is, get more profitable work and a better clientele.

B. There are also disadvantages. In addition to the carelessness and loss which are possible, there are needs for capital for payroll and for discounting trade invoices. This capital acquisition requires extensive and good accounting and additional overhead, such as bank-loan interest charges. Both buyer and contractor are vulnerable. There should be anticipation of some possible credit losses.

12-7   *Credit Information*

It is clearly evident that if credit information about a buyer is not available, other compensating insurance factors must appear, such as a payment bond to the contractor. No one can afford a loss.

All prospective buyers of construction should be checked regardless of how good their names sound. School boards, backed by municipal funds would certainly seem to be worthy of complete credit. Yet credit is seriously affected by contractual reliability, and certain boards and their employees are notoriously difficult to satisfy and slow to pay. (When profits are low anyway, a quick turnover of funds is necessary.)

Hospitals, places of workship, and charitable institutions certainly are morally sound. Yet frequently they have inadequate funds at the start of a construction project and depend on pledges and faith to raise additional money during the progress of the job. In addition, their directors may ask the builder for a financial gift to help the project. There is nothing wrong with such a procedure provided the contractor wants to so contribute and anticipates in advance what he has to do. Otherwise, it is distinctly unjust in that it forces contributions by assuming that all builders are well off and can afford a sizable money donation.

Certain builders pay their bills, live within the law, and yet are known in trade circles as speculators. They make a living on the work and credit of others. They risk a minimum of their own capital, take unfair advantage wherever possible, and are habituated to employing sharp practice as a way of existence. Their money is good, one can do business with them, yet contractually they are not of the best. As an example, the builder's agreement with a buyer might say, "The contract is between buyer and general contractor." In effect, even when the general contractor is paid by the buyer for work that includes items incorporated by a subcontractor, the subcontractor has no contractual standing. He cannot go to the buyer and ask that money be withheld to cover an unpaid invoice. The sharp builder uses the requisition money not to pay the subcontractor as intended but for the builder's own immediate purposes.[1] Precautions established by competent legal assistance are necessary (Section 7-3I).

---

[1] There is a rather painful construction answer to why a subcontractor acted as a pallbearer at a funeral: "I carried him while he was alive, and I'll be consistent now that he is gone."

Credit is not something to assume. Knowledge may not invalidate a contract but may modify its terms for safety.

Sources of credit information are readily available. Some of these are banks, supply houses, trade organizations, commercial credit agencies, the buyer's own representations, the seller's records, and the experience of subcontractors. Such enlightenment is *not* to be construed as actual knowledge. No one is willingly going to divulge information to his own discredit. Reports of any nature have to be interpreted in the light of other supporting facts, giving weight to business bias, personal information, and other circumstances. But any information, at any time, may prove highly significant. All material should be filed for cumulative effect in a separate credit file.

Credit information should be current and, if not utilized at once, has only limited use for future corroboration. If credit actions are indicated, they should be taken promptly. Quotations, negotiations, contracts, and any other documents or verbal promises require action. It is far better to be careful than to be injured. In certain cases, when reliance is made on contractual liens, legal protection is afforded only by filing a jurisdictional advance notice. Other cases affect the passage of title, the payment for material ready but not delivered, or any of many variations. They require different means of handling. *Competent legal counsel is a necessity.* Expense is required and must be anticipated to do a credit business. Losses should be minimized.

Management shortcomings are not often evident in actual construction but, rather, show up in the associated functions of the use of contract and credit, of trying to collect money, of keeping working capital free from too many fixed assets, of using advance planning—making up, in short, for uneven business experience.

12-8   *Quotation Follow-up*

The mailing or other delivery of the letter of quotation is only the first part of the sales effort required. If the bid is low, it will be answered. But if it is not the low bid, an answer is problematical. It can be assumed that there are others bidding, some of whom may be friends of the buyer or may exercise influence in other directions. Such competitors may be injected into the buyer's "will see" list. This is customary and nothing to warrant alarm. It is necessary, however, to make the quotation productive, and direct negotiation is wanted by the bidder. If the price and other offers are reasonably advantageous to the buyer, he also will want further extension of personal contact. The contractor does not need practice in estimating, but he does need a profitable job. He must follow up.

Of course, action on this important phase of selling should have started prior to this point. The person taking the bids may not be the one to give out the work. The *correct party* should have been discovered and personally contacted, his particular wishes complied with, and means of further contact established. Allowing some short lapse of time to get a possible voluntary reaction to the bid, an immediate follow-up is obligatory, regardless of the buyer's lack of reaction.

An ordinary sheet of copy paper firmly clipped to the office copy of the quotation will suffice as a memorandum. It will contain all names, telephone numbers, dates, and memoranda of conversations and results. A complete reminder is afforded, and anyone should be able to take over in case of necessity with a continuous record of what has transpired and with whom. The information may be kept in a loose-leaf binder, a large manila envelope, or any convenient folder. Note that sometimes conversations with a subordinate, such as a secretary, will precede contact. Her name is important to obtain because she shields the correct person. But the maintenance of the records in one place and the presence of this simple follow-up procedure will cover this essential.

An appointment for negotiation is required.

12-9   *The Contract*

After negotiations have produced a verbal contract, the agreement is written out in detail. In certain open-bid cases, the complete form of contract is originally published with the request to bid, and the bidder either assents to this form as part of his quotation or does not bid. Such condition in itself is adequate reason to have such a form carefully reviewed by legal counsel before estimating. The complete bid documents should be returned untouched if the contract form is unacceptable and cannot be changed. In many cases, however, the contract form will be drawn up later as part of the negotiating process by the organization of the buyer. The contract as drawn must thus be very seriously considered. It is definitely part of the makeup of the new job and one of the determining factors of profit and loss. And because a contract is a voluntary agreement between parties, the wording formulates the obligations and duties of each to the other.

Note that there are four essentials to a contract:
1. Mutual assent to the terms of the agreement
2. Competent parties
3. A valid consideration
4. Definite and lawful subject matter

In making up the contract, however, the process of drafting agreements can be, and usually is, biased. The legal advisor of the purchaser will rightfully endeavor to protect his client wherever possible, but occasionally at the expense of the rights of the contractor. This may involve withholding an excessive sum of money, denying legitimate protection for material delivered and labor incorporated, and sometimes even establishing a means by which the contract can be discharged at the option of the buyer only. Every transaction covers some different set of circumstances or possibilities and offers different pitfalls. The consequences can be so serious as to compel the specialized competence and advice of a good construction lawyer to review what has been drawn up by others. When a proposed contract is shown as being manifestly unfair, it will be changed because it is to the advantage of both the lawyer and the seller to get an agreement. Without an agreement *on the same thing*, there can be no contract. Thus, the time to make a change is when the contract is being formulated—not after it is signed. Thereafter it is plain to anyone (especially a judge or an arbitrator) that what has been signed is what has been agreed to.

The description of the work can be important as reflecting negotiation agreements. Very frequently the buyer, for his own reasons, has directly given out lead-time items, such as piling or structural steel. These are extensive and expensive items. The buyer may have verbally told the contractor during negotiations to eliminate these items from his bid, which he did. Yet the plans and specifications were not changed, and such trades will remain the contractor's obligation unless other proof releases him. A verbal agreement can be verified by outside circumstances. But suppose the buyer has suddenly left this vale of tears or has separated from his organization in a less final but just as complete manner (possibly involving strained relations). Who is to testify for the contractor?

The contract must specifically spell out all negotiated agreements, including changes to plans and specifications.

Unusual or not understood wording should be questioned. For example, in a request for a bid a definite due date for completion was specified, *plus* the clause "time is of the essence." This double coverage seemed merely redundant. Actually, the buyer obtained the advantage of a dangerous open-end liability clause. The contractor was put on notice and record that no extension would be given because of bad weather, delayed delivery, or other cause which might normally serve to obtain an extension of time. If possession and completion for any reason were not given on the due date originally specified, the buyer could sue for loss for any amount of money. Even if the job was complete but some minor item was unsatisfactory, such as some defective flooring, the buyer might refuse to accept the completed job. His reasoning would be that to get completion on the due date would have meant allowing the contractor to speed up and thereby turn out more defective work. The buyer stated that he did not intend to use these powers. Why then was the clause in the proposed contract? A damage claim for delay in delivery is possible even if the contract wording lacks a daily penalty.

Note that the opposing attorney has written this clause for the benefit of his client. The fact that a document is typed in finished form does not make it obligatory to sign the document. The buyer will amend the wording if the balance of the contract makes such action worthwhile. It is far better to object at once and openly to remove any such dangerous clause. It can be replaced with a penalty and bonus clause, which sets a penalty for delay and also makes it worthwhile for the contractor to finish ahead of time. Or a completion bond in a definite amount may be furnished, for which the premium cost can be measured and recognized in the bid; the amount of the bond sets the maximum liability. An alternate method can generally be found which will be just for both parties and will recompense them for what they are contracting to do.

The payment terms of a contract are important. The buyer may insist on retaining a considerable sum with every payment. This retainer will be released to the contractor a certain number of days after completion. In order not to impair his working capital and yet obtain the benefit of material invoice discounting if he accepts this arrangement, the contractor may have to get a bank loan. An interest charge becomes necessary. Although it may be good business to allow a bank to make money, there is still an added expense which would not have been necessary. Actually, to obtain the job, the contractor is financing the buyer.

Advantage may be taken of this payment requirement by asking for something for the contractor. The contract might allow, for example, that the terms of payment include material ready for delivery to the site but not necessarily on the site or incorporated in the structure. The law concerning sales varies from place to place. In general, title passes only upon delivery unless specifically modified. The contractor is giving up something valuable, but in return he gets the right to invoice for additional material. The trade discount for prompt payment is worthwhile. This type of proviso may be debatable, but it is useful when expensive material is ready for delivery and for some reason cannot be accepted on the job.

The retainer may be a most reasonable protective device of the buyer. It protects the buyer to some extent should he have to complete the job with another contractor to replace the original one. Percentages retained, however, can be overdone. If the buyer is overprotected, the working capital of the contractor may be unreasonably tied up. On any job, money is expended by the contractor in necessary cash payrolls and in the continuous running expenses of doing business. If the contract calls for a fixed percentage retainer of work in place throughout the life of the job, toward the end of the job this amount will be far in excess of any amount required for completion. Such a protective contingency is not a justification for excess. The contract is a two-way document. It should include text favorable to both sides. The retainer percentage should decrease as the incorporated value of work increases. Upon receipt of the newly drawn-up text, it should be examined and corrected, not only for what it includes but also for what it should include.

Note specifically that contract wording is sometimes indefinite. The preceding discussion mentioned successive payments to be withheld and to be released sometime after completion is attained. What is the definition of "the date of completion"? This important date generally starts the procedure for releasing the retainer. The date also effectuates changes in responsibility, maintenance, and supply and is the starting time of guarantee periods. If the date is subject to the willful actions of interested persons, it may be unnecessarily delayed. It should be contractually defined, as should similar matters. For disputes of any nature, the right to establish arbitration procedure should be in every contract.

12-10   *Modifications*

In making up the contract, all the bidding documents become part of the agreement. Quite customarily, both plans and specifications carry notations in small print which have as much legal weight as do those in large print. Such obligations may also be outlined in the supplementary general conditions of the specification, the proposal requirements, or any other bidding document. The size of the notation is no indication of the expense involved.

One small note existed on one alteration plan regarding a new wide door opening in an old bearing wall. The existing roof trusses were to be shored up as a necessary preliminary part of the steel work. The general contractor was then to cut the new masonry opening, including horizontal chases for new lintel beams under the shoring pins, and set the lintels on the old masonry walls bearing on end plates. After the new masonry had set, the shoring pins were to be removed. This was a logical way to handle an existing situation except for certain mistakes. First, the estimator for the general contractor did not see the note about the shoring and allowed nothing for all the work involved. Second, the steel specification did not call for any shoring, and this item, therefore, was not covered by this subcontractor. He refused responsibility. The general contractor paid the cost and took the loss.

In another specification, watchman service was specified but the time of discontinuance was delimited only by the words "at completion of the building." Long before that time, small steel window frames and miscellaneous openings, including doors and respective hardware, were scheduled to be set and the building closed in—and the watchmen could then be dispensed with. This modification was noted and clarified in the contract as to the time of completion of watchman use. The general contractor here obtained a payroll benefit.

Some member of the contracting organization definitely should examine all bidding documents from a contractual standpoint to determine where changes may be advisable. The time to correct or develop such matters is prior to final negotiation and contract signing.

12-11 *Insurance Policies and Surety Bonds*

Various risks must be taken as part of the construction business. The chance of loss is, in effect, spread to others by paying an insurance premium to someone reliable and able to pay if there is a loss. For this premium, these others, known as the insurers, agree to assume a contingent liability to meet a limited loss. Should the contingency not occur, no payment is made and the premium is considered as earned for services and is not rebated. Should the risk materialize and threat of loss occur, the insuring company will defend any legal action brought against the contracting company, using any necessary effort to keep low the possible money loss. If, however, a legal decision against the contractor is made by court action involving an amount in excess of the insured sum, the insurance company will pay only its obligated amount and the contracting company is liable for the overage. Risk, therefore, may not be completely eliminated but only lessened.

Thus, insurance premiums are a necessary expense but not necessarily a complete expense. Contingencies happen to everyone, and protected or unprotected possibilities can be hazardous to business survival. Insurance coverage does help, but it is made for limited amounts and time periods only. It should, therefore, be regularly checked to make sure that it is in force and that it is adequate. Due to the fact that types of insurance and amounts required vary with every job, the usual costs should be known to the office staff to give to the estimator. Should something special be required, the insurance agent should be called in to make sure that the risk can and will be covered and to establish the cost.

Note that premium costs cover both office and job. For the office overhead, there will be automobile costs covering passenger cars, dump trucks, and station wagons for deliveries. There will also be fire, public liability, and theft insurance. For the job (and to be charged in the estimate for that job) will be the same and additional insurance, such as property damage, freight loss, and especially, workmen's compensation. The latter is in a class by itself for two specific reasons:

1. Court damages and costs levied in behalf of workmen for physical

or health damage are so astronomical in amount that in some localities companies are loath to write such insurance and the state must support its own insurance organization. As a result, some construction companies must pay premiums to the state. In many localities, no local building permit will be issued unless a notice of current coverage is presented with the application.

2. Premiums for this type of insurance vary with the trade and with the experience record of the contracting company itself. Due to the hazards of respective trades, a structural-steel journeyman will pay a higher rate than a tile setter. Also, the general contractor is contractually obligated to act for the safety of the entire construction job, including such items as enclosing stairwells, planking over floor openings, or establishing illuminated street bridges to protect passersby. An experience rating is built up with the insurance company based on the accidents occurring to any construction company in some time period.

The premium rate chargeable to a construction firm, therefore, is not fixed but is arrived at by the insurance company for every job to be estimated. It is formulated from a description of the work to be done with the tradesmen involved and also from past experience. And because this experience record can be improved and the premium thereby cut down and because the premiums constitute a considerable part of the total job payroll cost, this becomes a place where money can be saved. Conversely, the premium can increase. (See Section 3-7 for further details.)

The entire subject of premium makeup, such as for fire, public liability, or maintenance insurance, should be studied for every estimate. Sometimes a small installed cost will produce a long-term yearly saving. Sometimes a good selling point is produced for negotiations.

A surety bond covers another type of risk. The word *surety* here means that one is jointly bound in an obligation with another to a third party. The word *bond* here means that someone is obligated by a legally enforceable written instrument, under seal, to do or abstain from doing some action. As indicated, the surety bond then is a long-lasting document to add the strength of the second party to that of the contractor in order to safeguard the rights of others.

As employed contractually, the request to bid of the specification used in making up the estimate calls for certain bonds to be furnished to the buyer to act as surety that work will be done. (The general contractor pays the cost of the bonds if he gets the job; hence he must include the cost in his estimate.) Such instruments are quite varied. There may be a completion bond in a large amount to the owner of the land, who has granted a leasehold, including the right to build a structure, to another. There may be a paving bond to a municipality to insure payment for repairing street openings. There may be a bond used as a surety for possible lien-law amounts filed against public construction to eliminate the necessity of filing against the real estate. The real estate is the actual security, but the bond may be accepted in its place.

Because of the wide variation of risk, time, and amount involved—and definitely dependent on the reputation and financial standing of the construction company—costs of this protection vary. As a matter of course, therefore, a financial statement or similar credit information is submitted to some good bonding company at regular intervals before being needed. The ability to obtain such bonds and the extent to which bonds will be granted definitely limit jobs which can be taken.

Without exception, a general contractor should have the relevant phrases of all bidding documents, for every job being figured, read immediately on receipt by a competent insurance representative. (The office photocopy machine and the mail are quickly effective.) Very real differences in liability can be expressed in the different ways the wording is put together. Either the insurance company (the bonding company) will accept the preset obligation, or it will refuse at once. In the latter case, unless the general contractor can get something modified, he is only wasting time and money in bidding. Also, if existing insurance is not adequate in any way, there will be an added cost to obtain what is required, which will have to be added to the estimate.[1]

12-12   *Liens*

A lien is a claim which one party has against another. Property involved may act as security, or an acceptable bond may release the lien claims.

This claim, therefore, is a legal and statutory creation for the protection of something—which might be earned pay, material furnished, or service provided. Not everything is protected, nor in the same manner everywhere. Such protection as is afforded must be attained strictly in accordance with the statutes of the locality having control.

In addition, on different occasions the same facts may afford a claim for and also against one or the other party. The rights of the owner and buyer, the architect and engineer, the general contractor and subcontractor, their employees and suppliers—and the public—are all intermingled. Where action may be brought to obtain the protection of a lien, in some cases the amount is contractually limited to the inadequate sum which one party originally agreed to pay the other. If mortgages or other encumbrances were attached to the property prior to the time work was started or material delivered, they will take precedence over later liens. And when a valid lien is filed, it must be perfected by other ac-

[1] F. S. Merritt, *Building Construction Handbook* (section on insurance), McGraw-Hill.

tions before it can be collected upon. For example, in some localities a notice of intent must first be filed before a lien may be filed.

Just as liens may be created, so may they be waived or discharged. But to be effective, the action must be in accordance with the law of the locality having jurisdiction. In a contract under which all liens must be waived to secure payments, disregard of local law may be a breach of contract. The filing of a lien by any other party after such payment is made is venal, as against the contractor.

It is not here the intent to teach business law or how to become a lawyer. Knowledge that certain fundamental laws exist is essential to guide a contractor properly. Particularly is this preparation necessary in situations such as negotiation, in which normally a contractor may act alone. But his actions are (or should be) reviewed and guided by a lawyer. Because of the number of questionable situations which arise in a normal construction-business existence, it is advisable to have and use a competent lawyer on retainer. Money will be saved, and trouble minimized.

An additional function of the lawyer would be to advise his client concerning new modifications affecting the construction business. There is a constant stream of local, state, federal, and foreign laws which may be of considerable importance in many phases of work. These items range from the manner of setting up corporations for the redevelopment of blighted areas to the granting of tax exemptions for certain actions. Advance information and competent advice are obtainable.

Many actions require signed documents for positive verification. These legal forms are carried in stock by business stationery stores. The forms have the distinct advantages of long use and of being printed with the correct wording. They allow space for inserts and particular phrasing. Important forms—such as the general release, individual and corporate; the subcontract; and others of similar nature—can be inexpensively and quickly obtained in individual sheets. Only enough need be purchased for current requirements.

13

NEGOTIATION

In the competitive struggle for construction sales, the time comes when the buyer has compared quotations and decided which of the various bidders he wishes to see. He assumes that all bidders are equally acceptable for bargaining purposes and that he can protect himself. Therefore, to minimize the field and to make easier the task of trying to reduce the quoted sums, he will generally make appointments only with the few bidders who are lowest in price. The greater the price differential between the low bidder and those over him, the greater the difficulty in eliminating that disparity. Hence the importance of the original base price to all bidders and the buyer.

13-1 *The Chosen Competitors*

Of the few selected contractors, the one with the highest price will be seen first, with the low bidder last. This stratagem will allow the buyer to attempt to reduce the quoted price of this first-interviewed contractor to below that of the low bidder. If he succeeds, this result is fine from his viewpoint. If he does not succeed, the buyer has the original low bid, which he can get without negotiation. With negotiation he hopes to get a yet lower price.

When the low bid is not so low as to indicate a serious error, which may later hurt the buyer, an attempt will be made to reduce the price of the low bidder also. This contractor is presumed to have a markup over cost which can be cut. For a buyer not to pursue a reduction would be an indication that the particular contractor being interviewed is the low bidder and does not have to compromise to get the job. This course, naturally, is not to the interest of the buyer.

An appointment to see the buyer toward advancing a quotation is, therefore, only an opportunity to fight further for a job. Other, somewhat higher-price bidders will not even have that opportunity—unless, of course, they are favored for some reason despite their bids. (There are rare cases of collusion between buyer and contractor; they are difficult to discover and normally unnecessary to consider.) This severe culling-out process of reducing many bidders to a few is a real hazard of the contracting business. The time and money spent in making up a bid are frequently wasted without even an opportunity to show the goods. It is one of the prime reasons why such a small percentage of work is obtained for such a large number of jobs figured.

The harshness of this immediate elimination does emphasize the importance of a perfectionist attitude for correct takeoff, pricing, and quotation. Yet a defeatist attitude is uncalled for. Work *is* obtained, and people stay profitably in business for long periods of time. Better contractual devices are evolved, such as negotiated bids, the addition of supplementary services offered, or ownership and contracting in one organization. But they are all predicated upon knowledge, experience, and the ability to cope with the negotiating process in developing a completed cost.

Both buyer and contractor should prepare for the negotiation meeting. Facts and figures, plans and specifications, documents and exhibits should be studied and compared. Anything necessary, including summaries, should be set aside and taken along. Points to be emphasized and general procedure should be tentatively outlined—subject, of course, to what actually materializes. In previewing what may be said, the use should be eliminated of descriptive but possibly objectionable phrases, such as "a pregnant situation," or redundant phrases, such as "May I ask this question?" (that is what one is there for). A man should be neither smart nor inept, neither obsequious nor blustering—just businesslike.

He should take as much time at the meeting as is necessary. The amounts involved are large, and the results of one confrontation are important.

13-2   *The Negotiation Meeting*

The negotiation meeting brings out the peculiar relationship which now arises between buyer and bidder. There is both *a common interest in reaching a successful conclusion* and *a conflict between opponents.* This relation is complicated by the intentional lack of straightforward communication between the two parties. Each tries to mislead the other so as to get as much as possible while giving as little as is necessary. To solve such problems requires (1) communication, although imprecise, (2) understanding, although based on both facts and assumptions, (3) meaningful actions designed to modify the original proposal. A bargaining procedure is established which permits progress toward a mutually profitable arrangement.

Communication is generally thought of as speaking and hearing. But that is not all.[1] A speaker makes a motion, and the recipient sees. A speaker evades, and the recipient mentally notes the evasion. A speaker includes some proposal with his exposition, and the recipient tries to understand the meaning of this action. There are other communication methods, such as deliberate silences and just as deliberate wordiness. There are other communication means, such as photographs, writing, or tape recordings. But all have a function in common—that is, as a transmitter of information which can be integrated, summarized, and interpreted.

During bargaining, the opposing participants are affected by the actions of each other.[2] Their respective interpretations and reactions in response are not predictable. There can be no preestablished fixity of position, but instead a mental flexibility is required. The importance of concentration on listening, seeing, understanding, and interpreting is emphasized. Included in this process is the conscious elimination of a serious fault—anticipation.

The thinking process is many times faster than the speaking process. While one party is talking and has partly developed a thought, the other person has time to think about what he will answer, provided the speaker says what the recipient decides he will. This conduct is dangerous. The recipient does not pay attention to all that is actually said and done. He may miss something of importance which was not in accord with what he had anticipated and which changes the import of the statement. Patience enters into every confrontation. There is always time and reason to ask if this is what the speaker meant. There is time to

[1] T. E. Anastasi, Jr., *Face to Face Communication*, Management Center of Harvard, Cambridge, Mass., 1967.
[2] T. C. Schelling, *The Strategy of Conflict*, Harvard University Press.

formulate an answer after making certain that what was said is correctly understood.

13-3 *Inducements to Action*

There are motivations for the actions and reactions of the opponents. The pressure items described below affect both buyer and contractor.

A. The buyer is responsible for his actions to his directors, to himself, to his coworkers, and to his bidders. Profitable business dealing by the buyer for his firm is necessary to maintain his self-confidence, his job, and his standing among those for whom and with whom he does business. Whether a target price has to be met or the objective is merely to obtain as low a price as possible, he feels obligated to get a contract price under what was originally quoted. If possible, he wants to be fair within limits to the various bidders.

The buyer may be under strong influence within his own organization, tending to sway him toward giving a job to some particular individual or company. But as a responsible and experienced executive, he knows that to continue to receive good bids he must distribute available work fairly. In most cases he will not select a favorite if legitimate business reasons indicate another determination.

The buyer may be influenced by time. Few jobs progress until the facilities are actually needed. The subsequent delays in design, approval, and bidding make urgent the necessity of quickly giving out the work with a guarantee of a definite delivery date for the completed structure. The productive use of the new facility is the required result. Of course, financing is involved.

Few individuals or organizations have enough money available to be able to or want to pay completely for construction from their working capital. It may be necessary to arrange for bank loans, the issuance of securities, or the obtaining of money in some other manner. In negotiations, the buyer is interested in keeping interest charges against his regular business at a minimum. He also wants to protect his cash investment in a structure against the contingency of a contractor who might not complete his job. Therefore, payments and retainers are of importance to him.

The buyer has a particular problem because of his dependency on others to create what he requires. He needs good workmanship and material, skill and managerial ability, and reliability, which entails getting a contractor who will not victimize him—and all this at as low a price as possible. A low bid is, therefore, a dangerous bid to the buyer. He knows that the low bidder who gets the contract must take advantage of any weakness in plan, specification, documentation, or supervision to come out without losing money. The buyer must look forward to exerting constant vigilance to get what he is entitled to—and would get if he were not trying so hard to take advantage of the contractor. Actions do come back to plague the perpetrators.

B. The contractor is responsible for his actions to himself, to his directors, to his coworkers, and to his subbidders. But his objective is to obtain a job with a possibility of profit. Because to get to the negotiations he has already cut his overhead and profit margins and left little or no allowance for adverse contingencies, he starts with but a small margin over cost. Therefore, he must know his cost break-even figure. This price is the point below which he cannot cover costs and will surely not make a profit (unless starting conditions are changed in some manner).

Occasionally a more compulsive reason will materialize and cause him to cut even the break-even price. His makeup sheets indicate that the prices he has used are predicated on the high production of his regular employees. He will lose them if he does not pay them, yet he has no backlog of work. He must get a job to keep these steady employees working and minimize their payroll drain on his capital. He must also give work to subcontractors who have given him subbids. If they get no opportunity to obtain work from him, they will concentrate their efforts elsewhere in order to exist. Yet his continuing in business depends on his ability to get good prices. Also, being in business means a continuous overhead expense, and meeting it even in part is a help.

The situation may be worsened by financial stringency. A contractor who takes too low a price must pay for one job with the proceeds from the next one, and he must obtain a next one to survive in business. Surprisingly, sometimes he does work out of difficulty. By getting work, his total yearly volume of business increases. By cutting his overhead in any way possible, he decreases his cost of doing business. In so doing, his competitive position has improved (but at his own very considerable effort). His next job may be a profitable one. Such individual necessity explains many below-cost negotiations.

Unfortunately, this type of situation will be misused. A deceitful buyer may falsely claim during the negotiations that he can get such a below-cost price. Unless this statement is proved untrue, the job will be taken by someone at too low a price. The so-called "successful" contractor may be forced out of business—owing subcontractors, material supply houses, insurance companies, and the community in general. Everyone suffers, including the bidders, and the failure is no satisfaction. Everyone lost previously.

The contractor is also faced with another fear. He is afraid to charge legitimate prices because he does not want to lose a job to someone else. Yet the contractor is not running a charitable organization, and he must profit in some way. He must realize that the buyer does not deserve any thanks for awarding a job to him until each party benefits.

13-4   *Tactics*

The tactics used in negotiation are infinite in their variety, but there are some basic forms. A few of these are discussed to forewarn, to stimulate, and to have them become recognizable. Their purpose is to effect a transaction. Both buyer and contractor are involved.

A. The buyer, in entering any negotiation, assumes that a previous comparison and weeding-out process has led to competitors who are equally competent, reliable, financially able, and honorable. This assumed contrast may or may not be so. The buyer, however, is then faced with the necessity of comparing the actual value of the bids. Have the competitors figured exactly according to plans, specifications, and bidding documents, or are there inclusions of something different or exclusions of something called for? His first concern is to question the contractor who is with him about the latter's quotation.

Note that when all bids are on the same printed form, as in open bidding, they can be easily compared because there is no negotiation permitted. For closed bidding, in which there *is* negotiation, however, the buyer has a tactical advantage in permitting a variation in the quotation form from each bidder. Each bidder is afforded complete freedom to write up his quotation as he sees fit. This method results in a considerable variation in bids as each competitor attempts to enter the bidding at as low a basic figure as will meet his objectives and as the wording and interpretation of the plans and other documents will allow. For his own financial safety, the bidder must call attention to what he is excluding or otherwise changing—and, by inference, point out that he is including everything else which is called for someplace on the bidding plans and documents.

The buyer has here an opportunity to find facts and figures. No two contractors will word their bids in the same way. Given different wording and pricing, the buyer can find by direct questioning how much a specific contractor will charge to include something which he has excluded but which a competitor has included. The buyer can and does also ask about the worth of including or excluding certain work as a possible construction intent. (Note the importance to the contractor of his take-off.) The buyer will thus quickly find what certain individual items are worth. Comparison will quickly determine at what price individual bids should be.

Such questioning affords the further opportunity of discovering what an individual contractor thinks is essential and what he thinks may be changed, eliminated, or postponed. These possibilities may be important if the quotations are higher than anticipated and originally budgeted. Changing of plans and specifications may be necessary later to get the price down.

At this point or before, the buyer may bring into discussion a device which sometimes works: he states that he can get more from an unnamed competitor and at a lesser price than from the contractor who is with him. This statement may or may not be true; the lack of ethics in such horse trading is condoned by many otherwise honest and upright individuals. It is definitely an attempt to scare the bidder. The contractor usually will not cave in readily and will come back with questions of his own to develop his further actions. He is certainly entitled to obtain further information before making any important concession.

B. The contractor, in turn, has options open to him, dependent to some extent on the buyer's prior attitude. The buyer may have shuffled papers as if looking for a subject of greater interest than the existing meeting, may have actually attended to many other matters during the interview, or may have seated himself behind a desk and placed the contractor's chair behind the barrier at a distance—just as if a schoolboy were facing the master. These studied and impertinent tactics are meant to attack the contractor psychologically and make him feel on the defensive. This situation is an opportune time for the contractor to ask for an assurance from the buyer that he is authorized to act for his firm. Such an inquiry is essential at some time, but at this point it gives the buyer the same aggressive treatment to which he has subjected the contractor. If the buyer allows himself to get insulted and terminates the interview, it is because he cannot stand investigation. The contractor has lost time and money but has saved a bad entanglement.

Should the interview continue on a businesslike basis, however, the contractor is faced with the necessity of attempting to penetrate the misleading verbal screen raised by the buyer to conceal the truth about relative quotation positions. Such analysis, even though tentative, can be most important in directing the course of negotiations. If the contractor's price is really high, he must make concessions to get the job. If his price is already low, any substantial concession is unnecessary and will mean a needless loss of income.

Possibly the contractor will first ask a series of questions about whether this, that, or some other uncalled-for item is included in the bid of a supposed lower competitor—or any competitor. If the buyer knows and gives a direct affirmative, one price is indicated. (This also is evidence that there were other contractors interviewed before this one.) If the buyer has not obtained the information from any other competitor and says he does not know, the contractor assumes that it is not included and his bid can be higher in actual value. (Also, since there are other bidders yet to be seen, he is probably not the low bidder. Future developments will corroborate this assumption.) This exchange has had the added effect of warning the buyer that the low bid does *not* mean a cost-free or correct bid. The buyer becomes uncertain as to the integrity of the competition, without a word from the contractor questioning their worth. The buyer will definitely check inclusions and exclusions should bargaining be prolonged beyond the present time.

Note that the freedom of quotation form can be advantageous also to the contractor. The written bid is not compelled to mention the necessary inclusion of certain essentials which examination of the site, the plans, and bidding documents have made evident to the contractor. When done later during construction by anyone, the price obtained will undoubtedly be higher and will have to be added to the contractual amount. This possibility does afford a possible offset in making concessions.

The takeoff may be used as a negotiating tool. For example, the contractor herewith involved may do his own masonry work. Knowing that many of his competitors sublet this trade enables him to use his allowed profit on this work. As previously noted, the profit percentage for one's own work is about twice what is customary for using subcontracts. Taking this profit out of the estimate sheets and cutting it in half allows a sum of money which he can offer as a concession and proposal to the buyer. The contractor has every appearance of being practical in wishing to get on a better cost-comparison basis, even though every concession hurts. But in addition, he is also getting the buyer's reaction. If the buyer accepts or asks for a somewhat greater amount, the contractor becomes aware of the price range of the cut which will possibly be acceptable. If the buyer rejects the price offer, he may well be in a strong position with an actual lower bid—and the contractor may have to really cut the price to get the job.

The contractor can also use an exact knowledge of who his competitors are. Determining the competition in advance of the interview is possible. All active competitors necessarily go to many of the same sources to determine if a supply quotation or a delivery date can be bettered in any way. Some suppliers and subcontractors will, therefore, have current information about who is participating in negotiations for a particular job. Intelligently directed questioning will probably unearth the answers. There undoubtedly are other means available.

Knowing the competition, the contractor should also know their business rationality and objectives, as evidenced by their past bidding records. Similar types of contractors use about the same sources of labor, equipment, subcontractors, and material, so that their basic costs are about the same. Only their overhead and profit are not the same. Therefore, if the contractor will take his own cost figure and add the overhead and profit customarily used by his competition (and there is a distinct pattern), he will obtain corroboration of other price indications.

Knowing the competition, he should also know what they do themselves and what they sublet. As an example, the competition do not do their own masonry, but the contractor at the negotiations does. This is a valid basis for a sales argument. It involves proficiency of workmanship, reliability of attaining the completion date, and correlation with other trades. The contractor herewith may further influence the buyer without attacking the competition directly. The buyer is ostensibly covered in such a situation by the completion bond which is specified to be provided under the contract. This coverage is inadequate. A bond does *not* guarantee workmanship, material used, or the time required for starting and completion. A surety *cannot* be depended on for anything except outright default by a bonded contractor (and almost any overestimated contractor can obtain a bond). A bond does *not* repay loss of occupancy time and money or damage to the reputation of the buyer in having picked the wrong party.

Mention of the exact names of the competition by the contractor may cause the buyer to wonder how the contractor knew these names. (Is there a leak of information in the office, and what else is known?) This uncertainty might also be of influence.

13-5   *Selling the Job*

During the process of negotiations, attempts will be made by the buyer to change prices in another way. The buyer is aware of the customary method used in arriving at a quantity of work and multiplying the summation by some unit price to obtain a cost figure. Therefore, if the buyer can convince the contractor that the units he has used are high in comparison with those of the competition, a price deduction may be obtained.

Possibly this particular quotation has been specified to include unit prices for doing certain work which may be necessary at a later time. The buyer may contend that comparison against the competition indicates that the quoted prices of the contractor are high by some percentage. Even if this percentage does not hold for the job in its entirety, the difference indicates a bidding variation. Or the buyer may use a specific subcontract, such as electric work, and ask how much the contractor has allowed per unit (which should be known). The buyer may contend that comparison with the competition indicates that this particular item is also high and can be lowered.

In effect, the buyer is actually trying to sell the construction at a lower price to the contractor than his quotation shows. If the buyer knows his facts and the contractor is willing to be convinced, this result will take place. Actually, it is camouflage for the cementing of good relations—at some expense to the contractor. Such action may forestall one reaction by the buyer which may be harmful to the contractor. This reaction is that the buyer does not have to make an immediate decision. He may defer giving out the job until he has determined if he can obtain a better deal from the competition. However, if this device has been previously used by the buyer and the present meeting is a second and final one, emphasis is directed to the negotiating process as having to be mutually satisfactory. The contractor has made a concession. It is up to the buyer also to concede something. He can show latitude in other ways.

The contractor also attempts to sell the job to the buyer. In addition to selling the good points of his organization and manner of construction, he attempts to make the buyer feel that the contractor is flexible and a good person to deal with. Items may be thrown into the negotiations which are not specified or necessary but have been indicated in conversation. Such subjects might be outstanding name lettering applied to a factory structure on the wall next to the main entrance, an exterior waterproof electric spotlight at the entrance step, or a mat recess and lettered mat for the front vestibule. The cost in each case would be a very small percentage of the total contract. The effect might be worthwhile.

During negotiations the contractor may offer suggestions for possible savings and improvements in the plans and specifications. As previously noted (Section 12-4), this sales device is dangerous. It tends to impugn the worth of the results achieved by the design of architects and engineers. They are among the contractor's best friends and are continuing sources of new information and new business. In addition, an unscrupulous buyer may misuse such suggestions by adopting them while giving the job to another. Should the contractor have any such ideas, possibly he will do better to withhold them until he actually gets the job. They usually do little to sway negotiations and may be a source of additional profit later when used with the prior approval of the designer.

Emphasis is again placed on offer and counteroffer, action and reaction. Negotiation is just old-fashioned bargaining with an impressive name.

13-6   *The Job Award*

There comes that time during the bargaining procedure when the parties arrive at a decision. The contractor has decided that further concessions will jeopardize his welfare. The buyer believes he has gotten a good deal. Each has come to the conclusion that certain profitable objectives have been obtained.[1]

---

[1] W. R. Park, *The Strategy of Contracting for Profit*, Prentice-Hall.

These objectives are as follows:

1. Facts have been ascertained, where necessary.

2. A limitation of plans and specifications has been arrived at, including a time for completion.

3. There has been a mutual accommodation leading to compromise. This conduct evidences a flexible manner of doing business, necessary for continuing good relations.

4. There has been a definite commitment by each.

5. Each believes he cannot get a better offer.

6. Each believes his objectives are substantially met.

This time of decision is confirmed by using another tested device found in every book on salesmanship. At such time as he believes he has obtained the job, the contractor starts discussing items which would normally come up after contract closing, such as whom to contact for a survey of the property, when insurance certificates are to be delivered, and how soon work is to start. If the buyer is not ready to close and is not receptive, a direct denial has been avoided and the matter is still open. Should the contractor wish to make some further concession, he can do so. If the buyer responds affirmatively, the job has been won.

13-7   *Summarization*

While negotiations are fresh in mind, regardless of the results, they should be summarized and dated in a record book. Names, titles, actual positions, addresses, and telephone numbers of everyone contacted at any time are entered. All are valuable for future contact. When the same person is dealt with from time to time, a precedent now exists as to his customary values and techniques.

When someone new is to be faced, a study of past efforts will help future negotiations. Sales effort can be strengthened. As an example:

The buyer's objection—The other firm presently doing our design and building does the complete job for a very low total fee which is below yours.

The seller's answer—The amount of the fee may be lower than ours, but the overall cost of construction to the buyer is the criterion. We are experts in this field. Our skill in design and in using material well and our workmanship and management cut the cost to you per cubic foot of structure, which we can prove. You will be paying less and getting more.

The strengthened sales effort—The seller should have the proof made up, illustrated, and added to the sales presentation for immediate use to everyone.

A study of past negotiations stimulates thought, improves proficiency, and offers sources for obtaining additional business.

14

OFFICE PROCEDURE

The obtaining of a construction contract offers an opportunity. How the details are handled determines to a large extent whether profit or loss is the result.

14-1 *The Letter of Intent*

At such time during negotiations as a verbal agreement indicates that a new job has been obtained, the status and location of all bidding documents change. The estimate folder is given a job number for reference and transferred to production. Of prime and immediate importance is a preliminary work and time schedule. It will determine the necessary delivery of material, equipment, and men to the job. It will emphasize the key items to be ordered out—but ordering also entails entering into obligations to make payment.

Since a verbal promise prior to the actual receipt of a signed contract is not considered adequate basis to start ordering, written protection should be obtained at once to ensure against loss. A *letter of intent* from the buyer will serve this purpose by stating that a contract is being prepared for certain work to be done by the contractor. Pending receipt of the signed contract, the letter will offer some protection. The buyer must be impressed with the necessity of getting this letter out immediately. For example, an immediate steel-mill date may be involved; the next rolling of a wanted member size may be months in the future, and a definite order may have to be placed to get on the present mill rolling schedule. Or the lead time and the actual cost of designing, ordering, and building special turbines may require a contract at the earliest possible date. Or permits, street-opening bonds, insurance certificates, and similar time-consuming details may have to be ordered out. Until a contract is signed, the letter of intent *is* a contract. The wording must be checked to ensure that it is the same as the verbal agreement.

The makeup of an exact production schedule is the first construction requirement for the new job. This is indicated in the progress schedule (Figure 14-1). Separate contracts of the particular job being considered may have been given out by the buyer for the owner, to be coordinated by the general contractor. Such a condition is shown on the schedule, which also notes that the start of erection of the structural steel is the key date around which construction is predicated. The start and the dura-

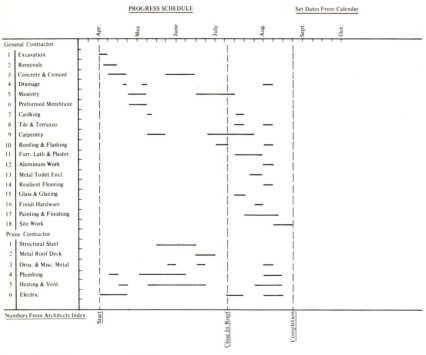

figure 14-1. Progress schedule

tion of erection are noted in the contract. (In any other contractual condition, such a key time for any trade should be established first.)

At this point it is essential to note that the designer controls the basic time schedule for progress of the structure. He must weigh the relative advantages to his owner-client in obtaining material in delayed fashion and paying a minimum market price for it or speeding up procurement and paying more for it. This is done through the building-supply facility known as warehousing. Structural-steel warehousing is a good example to explain the process.

Structural-steel shapes are produced at a mill in an intermittent fashion, depending on supply requirements. The rolling mills must be adjusted to produce differing sizes and quantities on the same machines at differing times. A mill rolling schedule is set up for turning out these products, together with a time schedule specifying when the work is to be done and a total quantity reflecting the orders on hand at the mill. If, for any reason, a required size has not been on a rolling list for some time, an entire otherwise completed order might be delayed in shipment, fabrication, and erection, waiting for that one piece.

To prevent such delays, a service has developed whereby every size as rolled is bought in standard lengths by a warehouse, stocked, and sold at an increase over the normal market price to cover financing, handling, cutting, and shipping charges and a profit. By specifying in the request to bid whether the material is to be mill or warehouse, the designer thus controls approximately the time at which erection can be anticipated. The estimated price, of course, immediately reflects the accommodation which has been bought. The progress schedule, when made up, reflects the designer's decision.

In making up the index numbers and other designations, the information used is the same as the architect's specification index for ease of cross-reference. The plans or other contractual documents should also be referred to so that everything is included. Occasionally the buyer for the owner may find it worthwhile to give out one specification trade to several different companies. In this case, the specification and progress schedule will also change, and these trades will be noted as prime contractors, with additional index numbers not heretofore used by the designer. The general contractor will then generally become job coordinator at an additional fee.

The time intervals of the progress schedule will allow for seven-day subdivisions to permit further monthly marking. In many cases, one trade is interdependent with another. Therefore, arrival time and the number of men on a job are set by the required date of completion of the preceding and the following trade. Thus, the important item 10, roofing and flashing, cannot even start until the metal deck (contract

2) is well under way, yet the roofing makes the job weathertight for most of the following finishing trades.

14-2   *Purchasing, General*

The purchasing agent for the construction company may be a member of the firm, part of the engineering department, or a specialist. Among his problems is maintaining interorganization communications. He must be advised of estimating decisions and other requirements, job happenings, and office results. In turn, he should advise others as to purchasing developments affecting money, men, material, and equipment. His job requires getting the best return for the lowest total monetary outlay but not necessarily the lowest first cost.

Receipt of an approved progress schedule will supplement efforts which the purchasing agent has already made. The material, such as face brick, may be subject to a specification requirement that the architect's approval be obtained before ordering. Such culling over the market, getting samples, and transmitting and obtaining approval before ordering take time. Thereafter, the brick will have to be contracted for, to be furnished or made specially by the one factory having the material and other qualities which are wanted. Occasionally, not every type or required quantity of brick is in stock. Since the brick is run through the kilns at intervals, it is necessary to get on the production rotation, which requires additional time. Thereafter, the brick must be made, stored to cure, shipped as needed, and paid for.

When definite characteristics for a material are noted in the specification, they must be furnished. In addition, the tensile strength of reinforcing rods may have to be guaranteed, lumber may have to be grade-marked, or the color, quality, and texture of limestone facing may have to pass later job inspection. Reference must be made to the office file for any specification item referred to only by the designation description of some trade or standards association[1] or some other source. If not on hand, this information must be obtained immediately, before purchasing for this job. The purchasing agent here comes up against the question of the foreign supplier offering a lower price than the domestic provider. There is often a dissimilarity of quality, workmanship, and finish which may or may not be acceptable. Time of delivery is also of importance. Even a small job delay may offset a saving in material cost, and considerable delay can be a disaster. If advance delivery is resorted to, the question of payment arises. The purchasing agent must be careful.

Of course, this obligation of money going out requires that top man-

---

[1] F. S. Merritt, *Building Construction Handbook*, McGraw-Hill.

agement be constantly advised as to actions. Not only should money be available when needed, but there is here a very important means of making money—the trade discount. Customarily, time is allowed to make payment on such diverse items as medicine cabinets, doorframes, and memorial plaques for the front vestibule. Many of such items are delivered in advance and used as necessary. However, if they are paid for promptly upon delivery (within a certain few days), a discount is offered by the supplier. The size of this discount is always of interest as an addition to the profit originally figured on a job. If the contractor does some of his own work, he can also get a discount for material for that trade. If working capital is limited when such deliveries are anticipated, it may be advantageous for management to arrange for a bank loan in advance (to be repaid when material is incorporated in the structure and then paid for by the buyer).

There are occasions when the beneficiary of a trade discount will deliberately take advantage of the time terms of the offering party. He will deduct a discount even though he pays at a later date and is not entitled to a deduction. The seller of material must bring this matter to the attention of the purchaser or face the collapse of his selling structure. Yet he cannot antagonize that customer by assuming an evil intent. Although the deduction is a typical sharp business practice to be avoided, it might be an error which could happen to anyone. The seller must consider the interest and feeling of the buyer. Again appears the importance of a good business letter (Section 7-7). For example, the following method of handling by a subordinate is conciliatory and allows any action later decided on by management:

"Was the discount of $_____ allowable on our invoice #_____ if paid on or before _____ deducted in error? Your payment was made on _____. If an error was made, please send us an additional check. If the error is ours, kindly let us know wherein we are at fault so that we may adjust our record. Please let us hear from you."

When certain subcontracts, such as for heating and ventilating, are to be given out, negotiation and acceptance should be immediate. The subcontractor, in turn, will have to place submaterial orders, such as for fuel tanks, oil burners, boilers, cooling towers, radiators, and other fittings. (Most of these require time for getting approval and delivery.) There is manpower which will require insurance and scheduling. There are preliminary requisitions to make up and be inserted into a time schedule, including inspections and work approvals.

Specifically, note that every proposal submitted by a prospective subcontractor demands attention and understanding. *The conditions of sale affect the purchase.* Whether those conditions are typed into the bid or are printed on the reverse side of the form and merely referred to on the face, they will become obligations which the purchaser accepts to get whatever he is buying. There may be an omission of a sales tax, which would make the quoted sales price appear lower than that of the competition. There may be a time limit set for acceptance, an accessibility clause of a road to the site, a time allowed for unloading by the purchaser without charge, or some other clause involving responsibility and action by the purchaser. Even inaction by the purchaser may cost additional money since it may lead to more than one erection visit. Such conditions are customary but require detailed care. Sometimes the purchaser must have the sales conditions changed in order to accept a bid.

Occasionally the subbid will include modifications of the plans and specifications. These changes may appear as additions, exceptions, or outright modifications (in which cases the designer may later refuse to accept what is proposed as an unacceptable substitution). The purchaser may have to get something separately which should have been included in this subcontract. This may be advantageous or disadvantageous, but again the purchaser must be wary.

There will also be modifications which the purchasing agent will insert to improve the job for his company. An example might be to use masonry block which is more expensive but lighter in weight and more uniform in manufacture than the specified material. In this case, there will actually be a saving in more blocks laid per day, plus a better job.

14-3 *Purchasing, Time*

Time is a distinct requirement of ordering. It affects the desirability of one supplier over another. Take, as an example, steel floor sheets spanning between the steel beams of the framework to support concrete floor slabs.

There does not seem to be much difference between competitors besides a small price variation. Both offer delivery only. Their terms of sale, however, sometimes make one bid preferable to another. From experience, the material seller may in his bid disclaim responsibility for transportation delay or for the additional cost caused thereby to the construction-company purchaser. Should this material come in to the local railroad freight terminal just before a weekend and require a demurrage (delay) charge before being unloaded, there would be an additional unestimated freight charge to be paid by the contractor. And if the construction company accepts the standard terms of sale because of the benefit of the overall delivered price, they will be obligated to pay the penalty should conditions develop adversely.

In this particular case, a separate erection contract (not in the designer's specification) will have to be entered into with a steel erector to pick up the material at the freight yard, truck it to the site, and erect it into place. A possibility of a saving also develops here. If the size of the job entails a number of tiers to be installed at different times, it is conceivable that the job can be operated to save money on *steel floor-form erection*. The steel frame will then be completely erected first, with floor material delivery held for a one-time construction job. To cover this possibility, the steel-erection contract will note one price for doing the subcontract in several visits to the job and a lower price if only one visit is required. Should the job work out as planned, a saving is possible.

To carry this simple case still further, although this floor sheet material comes in standard sizes, it is not generally carried in stock. The material to fill particular types of orders is rolled at regular time intervals, known as *mill schedules*, for a particular size and a particular location. If the job erection schedule calls for material to be on the site on a particular day, the order must be given out sufficiently in advance to provide the lead time called for. This leeway may have to provide for getting the order details approved by the designer. The order must be inserted on the mill rolling schedules, made up to form and size, painted or galvanized, shipped, delivered, and transported to the site. Other material will have other prior requirements.

Especially when approval of details is called for in the specification, a time delay automatically comes into being. Unless expediting of everything (including the checking process of the designer) is made part of the construction job from its very inception, there will be loss of time and money.

It is very evident that as soon as a letter of intent is available, a list will have to be made up showing everything that is required. At this stage, the person most familiar with the job and how it was figured is the estimator. In accordance with the individual job, he will therefore make up a purchase summary of *all* the items which are necessary, together with plans and specifications, subbid information and queries, and all other pertinent details. These data will go with the estimating file to the purchasing agent to complete any previous information he has been working on. Because the purchasing agent will modify his buying as pertinent facts are developed, the purchase summary is to be construed as a starting point only. Undoubtedly it will be modified by addition or deduction of items whenever an opportunity is afforded to save money.

Follow-up of orders is so important that the purchasing agent should give a daily report to management on results.

Time also enters into the dating of orders. One of the big money wasters on any construction job is moving material around. The lack of storage space on a work site and the necessity of having some quantity of material on hand for normal working leeway necessitate storage wherever possible. Should the storage location be away from the place of material use, considerable manhours may be wasted. If storage space at the right location can be arranged as an ordered function and material delivery and moving into place coordinated with structural erection, a saving in erection manpower can be made. This procedure may not be feasible for the entire job operation, but it may well prove practical for a part of the work.

14-4   *Purchasing the Subcontract*

When the primary contractor is faced with giving out subcontracts, certain considerations are essential.

A. *Reliability*

The value of any job as a money-making instrument depends upon the economical completion of the work. The construction progress, in turn, depends on the work of many trades. For example, when the roof sheathing is finished by one trade, the roof itself must be laid by another. This work will provide an interior waterproof building where other trades can work during inclement weather and finished material can be installed. Thus many phases of the work depend on the labor and material of the roofing subcontractor. When his reliability is not personally known, it must be established as well as possible by recommendation, from credit sources, or in some other manner. A low price in the office does not necessarily mean a money saving to a firm. When material, men, and equipment are delayed in getting to a job, fail to progress satisfactorily, and do not do good work, further expense may be anticipated.

The workmanship phase of reliability, of course, is important. The quality of every item of the job is indicated by behavior, material, and appearance under inspection. Should anything not be in accordance with the purchase contract, the work may have to be removed and replaced. The loss of time, money, and reputation hurts the innocent as well as the guilty.

The purchasing agent or an assistant, therefore, should take time to make inquiries of material dealers, banks, friends in the business, and references supplied by the prospective suppliers and subcontractors. A penalty clause in a purchase contract is *not* a safeguard. Loss is not wanted, and the penalty can never repay the loss.

B. *Price*

Only after the purchasing agent has satisfied himself about the reliability of those with whom he is dealing should he compare material prices or other subbids. The comparative prices may be reasonably close, or there may be a large discrepancy. Under any circumstances, the purchasing agent views all quotations with scepticism. He sets up his own value as to what he wants and thinks is reasonable—and aims to get that figure.

From the competitive point of view, any comparison must be on exactly the same basis. The purchasing agent must consider not only material and labor but also such general conditions as are necessitated by individual conditions. These factors might be the cost of cleaning, safety protection, or unusual insurance or any of the innumerable implied or specified particulars of some definite future contract.

C. *Size and Financial Strength*

An organization comprising a number of workmen has a greater factor of safety for a purchaser than an individual subcontractor. An organization or individual who can offer assurance that money will not be asked for until rightfully due and payable is practically a necessity. (Of course, many worthy small contractors are helped financially. The benefits, however, are considered and discounted in advance as being worthy of the effort and risk involved.)

D. *Other Considerations*

Equipment such as modern steel sectional forms for concrete, an individually owned crane and engineer for erection without rental delays, or an engineering department to expedite shop drawings and approvals are all influential elements.

Good reputation will confer good credit, which may be of use in the assurance of bondability.

Time of completion is controlled by attainable skilled manpower as well as by contractual wording.

It does not pay for the purchasing agent to cut the bid to get the lowest price possible. He may think he is saving money for his firm, but actually he may be antagonizing those very subbidders on whom his firm depends for good quotations. The subcontractors may bid again, but next time they will furnish a relatively higher price to allow for such chiseling (and also, possibly, to make up for what they have lost if they obtained a previously profitless subcontract).

As a matter of importance, the purchasing agent will take the individual requirements developed for him by the estimator and use these items as the basis for a columnar purchase summary of *subcontracts actually bought*. Each necessary subcontract is listed, together with the *estimated money value* in the next column. Thereafter will appear a column noted as *cost actually bought*. The next two columns, headed *plus* and *minus*, give the pertinent money value as a difference. As procurement continues, the profit or loss from subcontracting becomes immediately apparent. On this same summary can be added items of general expense, overhead, and estimated cost of work which the construction firm does for itself. An immediate indication is given of profit or loss on the entire job. If management action is indicated, the facts have appeared.

For every subcontract involving labor, purchasing routine must include requests for immediate coverage by compensation insurance. These should include submission of a certificate from an approved insurance company showing job coverage, accompanied by assurance that there will be a ten-day notice given before cancellation. Should other types of insurance be required, they should also be taken care of at this point.

14-5   *Obtaining Equipment*

The use of one's own equipment or the rental of another's is an individual problem, depending to a great extent on the circumstances of the individual contracting firm in connection with the individual job being considered. On a long-lasting job, the rental fees may bring the cost far in excess of the purchase price and all connected expenses of a new machine. On a job of short duration, the rental cost may secure prompt use of a special machine at a cost well below that required as a down payment on a new machine. Advantages, such as the latest timesaving machine production, have to be weighed against disadvantages, such as tying up working capital. And sometimes there are counterbalancing factors of tax methodology which can be properly interpreted only by someone currently and directly involved.

Assuming that this matter is satisfactorily handled as a special case, a list of all contemplated machinery to be purchased or rented must be summarized at one or several advance office discussion meetings concerning the method to be used in erecting the structure. New machines usually require time for delivery. Rental machines may be available, but not always—and work schedules may have to be changed. Manpower is a requisite, and the premium pay required for busy-season operation can be quite a serious unforeseen expense.

The interaction of every phase of the construction organization is clearly exemplified here. The purpose of the office meetings is to set up a purchase-and-delivery schedule. The purchasing department will follow this timing.

14-6   *Purchasing, Accessory*

By acting to implement details, purchasing transfers a contract into an actuality. All the bidding documents require study and procurement. Fire insurance in differing amounts (and other coverages) will have to be placed on the structure during construction to protect the interests of both the buyer and the builder. A construction sign of fixed wording, material, color, and size will have to be erected, where designated, to advertise what is coming. A temporary construction fence around the site must be installed. These will be new items.

But there will also be changes and extensions to existing services and supplies. *This necessity may require a validating rider with a change of terms and limits to an existing insurance policy, to cover a new location.* Certain material already on hand in the stockyard may be satisfactory for use at a saving in cost. Or the existing electric service at the job site may be inadequate and need to be replaced. Regardless of amount or type, all needed items require attention. Some of these items are not trivial. But no matter what the amount, a saving here is as important as elsewhere.

The alert purchasing agent may also be of help to his firm in initiating specification changes, with the idea of getting an increased contract return. For example, steel window frames may be called for, requiring a painting subcontract and additional maintenance painting thereafter (a cost to the buyer). The substitution of aluminum frames will cost more initially but will allow the elimination of the painting subcontract and later maintenance. There may be a saving of overall cost which will justify requesting a specification change from the buyer, who also benefits.

As soon as a subcontract or a direct material order has been consummated, a photocopy should be given to the acting job superintendent by the office purchasing agent for *confirmation of insurance coverage* and for other materialization. The job superintendent will not allow any work to be done until proper insurance coverage is presented. Thereafter, he must know exactly what obligations each party has assumed and what benefits will be attained and when. Actual contracts will modify plans and specifications as agreed to by the purchasing agent for the construction company in a multitude of ways and for very definite reasons. These modifications may affect delivery and acceptance, passage of title, guarantees, arbitration of disputes, and similar essential items. The superintendent must be made aware that trade discounts can be obtained by prompt checking of material deliveries and transmission of receipts to the office. The superintendent must also arrange on the job for necessary actions, such as receiving and setting window frames, which may have been purchased on a delivered basis only.

Upon ostensible completion of his work, the purchasing agent should obtain a complete and independent check from the supervisory section of his organization to determine that office procurement is actually complete. In addition to subcontract changes, there is always the possibility of human fallibility in drawing up plans and specifications, leading to omissions. Such a check should include verification of on-time delivery of contracted-for items on the site. Representatives of the contracting organization should visit sources and personally check procurement, fabrication, and delivery. Unfortunately, every supplier is subject to the demands of other customers. Expediting deliveries becomes essential— and as a continuing process.

14-7 *Supervision of New Work*

Making a structure is often the work of many independent contractors and individuals, and all are working motivated by their own interests. They must earn to live. The actions that they take will advance the interests of the general contractor at the same time as it helps their own advantage. In practice this works out to an attempt to do their own work as inexpensively as possible. Whether subcontractor, journeyman, or laborer, each will do what he must.

The general contractor depends on the job superintendent for the constant inspection that will ensure a fair return for what is paid out in wages, in material, or contractually. In order to help the busy job superintendent, there should be an office representative on the job at frequent intervals. This supervisor provides a check on the many details to be attended to, is the transmitter of money and information, and acts as a planner and a director. (The authority of the job superintendent, however, must be maintained at all times.)

A. When the specification calls for the site to be kept clean by the general contractor, this work can be done either by having a laborer on the job constantly or only when required. This payroll problem can be handled readily by consultation. On the other hand, the specification *for a particular subcontract* may require that the debris from that operation be collected in piles on the various floors as directed. This operation in itself uses labor time and should be part of the subcontract which is being paid for. Attention must be given to discussing such matters and gaining the savings involved, if any are possible. If a subcontractor has contracted to do certain work, he should do it.

B. The specification for an alteration job may call *for a certain subcontractor to do his own cutting and patching;* that is, the work has not been included in the plaster contract. Possibly the plaster contractor will do it for the other subcontractor, *but* as a job order (possibly at a low price since he is a coworker). In any event, the purchasing agent has already paid out money contractually for this work, and it should not be spent again by a supervisory oversight. One hand should check what the other hand has done.

C. When coordination of subtrades is required, even though the job superintendent may do the necessary advance telephoning for job appearances, the office should also be involved far in advance. Approvals should be followed up and obtained, suborders placed, time and space and delivery arrangements consummated, and erection prepared for. When expediting is required, it should be done. When inspection is required, it should be arranged for. When requisitions need approval to meet certain payment dates, arrangements in advance may be necessary. The actual work involved varies with every job, but it compels alertness.

D. A detailed interaction of job and office is an essential toward successful construction.

For example, the specifications may call for a new survey to establish site locations and elevations. This effort may not be necessary. There may be an existing survey used in the previous transfer of property or title survey and in the possession of or obtainable by the buyer, who will undoubtedly turn it over on request. If there *is* a cost here, it will be in bringing the survey up to date as far as encroachments are concerned, replacing or refurbishing old markings, and furnishing a new plot plan for the job superintendent. Certainly the cost will be less than that of an all-new survey.

Or a job fence may be specified but not particularized beyond the customary clause calling for the architect's approval. Should the general contractor have reuseable fencing on hand, now is the time to make this clause effective, by requesting such approval.

Or inspection will reuse existing sewer lines and water taps, thus saving the cost of street opening and repair.

E. A very definite item of caution is: Whose is the responsibility? Whether it be the owner's responsibility or that of the architect's representative, an independent prime contractor, or a subcontractor, the tendency is to spend as little as possible and to get some other party to do whatever incidental work has to be done. When this work is a specified function of the general contractor, he will do it. The question, however, arises when it is not clearly specified. It is all too easy to be a good guy and do such unspecified work at the expense of the account of the general contractor. Unfortunately, one is paid by a contract which involves plans, specifications, and documents, and if the buyer refuses to pay any additional bill, as not warranted or authorized, there is a distinct possibility of loss and a certainty of hard feeling. The office representative and the job superintendent must be mutually protective of the rights of their own organization as opposed to just liabilities. Laxity here is another source of loss.

F. At the earliest possible time, checking actual production, material, and equipment pricing against the original estimate should be done. Should there be any discrepancy, the cause can promptly be found and corrected to save as much of the anticipated profit as is yet possible.

Should there be an error in takeoff or application, it can be noted for use in the next available estimate. But in many cases the men who have done the estimating and pricing are unjustly blamed because their own organization is doing something which was not figured. An organization foreman temporarily not working will be placed with some other working gang just to keep him busy and pay his salary. Equipment will be used, not because it is suitable, but because it is owned. Failure on the part of an office worker to expedite material may cause delivery delay.

Possibly, if such conditions occur often enough, they will be commonplace and the cost record will be changed to include their effect. Then the firm will become a high-cost producer, which is a very dubious distinction.

14-8   *Supervision of Alteration Work*

An all-new job is a desirable job to get, but it does not often appear. And as site conditions get more and more crowded, such jobs become less and less available.

A. *Construction Problems*

A large excavation for a new skyscraper has a public-transit tube tunnel exposed by construction. The passengers must have protection, emergency access, and no interruption of service during construction. Details may not be given, even though matters of such magnitude will probably be indicated. Or the design of a building allows the main lobby to exit to an adjoining building lobby for side-street access. This plan involves alterations for the main trades of plumbing, heating, electric, masonry, concrete, structural-steel, and carpentry work, in addition to the new finishing trades. The new construction exposes sidewalls of old structures, which must be soundly built up and made watertight.

Such work is not laid out fully in advance by a design engineer and detailed by a draftsman. It is usually only noted in general. Rather, an existing condition is exposed on the job and develops problems which must be solved. These conditions, of course, allow for preplanning to a large extent, but such planning never seems to forestall fully the possibilities for loss. Referring to the above design, in which an old wall must be cut to provide access for a new building lobby, several things can go wrong with this simple piece of work. The old plan may not have indicated a condition in which a concentrated bearing load comes directly over the new lobby opening and requires temporary shoring until properly reframed (yet in this case the condition is covered in the specification and is definitely the responsibility of the general contractor). The masonry joints may be so hard that the brick is the weakest part of the wall and must be actually broken apart by an unusual air-compressor and jackhammer operation, involving an engineer and several laborers. These men would not usually be required or used. In the wall itself may be several water and drainage pipes, steam lines, and electric conduit, which must be moved under conditions of use without disturbing service above.

The estimator cannot be faulted in not having foreseen all these conditions in his takeoff, because the site examination and the plans did not uncover them. The estimator only included a reasonable figure to get the job. The additional cost is a direct out-of-pocket expense—to be made up, it is hoped, elsewhere.

This instance is multiplied in many ways. It occurs differently every time. Its effects can be minimized only by efficient and proficient supervision.

B. *Violations and Other Jurisdictional Troubles*

On any construction job site which has previously been occupied by something else or which will be occupied, there may be something which has been or can be a source of present trouble. An old building which is to be reused frequently has a violation notice placed upon the record by a local building inspector for some past infraction of the law, and this must be corrected. Or a state health inspector may bring a lawsuit to compel new factory drainage in a definite manner. Obsolescence can be expensive.

Clearing up old violations is covered by most specifications. A change of plans, however, such as changing the drainage design, is not generally the responsibility of the general contractor. The office supervisor is the representative of his firm for all items of any nature. He must initiate checking of responsibility and must authorize any unusual work.

Supervision of any type of alteration work requires distinct knowledge of old construction, its strengths and limitations. The unusual development becomes expected and customary. Adding to old structures often requires not only strengthening or other repairing of faults but also revising changed ideas. A flexible, detailed approach and a great deal of personal attention are needed of both job superintendent and office supervisor.

14-9 *Accounting Necessities*

Factual records are a basis of the construction business. Although much construction has been done without records, a successful organization requires accurate and complete information. Such facts should be properly set up when the business begins and in such a form as to be most easily incorporated in the system. Unfortunately, many companies begin business without an accountant, and also unfortunately, when they are used, many accountants have not supervised a construction business and do not include all the items necessary.

There are two general methods for keeping books: on the *cash* basis or on the *accrual* basis. Because there are differences between these two methods in the makeup of statements and the payment of taxes (and other items), there are reasons why the accountant will prefer to set up a particular set of books by one method rather than the other.

Consider this difference in terms of taxes only. When books are set up on the cash basis, receipts and disbursements are entered as soon as they occur. Practically, unless care is taken to balance payments against receipts in one year, expenses may predominate over receipts at the end of the year (assuming at this time that the construction is near completion). This bookkeeping system will show that the business has operated at a loss, which is not so. There will be no relatively low tax payment caused by splitting the profits between two successive years at a low rate for each year. Instead, all the cash returns will appear during the early part of the following year. At this time they will overbalance the small volume of completion expenditures. For this next year, there will be an apparent considerable profit, at a higher rate of taxes. Actually, this second year may not be profitable.

Alternatively, when the accrual basis is used, bookkeeping accounts are set up. These entries show the prospective profit in a signed contract as an asset from the date of inception. Anticipated receipts are properly shown against payments. A true profit-and-loss picture is thus given, and upon this taxes are figured for payment. Because tax payments are so important to every business operation, accounting procedure is of concern. The accrual basis requires considerably more attention and expense, which may not be warranted.

In a delayed-payment situation, the accrual method offers an insurance factor against slow payment at the end of the year. Note that the fiscal year itself can vary and need not agree with the calendar year (although once chosen, it must remain in operation). This time variation offers an advantage for the office manpower. Most reports, statements, tax returns, and other fiscal documents must be worked on during the first few months of the year. Spreading the time for returns also spreads the work load and decreases the office payroll.

This brief discussion of but one phase of an accountant's responsibilities indicates the complexities involved. Only one limited case is noted. No attempt will be made here to inquire further into a very complex subject. There are many other factors which the accountant must consider. Some of the essential areas will be outlined to note their importance.

A. *Contract*

A complete record is made of every agreement entered into (including obligations as well as expectation) and is set up for every job. Payment terminology establishes method of payment and time. Completion terminology establishes possible benefits or penalties.

B. *Purchasing*

Formal purchasing orders are the basis for determining many of the obligations entered into by the construction company. They will vary with the subject matter they cover, such as whether they include material only or labor and other obligations. All receipt tickets at a job must be checked there for material actually received and then numerically compared in the office against the order for quantities, terms, and other details. This double-tally principle is a preventive of carelessness, dishonesty, and waste. As company policy, it is not questioned by suppliers, and it aims to minimize trouble. (Should any short-order delivery be noted, it can be entered on the original receipt ticket and immediately on the driver's copy—and claimed.) Other shortages should be checked.

C. *Job Account*

The superintendent is generally entrusted with some sum of company money to take care of unforeseen expenses. These might be labor payoffs, freight charges, or local emergency purchases. A special receipt book is kept for this purpose, giving the facts of each payment to enter later in the correct account by the bookkeeping department and to reimburse the superintendent.

D. *Stock on Hand*

Material previously paid for from various jobs tends to accumulate in the storage yard. A list of the quantities of the various kinds of material in stock (and their entry dates) can occasionally be utilized to dispose of surplus, with only the labor of picking up and trucking to the site as an immediate cost. Of course, in practice, this material is sold from the yard to the job in such manner and at such price as the accountant will consider necessary.

E. *Financial Information*

Quite often during the course of a year, a contracting firm finds it necessary to file financial information. Sometimes such statements are necessary to get on a selected bidding list, to file with an individual owner, or to submit to a banker. It is possible to make any financial statement look better in a perfectly honest and legal manner. The accountant need only conform to good practice in requiring of management liquidity of assets, no excess of outstanding debits or slow-pay credits—in short, good business management. This supervision is definitely the accountant's responsibility.

F. *Checking General Accounts*

There are many purchases made during the course of operations which are part of the cost of doing business. Such items as the cost of borrowing money, premiums paid for automobile insurance, postage-stamp purchases, and monthly typewriter service are all part of a variable overhead. Office labor may increase at one time and decrease at another. Field labor may be warranted on one job and not on another. Checking is necessary, not only to pay bills but also to determine if a saving is possible. A summation must be kept up-to-date for the use of management and the estimating department.

G. *Asset and Liability Accounts*

Other accounts take cognizance of the ownership of land, buildings, machinery and automobiles, tools, equipment, materials, and supplies. This setup includes provision for writing off the cost of such items over a period of time, known as *amortization*. (Note that land sometimes appreciates due to scarcity, change of use or access, or for some other reason. Inflation, however, affects both the asset and the liability sides of bookkeeping—and will hurt because of the unequal and unsettling effect of the development of the condition.) There are also partnership, corporate ownership, and other interrelationships to be considered.

There are not only tangibles but also intangibles to be accounted for. These intangibles might be an established business with some definite reputation (good will), patents, a dealership, or vested interest, such as a factory representative.

Frequently these records must be referred to in making requests for bank loans or obtaining credit. They become part of a business statement that includes the other facts involving the business, such as its operating results.

14-10   *The Accounting Extra and Credit*

When a contract has been increased for any reason during the course of a job, management must insist that the bookkeeping department be notified in the form of a written contract. Only in this fashion will such a contractual amendment be entered as a definite agreement and asset. And most important, no accident or neglect will cause an oversight, in which the extra is not billed out.

Just as important is the saving to be offered the buyer in the form of a credit. As a matter of fairness, when work has been eliminated during the course of a job, when material or fixtures less expensive than originally specified are approved and used, or when a saving has evolved through some effort of the general contractor, a credit should be issued. If properly done, such voluntary procedure is most effective. Preliminary discussion before a definitive figure is reached will disarm any possible criticism. It will bring to light the overhead originally expended to get the work, the assumed profit not now obtainable, and the work already done but not to be billed for. It is possible and necessary to get a profit from this type of credit, but the cost is well worthwhile. The personal relationship has a very distinct advertising value. It becomes a means of gaining entrée to future business or a worthy recommendation from a satisfied customer.

14-11   *Collections*

The collection and disbursement of money in accordance with the contract are a necessary part of the smooth running of the job and are worthy of constant attention. The advance planning of requisitions and approvals is, therefore, an important detail. The contractual terms control. In a speculative apartment contract, when a payment to the contractor is to be made after the roof goes on, the buyer-owner does not get his own money from the mortgagor until that point in construction. Thereafter, however, the buyer-owner must pay all accumulated bills of any nature from that first receipt of money. It is therefore part of the construction business, if involved with this type of operator, to ask for information and to be very aware of this type of situation. It is necessary not only to submit the requisition to the right party but to be on his doorstep to collect when the money comes in. To know the local privileges and recourses for nonpayment is a determination for a lawyer. To avoid the aggravation, expense, and monetary danger of being caught in such a possible loss situation is far better.

When the contract allows requisitions to include material delivered to the construction site and payments to be made monthly after approval by someone representing the buyer, the latter party might be the key to payments. Here an appointment on the site for inspection of the requisition together will give an immediate meeting of any divergent opinions, the establishment of facts and values, and an opportunity to settle on an agreed sum. The approved requisition will then need only to go through the mechanics of payment, as it has already complied with the contractual terms.

When payments have been prearranged in a definite fashion, it is still necessary to facilitate inspection and approval so as to get the money. The procedures, times, documents, or other necessities do cause loss of time and working capital. A stratagem can be arranged at the inception of the job to minimize this loss of payment time if it is not already specified in the bidding documents.

The general contractor sets up a value list of each subcontract making up the total. The value of each trade contract then becomes a percentage part of the total contract price. The value of each trade contract is broken up, in turn, into percentages for every major subdivision of that class of work. If, then, the requisition for any payment period is in percentages of work completed, a value may be arrived at readily for the composite sum of each requisition. The percentage completion is clearly marked and easily checked for installation and workmanship. There is no excuse for undue loss of time. The requisition processes shown in Figures 3-1 and 3-2 are descriptive of this method. Note that no exact determination is possible in any case, and approval of requisitions without some prior meeting or method to offset one person's mental process against that of another is difficult. This method requires that an unbiased third party, such as the architect or engineer, approve the original figured computation of the contractor for correctness and for use. The computation need not be absolutely correct, as the retainer is adequate to safeguard the owner.

Close attention should be given to every requisition sent out, and the buyer should be contacted under the terms of the contract after only a minimum reasonable time for payment has elapsed. By the beginning of the following thirty days, another invoice comes due. If the prior invoice is not paid by the time this next invoice is due, the first invoice is definitely in default. Some construction firms are hesitant about taking decisive action. They feel that they may antagonize a good client. Yet there is a very definite obligation of self-interest and business survival involved, and at the moment the client is not so good. It must be concluded that lack of funds is holding up payment. If the customer cannot pay for the invoicing of one month, how can he get money to pay for two, particularly if the general contractor is nowhere at fault? Unless very satisfactory assurance is received that the delay will extend only to an immediately adjacent set date, the collection should be turned over to the attorney for such personal action as he may consider necessary. Due to the importance of chronological time for action under some local lien laws, it is necessary to act promptly to obtain protection.

There are some speculative builders of good reputation who arrange beforehand to have contractors take interest-bearing notes in part payment of requisitions. The same procedure can be followed where advisable. Because the contractor's working capital is involved, he charges interest for any rediscounting costs needed to get cash for notes. As a contractual right, when credits are doubtful, the contractor, in case of payment default, should be allowed the same degree of protection afforded the buyer: he should have the privilege of stopping work without invalidating the contract. He need take no chances.

Keeping working capital in adequate quantity is an absolute essential. The party in responsible charge must give the collection function his daily attention.

14-12 *Contingent Obligations*

A job may be completed to the point at which all final requisitions or bills of any nature are paid. Yet contractually there are contingent obligations still in force. Specifications set standards of maintenance and repair, in the form of a construction guarantee, for periods of time from some definite date. Bonds are required covering certain replacements to be made if necessary and with longer time effectiveness. Or a buyer may later wish to replace or add to a mechanical installation of piping or otherwise unmarked material.

The general contractor wants to satisfy justifiable requests to maintain a client, yet he wishes to operate as economically as possible. Therefore, he should be able to approve and act on fair claims immediately (and there are such requests). Yet, like everyone, he must protect himself against unreasonable, inequitable, and costly impositions.

Complete records, indexed and summarized for use, are necessary. This leads to two file locations. In the *active file* should be photocopies of the specification or other contractual guarantee and also any actual bonds involved. This procedure can be a big time-saver in locating facts, names and addresses, dates, identification numbers, and sometimes monetary limits. There should also be a record of all documents separately filed in a *transfer file* and stored elsewhere to save office working space. The supplemental location should be fire- and water-safe, yet accessible.

All documentary material should be saved. Letters give names, companies, and dates and explain actions and installations. Catalogs describe equipment guarantees and replacement parts. Approved specifications are referred to for information. Job records, particularly subcontract names and telephone numbers, are included. Plans should be folded and filed, but only after marking on them *accurately the actually installed locations*. Particularly, mechanical plans may be diagrammatic in nature. Hidden installations, such as piping and valve locations, electric conduit and pull-box locations, and sewer and drainage locations, are always valuable to know. Leaks do develop, and sometimes repairs and additional construction are involved.

14-13   *Office-controlled Advertising (See Section 7-9)*

A business offering something for sale wishes to call attention to what it has to offer. Those firms altering existing private homes might advertise in the classified pages of the local telephone directory or in newspapers for customers. But for most construction work, clients do not look to such a source and such advertising would waste money. Advertising expenditures should pay for themselves.

Construction selling reaches limited audiences. In addition, advance and special knowledge of the planning of others is needed to help secure work. Cultivation of personal contacts, such as professional, civic, and business activities allow, is one manner of advertising. But it takes time and effort and is dependent on chance. Personal contacts afford sympathetic hearings which may be helpful. There is a type of advertising, however, which sifts out prospective customers from uncertainties, gets to the correct party, and is held for future reference when not answered immediately. It can be used successfully in a small way. The method is the use of the direct-mail letter with a photograph and with condensed reference information.

A list can be made up or purchased and directed to some one of the broad classifications of work which is wanted (and, if possible, to an influential individual). For the company doing new factory construction, a list of every factory in a limited vicinity might be used. For the company building only chemical plants, the list might include every factory in this category on a nationwide basis. (In every case, new material should go to existing customers.)

Using a printed letterhead on a standard-sized sheet and dating with the month and year only will allow printing and mailing from a letter-shop in this business. The use of lettershops for successive mailings will implement the message without impeding regular construction work. It is hoped that the material will be worthy of filing. The format shown in Figure 14-2 is a photocopy of a job recently finished by the construction company. The data given are from actual recent experience, presented in a simple manner and in such words as to suggest filing. The information is such that it will be of immediate interest only to a prospective builder. Anything of such importance will warrant a letter from the prospective customer asking for more information. This is advantageous. The lead is then obtained and can be followed up personally.

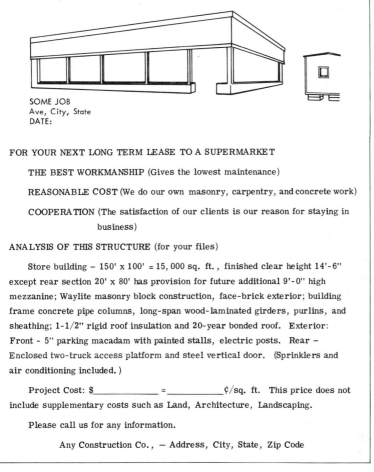

SOME JOB
Ave, City, State
DATE:

FOR YOUR NEXT LONG TERM LEASE TO A SUPERMARKET

THE BEST WORKMANSHIP (Gives the lowest maintenance)

REASONABLE COST (We do our own masonry, carpentry, and concrete work)

COOPERATION (The satisfaction of our clients is our reason for staying in
business)

ANALYSIS OF THIS STRUCTURE (for your files)

Store building – 150' x 100' = 15,000 sq. ft., finished clear height 14'-6''
except rear section 20' x 80' has provision for future additional 9'-0'' high
mezzanine; Waylite masonry block construction, face-brick exterior; building
frame concrete pipe columns, long-span wood-laminated girders, purlins, and
sheathing; 1-1/2'' rigid roof insulation and 20-year bonded roof. Exterior:
Front - 5'' parking macadam with painted stalls, electric posts. Rear –
Enclosed two-truck access platform and steel vertical door. (Sprinklers and
air conditioning included.)

Project Cost: $_____ =_____¢/sq. ft. This price does not
include supplementary costs such as Land, Architecture, Landscaping.

Please call us for any information.

Any Construction Co., – Address, City, State, Zip Code

figure 14-2. Sales letter.

And when a prospective customer has personally used effort to get information, he is apt to hold onto it.

When a series of mailings is used, this method does run into money.
Such a campaign should be checked at intervals for effectiveness. A
printed return-card mailing may be used to ascertain:

1. Whether the recipient is further interested in receiving mail
2. Whether there is anything at this time about which he would like
specific information
3. Whether anything about the addressing should be changed

There are other methods of advertising that are possibly better suited
to particular objectives. A distributed pamphlet on cold-storage-ware-

house construction by an expert in that field might be worthwhile. A pocket-size booklet on conversion factors or concrete additives might also carry a message. An impressive folder can be made up by an advertising expert to describe the larger construction organization and its work. Broadcast advertising in trade periodicals is used with success. In all cases the effort and expenditure should be carefully considered to ensure a. reasonable return.

Probably the best method of getting the best advertising return is to get the best available specialist, as in contracting. It is advisable to hire someone to spend efficiently and consistently. But he will be unable to sell the services of a moribund business unless it is first rebuilt in other ways. It must intrinsically offer as much or more than the competition. What is offered is important.

Yet after all the effort and expense, the production of a bona fide inquiry may be nullified. One uninterested employee can mishandle a request with disheartening ease and finality. There is only one way to manage this situation and prevent such a happening. Insist on personal attention, and follow up all inquiries, whether they come by letter, by telephone, or from any other source.

Productive advertising is a necessary part of staying in business and growing.

14-14   *Management*

Note that no mention has been made in this chapter of that most important item: office management. Every detail of the foregoing text should become part of the knowledge and skill of the person in charge—plus the experience attained by the successful assumption of responsibility. Good management is not inherited. It must be earned by working for it.

15

GRADING UP

To develop any business, one must offer something which others consider worthwhile. Therefore, the individual construction company must first propose to do the same quantity and quality of work as the competition at the same or a better price. Should the contractor obtain an additional price, it might be due to more service offered or a better quality of workmanship. The buyer does not offer the increase out of the goodness of his heart; the contractor must earn it. Due to competition, the profit margin is generally lower than it should be. Yet firms survive and make money. A man must have faith. One legitimate way to increase the profit margin by management is by using the stratagems discussed in the preceding chapters. Another way is to develop improvements. These can occur in many phases of the business. The necessity to improve is compelled by competitive coworkers and businesses. Competition is always there to take away some individual's position or a firm's construction job.

15-1 *Labor Possibilities*

The cost of labor continues to increase. People want to buy what others have and to improve their status. Our society approves the aim but pays increased costs with reluctance. The process is not easy for whoever hires others. The condition must be accepted, however, and to offset increased pay means improving the production of the labor force. This designation includes both office and job employees.

A. Office payroll, although an estimating overhead, is a management essential. Capable manpower and womanpower must be attracted and held to motivate individual situations properly. The office worker is influenced by personal benefits. If aiding the office worker adds something to the estimating overhead, it also gets good supervision and support to improve production. The added expense has an offset.

Taxes and individual expenses are universal problems levied against pay. There is little left over for retirement payments. (The union journeymen on the jobs may have such a benefit, and often their supervisors do not.) Reducing taxes for the employee by assuming some of them, cutting expenses, and adding benefits for workers will increase the worth of their affiliation with an organization. Supplying a valued employee with a gasoline payment card increases his real return by cutting his expenses. Yet it does not increase the take-home pay subject to tax. The gasoline tax itself is paid without evasion by the organization as a business expense. Or group hospitalization, retirement plans, and vacation funds may be insurable items with the premium paid by the employer. Or the discount privilege of buying from regular construction-supply sources may be granted an individual. New refrigerators, stoves, masonry building material, lighting fixtures are large-ticket items, and such a saving for employees is substantial and appreciated.

B. Field labor, theoretically, because of union rates and rules, should cost the same to one construction organization as to another. Actually, production is different. Only a few firms are luckily owned by a family of interested tradesmen who can produce enough to get any job they care to go after. Most firms compete by efficiently using unrelated hired hands. The fact that a good rate of production is already established does *not* mean that it cannot be bettered.

Solutions to the problem of obtaining greater production may lie in more efficient use of the number of men employed, in the tools and equipment supplied to them, or in the material and its location for use on the job. They may also lie in preparing in advance for rainy or freezing conditions or for the necessity of obtaining men outside the working district.

Those outside the business tend to think that new machines or methods will automatically give greater production. Of course, this "cure-all" is not the answer. Men must operate machines and apply methods. If men will be thrown out of work in an industry which they control, why should they allow the introduction of that which destroys their livelihood? Some way of safeguarding the jobs and money return of present labor must go with any new manner or method of increasing production.

Assurance and incentive are necessary before the workmen will agree to operate anything new. Also, if the machine uses some material not available in the present market, where and how quickly can the material be obtained?

There is no easy solution to these problems. Constant effort, study, and forethought are required to cope with changing conditions.

C. Management problems also are individual problems. To master a subject, to advance in one's business, requires not only study but thoughtful application of effort. Sometimes formal education through extension courses of limited-time seminars give the added advantages of example and necessary sustained effort (particularly if the course is paid for in advance by the employer). This type of study can be obtained through courses offered by local institutions and sometimes cosponsored by trade organizations. The effort facilitates forming friendships in the construction community for a possible later benefit.

Mental improvement, however, also leads to stimulation and a questioning attitude. Too often in the business, a bystander will be aggravating to the experienced man by having part knowledge. The bystander will comment on how much more profitable the business would be if it used one of the modern devices, such as a computer, or a modern method such as a systems approach. It is true that an advance in technology is worthwhile when it is properly used in the right place. But when it is misused and overly expensive, and also used in the wrong place, it can be more costly than what it replaced.

Consider the timesaving and mechanical computer. The machine has its place. But when the nature of the business does not give consistently correct results and the people who feed so-called "facts" into the machine do not consider the source, the results are suspect. Such results, if wrong, are expensive and heartbreakingly slow to correct. Anyone who has tried to have a computerized bill revised has suffered frustration.

The individual should not accept technical advances just because they have been successfully used by others. Are they applicable to his business? Will the results return a profit on all the cost involved? Is that profit sufficiently greater than is now being obtained to warrant the increased investment? The dependence on machines would be all right if it always worked. But the machines fail. Can the men take their place?

We have had, and are getting, specialists in various techniques, in the functions of material, and in other aspects of living—and many of these developments are good. A specialist, however, of the left knuckle or the right knee is too confined in his field to be a competent authority for the whole body. Every part influences every other part. Every development has its strengths and weaknesses and its dependence upon correlative parts. We need understanding of the whole project.

15-2   *Material Possibilities*

Problems invariably call forth efforts to solve them that involve new materials. Some percentage of this answer is usually thoroughly practical. Of necessity, it is advisable to consider seriously every new suggestion. Due to unexpected side effects, however, it is also necessary to job-pretest everything offered thoroughly under actual working conditions before ordering in quantity.

For example, when epoxy floor-patching material first appeared on the market, it was advertised as adhering to any open, porous, or cracked concrete floor. Truly it was a boon for the construction business. But upon being tested in the field, the plastic material also adhered to the mason's steel hand trowel and could not be worked or finished. This defect has since been taken care of, and excellent workable materials are obtainable. The necessity is evident of considering new items, but they should be self-tested before being recommended or ordered.

When materials new to the contractor are shown or specified for the job he is figuring or has contracted for, the responsibility is the designer's. The contractor, however, should obtain as much information as possible from the manufacturer in advance of purchasing. This knowledge should be in writing so as to afford a factual basis if future discussion or disagreement materializes. The means and methods of application can also be prepared in advance.

15-3   *Equipment Possibilities*

There are many reasons for using certain equipment. The ability to do a job is the motive, but with minimum time and effort and with maximum safety and durability. Equipment decisions, however, depend, in turn, on other assessments. The method chosen to do a job will determine what to use to do it. Sometimes hand erection is more advantageous than erection by machine, particularly for a few pieces. The machine will require using additional highly paid men. The total cost per erected member is what counts. The return on investment compared with the use of working capital will also indicate whether to buy or rent. This decision includes such complicating items as maintenance, obsolescence, and deterioration. Which of many competing sales claims is most favorable is always a question. For example, does the contractor have present equipment whose use would make or lose money?

Job equipment also includes nonmachinery items, such as individual small mortar tubs—and also suitable collapsible legs so that they can be set at an efficient working height. (One item and action always affects others.) Nonmachinery items such as wood scaffold plank or shovels and maul handles deteriorate, crack, and become unsafe with use and age and should be replaced. Physical equipment on hand, such as shoring timber paid for and left over from another job, becomes an asset which may be estimated at a low rental price to get a new job. The use of equipment entails thought.

Office equipment is another factor for consideration. Because of the vital necessity of accuracy, desk-top adding and calculating machines are modern necessities. The use of large computing machines in making out payrolls and other reiterative calculations is no longer the prerogative of only the very large organization. Because the telephone company provides rental connections for computer time sharing, it is possible to use such facilities whenever practical. And the marketing of the dry-type office photocopying machine has added immensely to accuracy of recording.

15-4   *Management Developments*

Management is becoming more of a science and less of a rule-of-thumb operation. As the money units involved grow in size, managers must also grow more professional in training and experience and must study to act in a quasi-public manner. This necessity arises because construction, in its economic, social, and environmental phases, is an instrument of public policy.

As problems of land utilization, housing, and environmental conditioning come up and are solved, they are publicized. Thus a technique is arising, *but it is based on large-scale operations.* Such methods are definitely advantageous on many smaller jobs. But when the money value involved does not warrant the additional expense also involved, successfully used existing methods are still adequate. For example, the progress planning of a structure has been, and is, done by establishing a chart similar to that shown in Figure 14-1. When monetary size, however, reaches a certain increased value, architectural designers begin to specify that certain new methods be used. These might be CPM (critical-path method, described below) or some similar method of analysis. It immediately becomes necessary for bidders on such jobs to know what is required and to add any additional costs involved to their quotations. Something new and advantageous is added but at an increased cost over what had been used previously.

A. *The critical-path method* and similar peculiarly named progress methods deter many practical men from attempting to acquire a knowledge of new developments. They are afraid that their education may not be adequate. This fear is a fallacy. The process of assembling a descriptive vocabulary for a new topic has the deceptive aspect of a pink whisker disguise at Halloween. It does not mean much if one knows the subject underneath. All these techniques are merely extensions of previous knowledge, used in a more extensive and hence a more costly manner.

There are a number of books and courses of study specifically written to understand these subjects readily (see the Bibliography). A commonplace term, for example, is *network*. A network is represented by a series of lines joining a series of starting or terminating points. Each line delineates an individual construction operation. And because each operation comes before or follows another, the simple sketch is known as a *sequence network*. So where, so far, is there something new? Actually there is something new, and that is in the use which has been developed for the next definition. *Critical path* indicates the longest length of total time on a sequence network which is required to do a total piece of work.

Emphasis is placed here on activities which are essential to the time allowable on the critical path only. Corollary work is not forgotten, but since it is not essential to immediate progress, it is temporarily neglected. In pointing out which of the many operations affect the final result on large work, the method pays for itself. The study of such a system takes time and requires considerable practice. There are additional possibilities in the utilization of these systems which will develop with use and skill, such as cost finding.

B. The *systems approach* is another name for a revised method of attaining efficiency in large-scale work. An endeavor is made to utilize already developed mass-production techniques to offset rising production costs. What is actually referred to is the use of systems of production.

Such an objective is not easy to obtain. Systems use requires:

1. Predetermined relationships to determine design
2. Design in modules and detailed for easy field erection
3. Design of modules for controlled, mass-produced, and economical factory assemblage and for practical shipping
4. Cooperation in advance between representatives of union labor and designer-purchaser teams so that job work rules will permit the use of off-job assemblage, on-job delivery, and methodical grouping regardless of the necessity of crossing trade lines
5. The financing of large-scale monetary units to permit the advantages of mass purchasing and production
6. The design of smaller elements to be used with the primary modules
7. The approval in advance of building departments, zoning districts, or other jurisdictional authorities to remove obstructions of any nature

As can be seen, there are many obstacles to be overcome before this procedure can be used. Changes of work rules today, however, may be commonplace tomorrow. And what starts only for the very large project may later be copied as a countrywide catalog item for general use.

Men in the construction business are not obstructive, but they are practical. Advances are theoretically as satisfactory in one business as in another, but abstractions in an intermittent business do *not* pay the rent, food, or clothing bills for a family of a wage earner. Developments are made under very different circumstances, with different aims and under other cost compulsions. The realities of existing employees in the building and supply trades, and their necessity to continue earning on the relatively small and individually personalized projects of the business as presently constituted, are of primary importance. *There are many more small jobs than big ones.*

Until the advances are brought into line with the present construction setup, or until the setup is changed, there will be little acceptance. We are living in a competitive society and must offer what is of value to the consumer, whether that person is a workman looking for a livelihood or a purchasing agent paying the smallest possible amount for a structure.

The building industry, as an independent group, has to work with others to establish this, or any, concept. The architect, as the buyer's agent, is the key to designing and purchasing systematized construction which is also aesthetically acceptable. The manufacturer will have to develop practical methods. Union labor is already actively involved and is aware of the necessity of cutting costs to compensate for increased benefits.[1] The contractor, in translating these ideas into actuality, must anticipate and overcome any restraining or disruptive forces which materialize.

Savings will come in such areas as structural and ceiling components, lighting fixtures, heating and ventilating units, plumbing assemblages—wherever inventiveness foresees an economy. The systems approach is not a panacea. It is only one attempt to improve on existing methods.

C. Another deceptive "pink-whisker" approach is the definition which is used with a new meaning. To a construction man, a *model* is defined as an actual scale representation. To a new technique theoretician, a model is an analytical description of a problem to be solved. Each man is capable and is working toward the same aim, but they are just not discussing the same thing. Until one speaks the language of the other, progress will be accidental.

Words and phrases used with a different from customary meaning or not clearly defined are very misleading.

15-5   *Improving Old Methods*

The fact that a construction firm has estimated and gotten a job predicated on a certain method of doing work does not mean that the produc-

---

[1] Battelle Memorial Institute, *The State of the Art of Prefabrication in the Construction Industry*, research report to the Building and Construction Trades Department, AFL-CIO, Washington, D.C.

tion will be obtained as figured, that the work can be done in the time originally estimated, or that a profit will materialize. There are so many necessary details to be supervised and so few men to do the work that management does not do a complete job. Management has not advanced, despite knowledge of its needs. Yet it is here also that money is made or lost.

For example, efforts have been made to lay out a cost-control system to be operated by the foreman, supposedly checked by management, and corrected when necessary. The system is poorly supervised and inadequate, although the basic costs developed are necessary for estimating. Some method must be developed to judge and to improve procedure as it is actually under way. A method to supplement the cost-control system is indicated. The building business needs practical research and testing, just as does the space industry or television. (And it, too, needs financial support.)

Fortunately, such action is already under way to a limited extent over the entire country. Described below is a cost-checking system which is the result of investigations and development by Henry W. Parker, Associate Professor of Civil Engineering at Stanford University.[1] His research and similar material were brought to the writer's attention by the Division of Continuing Engineering Studies, Newark College of Engineering, in a seminar which they cosponsored with the New Jersey Building Contractors' Association, who publicized the meeting.

A. Time-lapse Photography

Usually, the supervision of the foreman's cost-control system mentioned above is done by one person, who uses a stopwatch and paper and makes records by personal observation. It is practically limited in time by whatever a man can spare from other pressing problems and in scope because not everything is noted. In addition, the observer takes time off, notes matters which are not pertinent to the subject, and is otherwise distracted. His work is not complete or accurate.

The result of Professor Parker's research is a continuous series of frames of color-film pictures. The pictures are taken by an automatic camera. They are of one scene and are taken from one location but at varying time intervals, depending on the amount of detail to be included. An accurate observation is thereby obtained. Color film is always used because of the clarity, detail, and contrast obtainable. After the camera is set on a tripod and sighted on the scene to be recorded, it is started and will run unattended, using an electric-eye device to change exposure time as light conditions change. The exposed film is then normally developed and run through a projector with a variable-speed motor. This allows chang-

---

[1] Henry W. Parker, *Methods Improvement Techniques for Construction and Public Works Managers*, Construction Institute, Stanford University.

ing the speed of viewing, stopping for critical inspection, or reversing for an immediate replay.

Referring to whether there will be opposition from employees, management always has the option of trying to improve operations. If the workmen are advised in advance and promised an opportunity to see the finished film, there will be no criticism and no obstructionism. Where they have participated, they will help if a new method is possible and is devised. (After a few minutes of operation in plain sight, the men will forget the presence of the machine.)

A photographic system offers certain definite advantages:

1. The film may be viewed almost immediately, while action has just started on the site.

2. When shown, the film is the focus of attention and there are no other distractions.

3. Action can be stopped for examination at any point, or the same series of actions can be run through repeatedly.

4. During working hours, management may be constantly busy with other urgent matters. Then, when time allows, the actual job scenes can be completely and accurately reviewed for competent criticism.

5. A permanent and dated record is made and filed. Such a record will settle claims and arguments.

In teaching right and wrong procedures leading to money savings or losses, the following are but a few of the items which actually appeared on successive frames of one operation:

1. Carpenters could have built all the scaffolding at one time. They would now have to return because they built only that part of it being worked on and did not build that particular section wide or high enough.

2. There were not enough ready-mix trucks assigned to the job for continuous delivery. The entire gang. waited at times for the next truck to appear.

3. Even had there been a continuous flow of deliveries, there were too many men on the job for the size of the operation.

4. The prepared forms did not fit. They had to be taken out, refitted, and replaced. The forms were also inadequately marked for location and were delayed in erection.

5. The reinforcing bars were stored outside the structure. Yet the *outside* wall forms were erected first, and then the bars were lifted over the top of the forms by ironworkers so that they could be set before the inner forms were erected. To save this hand-lifting time, the inner forms should have been erected first.

All these items may be small or large, but when there is unnecessary erosion of profit, eventually there is no profit. Discussion at such viewing sessions is important and should entail no blame. Each participant depends on others for advance information, material, supplies, and equipment. Each gets to know of the problems of the other. The results are what count and what determine future actions.

B. *A Universal Measuring System*

Even as basic a matter as the use of measurements in drawing plans is subject to investigation for saving time. General contractors competing with others in many foreign countries must figure plans drawn there which use the metric system. The metric system is a system of measuring in units of 10. For example, 1 meter equals 100 centimeters; a scale of 1:100 means that 1 centimeter on the plan equals 1 meter in actuality.

When trying to compare foreign plans and specifications with a contractor's foot-and-inch measurements, it therefore becomes necessary to use a conversion factor of some nature to transpose from one system to the other. One centimeter in the metric system is the same as 0.3937 inch and can thus be converted to the system of feet and inches. An estimator can determine and visualize the size of an object by translating it to his own terms. However, why is it not possible to have one terminology used by everyone in order to save this needless waste of time? As the world effectively gets smaller and closer, this concept of a universal engineering language becomes economically more necessary.

Because the metric system has many logical advantages over other systems, there is an active movement toward making it the universal measuring system. The general contractor who is abreast of his time will take note of such developments and make them part of his required business study.

15-6   *Other Suggestions for Improvement*

There are many other ways for improvement to be developed as individually planned.

A. *Improved Advertising*

The fact that sales have been made by broadcasting letters, visiting designers, or subscribing to trade publications does not mean that the method cannot be improved. The direct-mail campaign can be sharpened in its aim by personalizing the addressing. The local chamber of commerce can be more effectively utilized by its advance knowledge that efforts to sell available property have materialized. The local railroad agent will know who is interested in a site with a railroad siding. The local public service company will know who has made inquiries about the availability and cost of power.

And the fact that attempts are made to influence others by giving them show tickets or merchandise for holiday gifts does not mean that there is not a better way. It might be better to give them subscriptions to trade magazines, which arrive many times a year as a reminder. Or they might be presented with a new book on the development of their particular industry, without the excuse of a holiday, when everyone uses the same old worn-out subterfuge of giving. It is always better to be strictly honest—about motives as about anything else.

Advertising should be personal and thoughtful, especially when there are relatively few customers. Present customers, incidentally, represent a capital investment. It has cost money to get their job and to open the account. When and if another job is received from them, a return is obtained on a previous investment just as truly as a return is obtained on money invested directly in the business.

B. *Solving Problems*

In every location, new sources of business occur because new problems develop. For example, potential power shortages in public service distribution systems become apparent at times due to a variety of causes. The increased cost of capital financing, public opposition to power-plant installation on ecological grounds, lack of rate increases warranting capital expenditure—all indicate further delay in alleviating the condition.

The situation of overloading leads to possibilities of very expensive shortages of electricity and damaging drops in voltage where such conditions can cause considerable loss. Factory process boilers do have safety-control switches, but they cannot be thrown into place at a moment's notice. Also involved is spoilage of materials, damage to containers, and innumerable health, money, and time losses. The need to the public utility company for continuity of electric load to maintain the balance of its system in operation leads to a very practical necessity. The lighting companies must shed part of their load to stay within their lowered productive capacity and maintain power. When such a condition is brought to the attention of necessitous power users, a possible customer is created for an emergency source of built-in standby service.

It is impractical to expect the public service companies to give up and stop selling the electric power which is their livelihood. Yet they might be willing to enter into a standby private plant-installation arrangement which is meant to overcome their supply difficulties and is built in accordance with their requirements. Of course, this type of supplementary source would also require standby rate changes by the controlling utility commissions to make the project economically feasible. Yet someone is going to get work such as this. Undoubtedly, the profit margin will be better. This example is only one of the many problems which will develop with overcrowding, new power sources for the use of the public, communication difficulties, traffic congestion, ad infinitum—but to the advantage of the construction business.

C. *Adding Services*

Additional construction services may be warranted. A manufacturing company furnishing air- and water-pollution control apparatus may welcome a representative who not only can sell but also can install the units and enclose them in a protective structure. Competition is much reduced for this type of work, with a corresponding improvement in the profit percentage. And when such opportunities are preempted, new developments and new opportunities always appear. Whoever said "The postman rings only once" was being misleading. He comes and rings once, but he does so every day.

D. *Personal Ownership*

Private corporations may be formed to include as members a general contractor, architect, rental agent, lender, and such other parties as will make an owning corporation self-sufficient in financing, design, construction, renting, and maintenance. This type of corporation will furnish the efficient and personally interested local management necessary to make a success of limited-income projects with social objectives, such as slum-clearance projects at low rents.

Of course, there are individual objections to any specific development. But opportunity is given to own a share of what one works on. The power of eminent domain is used to assemble and turn over large blocks of property. The benefits of mass purchasing and production are secured. There is afforded the result of bringing back inhabitants to large areas at a time, with subsequent improved personal protection. Again, the risk must be worth the effort.

15-7 *Summarizing Contracting Possibilities*

Problems and the opportunities to satisfy them will always exist, not only to meet present conditions but also to satisfy new developments. There are the following sources of business, among others:

1. Present unmet needs require fulfillment. For example, many individuals would like to own their own homes rather than rent. The increasingly higher prices is an obstacle which must be overcome.

2. Present fulfilled needs require alteration to offset obsolescence and deterioration.

3. An increase in production, using modern methods and equipment in modern factories, will be a management offset to increased job production costs. New erection will be required.

4. A predicted increase in the population will require more habitable space. It foreshadows increased distribution of earnings. It will change habitability patterns.

5. There will be correlative changes in social relations, laws, and distribution systems.

6. As concepts change and to level out a fluctuating business, construction men will build more for their own account.

7. New requirements offer new fields for building, possibly with better profit margins. Congestion, air pollution, water contamination, and noise disturbance are problems that become always more urgent. Decay resistance, food preservation, manufacture of new essentials are but a few of the topics which suggest themselves.

8. Old buildings will be replaced for better utilization. There is a relative change in importance between city centers and suburbs. The prospects seem good for construction requirements.

The opportunities are limitless. There are problems requiring solution not only in selling but also in many other cost fields, such as labor. The unions have been maturing, gaining stability, and achieving many of the objectives for which they struggled. These include a living wage, stability of employment, and the ousting of nonunion competition. Unions are also organized into specific types. Since the problem now is for productivity to offset costs, the unions are faced with a regrouping effort. As the necessity changes from complete knowledge, needing a long trade apprenticeship, to assembly techniques, which require less skill, their system will also change. Possibly incentive payments will be permitted on a group basis. This change will revive that personal interest which is so noticeably and disastrously missing. The need for keeping construction costs within the ability to pay for them is self-evident.

15-8   *Conclusion*

Every working day is a grant of time—time to plan, time to work, time to finish and to benefit. There is no one factor of the construction business which is most important; all are important. Selling should be not only on rainy days, but every day consistently. Because a delivery is delayed is no time suddenly to discover and follow up shortages; every day requires alertness. If a construction business is to prosper, the person in charge of any function, large or small, must do and get done *now* those actions which need doing. Tomorrow may never come, or when it does, it may bring requests for unfigured pay raises, strikes, or other increased costs.

It is necessary first to know and then to do the right thing immediately. The right thing, however, is not just to work but to work at a profit. The decisions to be made involve weighing differing courses of action as matters of judgment, based on facts rather than on guesses and gambling. This book has tried to expose what managers of construction should know and what personal skills they should strengthen.

The advantages are not only in making a livelihood but also in continuing to be in such a fascinating, individualistic, and worthwhile field. An immigrant laborer summarized the feeling of achievement and justification of all when he pointed to a home and said, "I built that."

BIBLIOGRAPHY

When individuals add to their knowledge of construction, they also improve their ability and the possibility of earning more than their present return. This happily to-be-desired result requires study—of both the principles and the management of construction. In addition to theory, the ability must be developed further to analyze actual problems and to act correctly.

Part 1 of the Bibliography briefly outlines a few of the many possible subjects, authors, and books suggested by the text. If anything else is available, one should use it. There are many excellent texts which are unknown to the writer and which may contribute a differing point of view and much of value. In using any reference, however, one should always compare the date of publication with the present date. If there is a considerable differential, some parts of the text may require revision.

There is always something to learn. The individual should know many trades to understand, contract and subcontract, and enforce plans and specifications. He should read up on those items which are not clear to him. For example, a vent pipe in a plumbing line seems to be superfluous, yet the designer inserted many of them at considerable expense.

Money has not been thrown away, and there is a very good reason for this installation. The vent pipe bypasses sewage gases to a point above the roof but is of real consequence in providing air relief to bypass plugs of waste falling in house sewer lines. These plugs might otherwise become stoppages due to trapped air and result in a serious health hazard.

Part 2 of the Bibliography refers to putting theory into practice. A library, whether it be federal, state, municipal, or private, offers a wealth of reference material and services. Questions are correctly answered, books may be borrowed, a copying machine is available, often at a small service charge, and a microfilm scanner may be used, usually at no charge. The library may have a reciprocal arrangement whereby a wanted text owned by another library in the same area may be borrowed for the use of an applicant. Knowledge gained can be focused on individual aims.

There is one practical method of paying for the continuance of this ready reference system. Publishers can continue to exist and serve their function of printing knowledge only by selling their books. If any library reference book or service is of continuous business use, it should be bought or otherwise obtained for private utility.

Part 3 refers to establishing a personal reference file from the daily receipt of one's own business information. Such news may come from a periodical, the mail, or conversation with another. Typical of such material might be an advertising postcard offering secondhand brick at a price and from an individual not otherwise listed. This information might later solve an architectural requirement for a job to be estimated. Or printed advertising explanatory of new materials, equipment, or services may be useful. Or for a contractor doing his own masonry, a photocopy of a set of coursing tables in a textbook may be worth filing.

Part 4 refers to information which may already be obtainable in printed form but not usually through regular sources. A commercial company may issue a sales manual which contains considerable worthwhile trade information about the product to be sold. An association may issue a handbook for its members which establishes grade rules, tolerances, and allowable defects. The local manufacturers' organization may publish tax-computation tables involving social security, unemployment compensation, and other payroll deductions.

Because of the many subjects of interest, the few items given here are merely examples (and the worth of any product or service mentioned is *not* implied).

To act correctly is based on knowledge but developed by experience. There is no substitute for actual experience in construction and the successful assumption of responsibility.

PART 1   SUGGESTED PERSONAL LIBRARY

Accounting

A.I.C.P.A., *Audits of Construction Contractors*, American Institute of Certified Public Accountants

Coombs, W. E., *Construction Accounting and Financial Management*, McGraw-Hill

Kellogg, I., *How to Use Financial Statements*, McGraw-Hill

Wolkstein, H. A., *Accounting Methods and Controls for the Construction Industry*, Prentice-Hall

Advertising

Adams, C. F., *Common Sense in Advertising*, McGraw-Hill

Danger, E. P., *How to Use Color to Sell*, Cahners

Arbitration

American Arbitration Association, *Dictionary of Arbitration and Its Terms*, Oceana

Bernstein, M. C., *Private Dispute Settlement*, Macmillan

Collecting Accounts

Beckman, T. N., and R. S. Foster, *Credits and Collections, Management and Theory*, McGraw-Hill

Schultz, W., and H. Reinhardt, *Credit and Collection Management*, Prentice-Hall

Communication

Anastasi, T. E., Jr., *Face to Face Communication*, Management Center of Harvard University

Aranguren, J. L., *Human Communication*, McGraw-Hill

Construction

Clough, R. H., *Construction Contracting*, Wiley

Huntington, W. C., *Building Construction*, Wiley

Medlycott, A., *Applied Building Construction* (courses), Chapman & Hall (distributed by Barnes & Noble)

Merritt, F. S., *Building Construction Handbook*, McGraw-Hill

Cost Control (For Costs see Part 4)

American Institute of Architects, *Creative Control of Building Costs*, McGraw-Hill

Carroll, P., *Overhead Cost Control*, McGraw-Hill

Credit

Classon, B. D., *Commercial Credit and Collection Guide*, Prentice-Hall

Credit Research Foundation, *Credit Management Handbook*, Dow Jones-Irwin

Dictionaries

Lipowski, B., and M. Bersten, *A Picture Dictionary. Building and Construction Terms*, Arco

Estimating

Benson, B., *Building Contractor's and Home Builder's Handbook of Bidding, Surveying & Estimating*, Prentice-Hall
Dallavia, L., *Estimating General Construction Costs*, McGraw-Hill

Information

Manley, M. C., *Business Information—How to Find and Use It*, Harper

Insurance

"Investments, Insurance, Wills—Simplified," *U.S. News & World Report*
Lucas, G. G., and R. H. Wherry, *Insurance, Principles and Coverages*, Holt
Pendleton, O. W., *How to Find Out about Insurance*, Pergamon
Williams, C. A., Jr., and R. M. Heins, *Risk Management and Insurance*, McGraw-Hill

Legal

Cohen, H. A., *Public Construction Contracts and the Law*, McGraw-Hill
Powell-Smith, V., *Modern View of the Law for Builders and Surveyors*, Pergamon
Walker, N., and T. K. Rohdenburg, *Legal Pitfalls in Architecture, Engineering, and Building Construction*, McGraw-Hill

Letters

Buckley, E. A., *How to Write Better Business Letters*, McGraw-Hill
Shurter, R. L., *Effective Letters in Business*, McGraw-Hill

Management

Chironis, N. P., *Management Guide for Engineers and Technical Administrators*, McGraw-Hill
Kazmier, L. J., *Principles of Management: A Program for Self-instruction*, McGraw-Hill
Miller, L. C., *Successful Management for Contractors*, McGraw-Hill

Negotiation (see also Part 1, Communication)

Nierenberg, G., *Art of Negotiating*, Hawthorn
Schelling, T. C., *The Strategy of Conflict*, Harvard University Press

Office

Cottom, T. W., *Contractors' Desk Book*, Prentice-Hall
Deatherage, G. E., *Construction Office Administration*, McGraw-Hill

Personnel

Beach, D. S., *Personnel, The Management of People at Work*, Macmillan
Bittel, L. R., *What Every Supervisor Should Know*, McGraw-Hill

Plan Reading

Bellis, H. F., and W. A. Schmidt, *Blueprint Reading for the Construction Trades*, McGraw-Hill
Kenney, J. E., *Blueprint Reading for the Building Trades*, McGraw-Hill

Prefabricates

Battelle Memorial Institute, *The State of the Art of Prefabrication in the Construction Industry*, research report to the Building and Construction Trades Department, AFL-CIO, Washington, D.C.

Collins, F. T., *Building with Tilt Up*, Know How Publications

Lewicki, B., *Building with Large Prefabricates*, American Elsevier

Pricing

Park, W. R., *The Strategy of Contracting for Profit*, Prentice-Hall

Purchasing

Aljian, G. W., *Purchasing Handbook*, McGraw-Hill

Bagot, K., *Profit Potential of Purchasing Negotiations*, American Management Association

Pooler, V. H., Jr., *Purchasing Man and His Job*, American Management Association

Real Estate

Casey, W. J., *Real Estate Desk Book*, Institute for Business Planning

Wendt, P. F., and A. R. Cerf, *Real Estate Investment Analysis and Taxation*, McGraw-Hill

Safety

Bendick, J., *Emergency Book* (designed for juniors), Rand McNally

Manual of Accident Prevention in Construction, Association of General Contractors of America

Siemon, K. O., *Directory of Safety and Construction Codes, U.S.A. States and Cities*, Code Publishing Co.

Sales

Corman, C. W., *Sales and Secured Financing*, Bobbs-Merrill

Prentice-Hall Editorial Staff, *Handbook of Successful Sales, Advertising and Marketing Techniques*, Prentice-Hall

Superintendence

Arco Editorial Board, *Construction Supervisor and Inspector*, Arco

Royer, K., *Desk Book for Construction Superintendents*, Prentice-Hall

Taxes

Atlas, M., *Tax Planning for the Construction Industry*, Bureau of National Affairs

Techniques

Gill, P., *Systems Management Techniques for Builders and Contractors*, McGraw-Hill

Johnson, R. G., *PERT for Managers*, Argyle Books

Levin, R. I., and C. A. Kirkpatrick, *Planning and Control with PERT-CPM*, McGraw-Hill

Parker, H. W., *Methods Improvement Techniques for Construction and Public Works Managers*, Construction Institute, Stanford University

Priluck, H. M., and P. M. Hourihan, *Practical C.P.M. for Construction*, Means

Terminology (see Part 1, Dictionaries)

Trade Unions

Barbash, J., *Unions and Union Leadership*, Harper

PART 2   SOURCES OF INFORMATION AVAILABLE FROM THE PUBLIC LIBRARY

Arrangement and Other Basic Information

Aldrich, E. V., *Using Books and Libraries*, Prentice-Hall

Gates, J., *A Guide to the Use of Books and Libraries*, McGraw-Hill

Morse, G. W., *Concise Guide to Library Research*, Washington Square

Sternberg, V. A., *How to Locate Technical Information*, National Foremen's Institute, Waterford, Conn.

(The following are examples only of the many which exist.)

Contractors

Contractors Register, 5 Van Wart St., Elmsford, N.Y. 10523
For Metropolitan New York area names, addresses, and telephone numbers of general contractors, subcontractors for various trades, equipment and material dealers.

Credit Associations

Associated Credit Bureaus of America—any local affiliate

Dun & Bradstreet—also publishes directories and miscellaneous publications

Directories

New Jersey State Industrial Directory
N. W. Ayer & Sons Directory of Newspapers & Periodicals
Scientific and technical societies in the United States and Canada
Thomas Register of American Manufacturers
Guide to American Directories

Encyclopedias

Ask local library for assistance.

Governmental Aid

Ask local library for assistance, and write to Supt. of Documents, Government Printing Office, Washington, regarding past publications and the subscription charge for the monthly *Catalog of Government Publications* for current and future publications.

a. Small Business Administration, *Starting and Managing a Small Business*
b. *Report on Private Employee Retirement Plans* (#20402)
c. *Public Policy and Private Pension Plans*
Schmeckebier, L. F., and R. B. Eastin, *Government Publications and Their Use,*
   Brookings Institute

Handbooks

Architects & Builders Handbook, Wiley
Electrical Engineers Handbook, Wiley
Kents Mechanical Engineers Handbook, Wiley
Standard Handbook for Electrical Engineers, McGraw-Hill
Standard Handbook for Mechanical Engineers, McGraw-Hill

House Organs

Printers Ink Directory of House Organs
   If any seem individually useful, ask to be placed on their mailing list.

Indexes

Engineering Index, Engineering Societies Library, 345 E. 47 St., New York
New Technical Books, New York Public Library
Technical Book Review Index (monthly publication), Special Library Service

Manuals

Ask local library for assistance. For example, in sewerage construction, the
Public Works Journal Corp., 200 S. Broad St., Ridgewood, N.J., publishes the
Sewerage Manual and also the *Public Works Magazine,* a material-source
periodical.

Miscellaneous Subjects

Maps
Newspapers and periodicals
Publishers and addresses
Reference tables, reports, research and development items, reviews, tests
Services
State and federal aids
Textbooks
Yearbooks

PART 3   SUGGESTED TOPICS FOR THE BUSINESS FILE

To locate filed material, it is recommended that the filing system and alphabetical
index of the American Institute of Architects No. E301 be used.

Advertisements	Equipment, material, methods, services, systems
Associations	Addresses, information, material, applications
Books	Bookstore and publisher addresses, reviews, literature
Brochures	People, products, other phases
Business	Statistics, charts, graphic items, other phases

Catalogs	Sources, informative details
Competitors	Public-bid results, other information
Cost data	Own material, economic material
Directories	Reference information
Equipment, material, and supplies	Sources, prices, stock and mill items, availability, quality definitions, quantity variations
Financing	Sources, rates, information required
Forms	Legal, membership, stationery
Insurance	Types, limits, costs, fire ratings of various items
Jurisdictional	Municipal, county, state, federal, charges, regulations
Mail advertising	Lists, printing, mimeographing, typing, mailing
Maps	Road, use, zoning, water, typographical, other
Periodicals	Construction, credit, economic, equipment, management
Sales material	Industrial parks, news, transactions, developments, other
Samples	Of future interest
Sources	Subcontractors, fuel, office equipment, repair, cleaning
Specifications	Standard, trade, other
Tax information	Withholding, sales, use, other
Trade details	Texts, associations, other details of interest
Training	School, college, extension, correspondence, seminar
Transient help	Quantity surveyors, office, job
Unit prices	Own computations, subcontractors
Wage rates	Localities, trades, hours, foremen, journeymen, laborers, fringe benefits (welfare, pension, vacation, etc.)

PART 4   SUGGESTED OFFICE REFERENCE MATERIAL

Advertisements	*Printers Ink Sales Promotion Idea Book*, Funk & Wagnalls
Associations	American Management Association, 135 W. 50 St., New York
	National Association of Credit Management, 44 E. 23 St., New York
Catalogs (trade)	*Construction Data Book* (admixtures, waterproof material), A. S. Horn Co., 730 Third Ave., New York
	Sweet's Catalog File, McGraw-Hill Information Systems Company, McGraw-Hill, Inc., New York
Costs	*Building Construction Cost Data*, R. S. Means Co., Duxbury, Mass.
	Construction Cost Manual, Box 8788, Denver
	Construction Pricing & Scheduling Manual (building-cost calculator) and *Costs and Trends* (periodical), McGraw-Hill Information Systems Company, McGraw-Hill, Inc., New York
Economic material	*N. J. Economic Review* (periodical), Dept. of Research and Statistics, Trenton
Equipment and rentals	*Blue Book, Equipment Guide Book*, 615 University Ave., Palo Alto, Calif.
	Construction Equipment Guide, P.O. Box 99, Abington, Pa.
	Green Book, Association of Equipment Distributors, 615 W. 22 St., Oakbrook, Ill.

Handbooks

Recommended Practice for Placing Reinforcing Bars, Concrete Reinforcing Steel Institute, 38 S. Dearborn St., Chicago

Steel Construction Manual, American Institute of Steel Construction, 101 Park Ave., New York

Marketing services

Brown Letters, Brown Letters, Inc., 101 Park Ave., New York

Dodge Reports, McGraw-Hill Information System Company, McGraw-Hill, Inc., New York

INDEX